Anne Cohen Kiel

Continuity and Change
Aspects of Contemporary Norway

To Arne, and in memory of Tom
who gave me the courage to carry on.
ACK

Anne Cohen Kiel

Continuity and Change
Aspects of Contemporary Norway

Scandinavian
University Press

Scandinavian University Press (Universitetsforlaget AS), 0608 Oslo
Distributed world-wide excluding Norway by
Oxford University Press, Walton Street, Oxford OX2 6DP

Oxford New York Toronto
Delhi Bombay Calcutta Madras Karachi
Kuala Lumpur Singapore Hong Kong Tokyo
Nairobi Dar es Salaam Cape Town
Melbourne Auckland Madrid
and associated companies in Berlin Ibadan

Oxford is a trade mark of Oxford University Press

Published in the United States
by Oxford University Press Inc., New York

© Universitetsforlaget 1993

Cover design by Ellen Larsen
Sweater design: Ellinor Flor
Photo: Guri Dahle

British Library Cataloguing in Publication Data
Data available

ISBN 82-00-21116-9

Library of Congress Cataloguing in Publication Data
Data available

Typeset by Sørlandets Satsbyrå AS, Kristiansand
Printed in Norway by Edgar Høgfeldt AS, Kristiansand 1993

Contents

Introduction

The purpose of writing this book has been to meet the absence of literature in English that describes present day Norwegian society and also looks towards Norway's future. I felt the need to avoid the coffee table type of literature which romanticizes and mystifies Norway through a model of rose-painted harmony and static culture. Norway is a modern society in a changing world and not an isolated iceberg in the upper corner of Europe.

The book can be used in a number of ways. For university students, it can supplement lectures on Norwegian life and society at both an introductory and an advanced level. For immigrants, visitors, and others interested in Norway, the book is a useful reference to relevant aspects of Norwegian society.

The authors chosen to write the chapters were given an understanding of the type of book the editor had in mind. They were then free to develop the chapters as they wished. My belief was that, given as much freedom as possible within a framework, the authors would produce both interesting and enthusiastically written articles. I feel this book is evidence of this.

Each author has managed to capture some of the more salient aspects of Norwegian society that are interesting from a foreign, as well as from a Norwegian, perspective. In addition, each chapter conveys basic information about Norwegian society and culture. The chapters do not necessarily represent the editor's point of view; the opinions expressed are those of the authors.

The chronology of the articles is not random; they have been grouped together so that they complement each other. This does not mean, however, that chapters cannot be read as separate entities, or in a different order. Finally, as some authors write in British English and others in American English, I chose to allow each author to write in the form he or she was most comfortable with.

The first chapter, by Thomas Hylland Eriksen, is, as the title suggests, a reflective look at Norwegian identity in a changing world. It is an introduction to the Norwegian way of life (*den norske væremåten*) as Eriksen sees it today, and it also looks at prospects for the future.

The second chapter is written from a cultural-historical perspective. Brit Berggreen successfully attempts to trace the creation of a modern Norway through a practical ideology. This ideology was developed primarily by Christopher Bruun (1839–1920), with the resonance of national romanticism found throughout Europe clearly heard.

Chapter Three is, in common with Eriksen, a reflection. However, it is a reflection from a foreigner's experience in the Norwegian capital. Ever since Branislaw Malinowski's diary was published, anthropologists have been forced to recognize and evaluate their feelings towards their fieldwork area and the 'natives' they encounter. This chapter represents the road toward understanding some of the more implicit rules for Anne Cohen Kiel, a foreigner and an anthropologist.

Richard Malinowski introduces the reader to regional politics. As one of Norway's most intriguing identity markers, regional politics emphasizes the post-World War II solidarity and community building, now being undermined by present political trends.

Another fundamental aspect of Norway is its welfare state. Kåre Hagen and Jon Hippe examine in Chapter Five, the welfare state from its beginning through to the present crisis. They discuss its future and speculate on the issue of 'farewell-to-solidarity' which we are facing today.

The sixth chapter guides the reader to political economy as an academic discipline. Lars Mjøset takes the reader through the development of the political economy from the end of World War II to the present day.

The seventh chapter is related to and complements both the chapter on political economy and the chapter on the welfare state from a more philosophical point of view. Erik Oddvar Eriksen expresses social democracy as an ideology in crisis through the history and development of the Norwegian Labor Party.

In Chapter Eight, Øystein Gullvåg Holter describes family patterns in modern Norway. In addition, he points to complex issues that will have future consequences for the family.

Chapters Nine through Thirteen take on a more factual approach to the subject matter: Tove Skotvedt outlines both the history and present situation of the oldest ethnic minority in Norway, the Sami. Long Litt Woon outlines Norwegian immigration policies and discusses issues and trends. Arne Fliflet introduces the reader to the Norwegian legal system. Oddvar Vormeland describes the Norwegian educational system and its trends for the nineties. The Norwegian Institute for Nature research (NINA), presents Norwegian nature and the conservation of natural resoures.

I chose Helge Pharo's article on Norway and the World since 1945, for the final chapter as it both sums up and directs us back to the purpose of the book: to melt once and for all the mythical iceberg and to depict Norway as a modern society in a changing world.

I would like to acknowledge the following people for their support: Anne Turner at the University Press, for her guidance and enthusiasm, and for renewing my confidence; Astrid Torud for her ideas and contributions to the realization of this book; Marit Solesness at Scan Foto, for her undivided attention and energy in finding suitable photographs; Kirsti Nøst from Oslo Sporveier, who found the original advertisement campaign referred to in Chapter 3; Arne Kiel for caring for the children and providing irreplaceable help in translating and editing; Aase Marie and Miriam Janice, for being such good children when I needed it!

Oslo, 1993

Anne Cohen Kiel editor

1

Being Norwegian in a Shrinking World: Reflections on Norwegian Identity

Thomas Hylland Eriksen

A desolate rocky cliff arising gloomily from the foaming, dark Arctic waters – the home of a small breed of stocky peasants and tough fishermen painfully eking out a living from their rough and hostile environment. Is this Norway? No? Then how about this one: It is the most perfect democracy in the world; along with Sweden it has the planet's only fully-fledged welfare state. It is technologically highly advanced and rich in natural resources, and its inhabitants enjoy the highest standard of living in the world as well as the least polluted environment. The German sociologist Hans Magnus Enzensberger wrote, in his small book on Norway (Enzensberger, 1984), that this country is simultaneously an ethnological museum and a future laboratory. Seen from the vantage-point of continental Europe, Norway is in many respects out of step, and Enzensberger's characterisation of the country as a place of contradictions – wedged between the turbulence of modernity and the inertia of tradition – may be a good starting-point for a reflection on Norwegian identity at the end of the second millennium, A.D.

The first part of this chapter outlines the contemporary domestic discourse about "Norwegianness". In the second part of the chapter, critical light is shed on the cultural construction of modern Norway, and some recent challenges to the customary perceptions of Norwegian identity will also be discussed.

The Ongoing Invention of Norwegian Identity

The making of the Norwegian nation

Foreigners are often at a loss at describing the country in simple terms, but so are – alas – Norwegians. Since the advent of Norwegian nationalism in the 19th century, discussions concerning the Norwegian national character have periodically been at the forefront of public life in the country, and they never fail to arouse great passion. What does it actually entail to be Norwegian? What are the Norwegians "really" like, and in which ways are they different from other peoples? In the early 1990s, these issues have flared up with almost unprecedented intensity. There are several causes for this strong interest in Norwegian national identity, and we shall look into some of them in greater detail below. Let me nevertheless mention the recent wave of non-European immigrants, the Sami ethnic movement in the north, the prospect of membership in the European Community (EC), the globalisation of culture, and the planning of the 1994 Winter Olympics at Lillehammer, as some concomitant processes which inspire many Norwegians to scratch their heads and ask themselves: Who are we, and why is that so?

When we try to understand the contemporary concern with Norwegian national identity, we should keep in mind that the country's history has been construed so as to distinguish it crucially from every other European country, including its closest neighbours, Sweden and Denmark. Although there was a mediaeval kingdom roughly where Norway is presently located, its history as an independent nation-state is short, dating from its peaceful secession from Sweden in 1905. Sweden, being among the winners of the Napoleonic wars in 1814, had in turn taken over Norway from one of the losers, Denmark. Norway had then been a part of the Danish kingdom for more than four hundred years.

A peripheral country in Europe as well as in the world-system until the 20th century, Norway was scarcely affected by the many upheavals and conflicts unfolding on the Continent from the Renaissance on, and its development followed, in many respects, its own course. Notably, Norway was never an independent colonial power, nor did it have a widespread feudal system. For centuries, the only sizeable town with strong links to Continental Europe was Bergen in the west. With no powerful city bourgeoisie and no strong landed gentry, burgeoning Norwegian nationalism took on a different character from that of other European countries in the 19th century. It was emphatically rural and egalitarian in its orientation, and it tended to glorify the simple ways of life of the countryside rather than revel in urban grandeur or the military pride of the state (see Berggreen's contribution to this book). There was, after all, little grandeur and military pride to attach oneself to, since the country had been a peripheral part of the Danish kingdom for centuries.

An irony of this invention of nationhood is the fact that those

individuals who most strongly promoted the idea of Norwegianness as a rural form of life, were themselves urban and highly
educated people – their daily life was very far removed from that
of the simple peasants whom they defined as the carriers of
national identity. It was the urban middle-class, riding on a pan-
European wave of 19th century romanticism, which decided on
rural folk costumes, folk dances and fairytales as central national
symbols towards the end of the nineteenth century.[1] The farmers
who actually wore the "typical" costumes and danced the "typical" dances were less likely to see them as "typically Norwegian"
(Østerud, 1984). This creative production of a national identity
consists in what an anthropologist might describe as a form of
bricolage (following Levi-Strauss, 1962), whereby one appropri-
ates a set of known objects or symbols, and combines them in
new ways in order to create new forms of meaning. Thus the old
dances, tales and handicrafts of the Norwegian countryside took
on a new meaning when they were juxtaposed with the trappings
of a modern state and a nationalist ideology.

Nationalism

Nationalism is a kind of ideology which proclaims that the political boundaries should be coterminous with the cultural boundaries of a given territory; in other words, that a state (a "country")
should only contain people *of the same kind* (Gellner, 1983). The
idea of the Norwegian nation was born the moment a few people
decided that (i) the area contained a *distinct culture*, (ii) the area
should have political self-determination. Neither of these as-
sumptions were evidently or "naturally" true at the time. During
the formative stage of Norwegian nationalism in the mid-19th
century, Norwegian nationalists had to compete with Scandinavi-
anists, who regarded Scandinavia (or at least Norway and Denmark) as a single cultural area.[2] That fusion of a cultural identity
with a state which is implied in nationalism, is not in itself
"natural" either, as recent writers on the history of nationalism
have reminded us (Gellner, 1983; Anderson, 1983). Before (and
indeed after) the French Revolution in 1789, few states were
nation-states: they were multicultural states. At the court of the
Ottoman empire, to mention but one example, three languages
were spoken – Arabic, Turkish and Farsi (Persian). At the royal
court in Copenhagen – the capital of Denmark-Norway – German, French and Danish were used.

Nationalism and nationhood are cultural products, imaginatively created by nationalists. Nationhood is a social fact in so far as the inhabitants of an area believe in the existence of that *imagined community* (Anderson's, 1983, phrase) which is proposed by the nationalists. They hold that they have something profound in common, which could be phrased as *metaphoric kinship*, with a great number of people whom they will never know personally. It is in this sense that the nation may be spoken of as an imagined community; it is no more "imaginary" than other kinds of communities, but it is abstract and depends on ideological justification – it must be "imagined" by its members – in order to exist. In the case of Norway, Norwegianism was eventually to win out over Scandinavianism, and by today, surely, few Norwegians claim that they belong to the same nation as Danes, or Swedes, for that matter. Nationhood need not be strongly related to "objective cultural traits", although nationalist ideology tries to persuade people that it is. So although it could be argued that people from South-eastern Norway have more in common culturally with people from Central-western Sweden than with people from Western Norway, such a similarity has little consequence in so far as people from Eastern and Western Norway insist that they belong to the same nation and exclude Swedes from it.

The nation is, in other words, a historical and cultural fact; it is not a fact of nature. Nationalism is also a modern phenomenon, and this has been poorly understood until quite recently. Since nationalists are eager to present their nation as ancient, and since they draw on traditionalist symbolism (such as folk costumes and myths of ancient wars), many have been led to believe that nations – such as the Norwegian one – are indeed very old. In fact, the use of old symbols (some dating back to the Viking era) in Norwegian nationalism can be quite confusing since it seems to suggest that the Norwegian nation can be traced back to the Viking era. We should therefore be aware that these symbols had a different meaning in their original context, before that creative *bricolage* which built a bridge between past and present. At that time, the *springar* (a typical dance) was not an expression of national identity, but an imported weekend pastime, or a part of a wedding ritual. It is only retrospectively that it has become an embodiment of nationality.

Looking critically at the historical sources of the nationalist project, one will find that they are ambiguous. For example, the history of the Nordic region may just as well be used to justify a

Scandinavian or regional identity as a Norwegian one; the history of each country is intertwined with that of the other Scandinavian countries, and at a lower level, people from Sunnmøre may feel that they have little in common with people from Oslo. We should therefore be aware that history is a product of the present, not of the past. The contemporary view of say, the Viking era, is quite different from the view which was current in the sixteenth century. These and related aspects of nationalism and national identity will be dealt with in the second half of the present chapter. At this point it should be kept in mind that the nation – as a community of citizens regarding themselves as culturally similar – depends on *ideological justification* in order to exist. And – since nations are historical products – the definition of nationhood may change. It is with such a context in mind that the discourse on Norwegian national identity can be properly understood.

Dano-German and Norse trends

Perhaps a feeling that their nation-state and national identity are vulnerable, can account for the widespread Norwegian interest in discussing the content of domestic "national character". The country has a small population, it is geographically peripheral, and it has a comparatively short history as an independent state. Today (1992), there seems to exist a real fear of the imminent disappearance of the "Norwegian way" if the country is to join the European Community, and the organizers of the 1994 Winter Olympics in Lillehamrner have vowed to take care of the national heritage in their choreography of the event. However, Norwegian identity seems to be contradiction-ridden. The Norwegian language issue is a strong indicator of this. Since the invention of the Norwegian nation in the mid-19th century, the country has been divided into adherents of *Nynorsk* (New Norwegian) and *Bokmål* (literally, "Book language") or *Riksmål* (State language). Nynorsk, a standard script based on certain rural dialects, was invented by Ivar Aasen in the mid-19th century, and rapidly gained popularity among certain segments of the population, particularly in the west and extreme south. Claiming that the users of *Riksmål/Bokmål* were really writing Danish and were thus unpatriotic, *Nynorsk* users saw themselves as the more authentic carriers of nationhood. Even today, all schoolchildren have to write compositions in both variants of the language, which are, incidentally, closely related. Although the language issue, virulent for decades, has abated, the persistence of the division indicates a widespread self-conscious and contradiction-ridden reflection over one's national identity.[3]

The Norwegian language issue could be articulated as an expression of a cultural division between Dano-German and Norse currents in Norwegian cultural history (Øyvind Østerud's suggestion), typically represented by EC scepticism and Nynorsk on the Norse side, confronted with the modernism and extroverted tendencies of the Dano-German trends. A passionate defence for the Dano-German trends is a small book by Jørgen Haugan (1991), where the author laments the lack of Continental manners and an exciting intellectual life in his native country. Strongholds of "Norse" trends are the western parts of southern Norway, while the "Dano-German" trends are strongest in the larger cities, particularly Bergen and Oslo.

Despite such internal divisions, it could be argued that Norwegians are generally concerned to retain their distinctiveness, and moreover, that most of them insist that they are a single people. Trine Deichman-Sørensen (1988) has suggested that in a small country such as Norway, nothing unites the population more strongly than the general interest in "Norway". But what does this distinctiveness consist of? Instead of providing a more or less random checklist of "Norwegian cultural traits", I shall outline the recent public discourse on Norwegian distinctiveness. Frequently anecdotal or satirical in character, much of the popular literature on "Norwegian character" should perhaps be read as political statements in their own right, and not necessarily as "scientific" work. It nevertheless contains many valuable insights as well as itself being a contribution to the ongoing definition of Norwegian identity.

Egalitarian individualism

Most of those writing on Norwegian national identity seem to agree that politics in the country are marked by a peculiar democratic ideology, which we may tentatively label egalitarian individualism. Equality and the integrity of the individual are in other words believed to be highly valued. Historical and geographic reasons for such an ideology are often evoked – for example, Norwegian farms were scattered and did not invite the communal form of organisation more common in other parts of Europe, and the country lacked a strong aristocracy and related hierarchies – but we shall not go into such arguments here.

The ideology of egalitarian individualism, it has been argued, expresses itself through a strong suspicion against social climbers and rejection of formal social hierarchies. In political rhetoric, *equality* is a positively valued word, whether it concerns gender, class or town and country. Few politicians would venture to say that they favoured inequality. The social democratic ideology which has guided post-war Norwegian politics expresses such values, which are embedded in the concept of the Welfare State (cf. Andersen, 1984). The author, Aksel Sandemose, an immigrant from Denmark, coined the *Law of Jante* (*Janteloven*, cf. Sandemose, 1953), which presents such an egalitarianism in a less charitable manner. The Law of Jante proclaims in a variety of ways – that "Thou Shalt Not Think Highly of Thyself". It expresses, in other words, an ideology of equality which deprecates the original and the unusual. It is widely held that the Law of Jante is a deeply embedded aspect of Norwegian culture, and that it discourages brilliance and high achievements. Indeed, the Law of Jante has repeatedly been mentioned by local businessmen as an obstacle to economic growth and prosperity. (It is true that Norway contains fewer very rich people and thus has a greater measure of economic equality than most other countries, but it is not true that the country has had an unusually low economic growth rate.)

Be this as it may, the idea of Norwegian egalitarianism has inspired, and continues to justify, legal provisions for equality between the genders, a progressive system of taxation and a highly subsidised rural sector. Egalitarian individualism is also frequently mentioned as a driving force behind the strong resistance to EC membership, which reached a temporary peak in the 1972 referendum when 52.5% of the population voted against membership. The idea of decentralisation, a related aspect of this ideology, will be discussed below.

Consensus, compromise and formal justice

The Argentinian anthropologist Eduardo Archetti, who has lived in Norway for many years, has compared the Norwegian *style of discourse* with that prevalent in Catholic countries (Archetti, 1984). In his view, Norwegians are consensus-oriented and issue-oriented (*saklig*) when they are forced to solve tasks together, for example, in discussions at meetings. This entails that (i) they tend to be unwilling to accept disagreement; (ii) they stick to the facts and avoid including personal or other formally irrele-

vant aspects into the situation. Regarding the consensus orientation, Norwegians would, according to Archetti, tend to prefer a
poor compromise to a violent quarrel – even if they were eventually to emerge victorious from the latter: They strongly wish to
agree.

As regards the "issue-orientation" of Norwegians, Archetti
links this with a related observation of Norwegian culture,
namely a concern with formal justice – or, as an anthropologist
might say, *balanced reciprocity*. This means that one returns a
favour or a gift almost immediately, and measures the return
virtually with mathematic precision. In other societies, people
might buy each other drinks, cups of coffee or meals without
demanding an immediate return of the favour. In this way, they
establish a lasting relationship. In this country, it is uncommon
that people do not split restaurant or bar accounts, pay their own
entrance fees, and so on – even if they know each other well. Are
Norwegians afraid to develop informal commitments or obliga-
tions vis-a-vis others? Are they simply afraid of making friends?
So it may seem, if Archetti is correct. It may be the case that
Norwegians (and, it could be argued, other Scandinavians), imbued with Protestantism and Puritanism, fear the consequences
of a friendship with a person whom they do not already know
well. Since honesty and sincerity are important values in Norwegian definitions of self, it could be argued that Norwegians may
be afraid of making promises of friendship which they might
break in the future. Further aspects of the discussion of Norwegian identity seem to confirm this assumption.

The rural connection

"You can get me out of Valdres, but you cannot get Valdres out
of me," writes the native social anthropologist Tord Larsen
(1984) as an illustration of the intimate identification of Norwegians with their place of origin, even if they have long since
migrated from their native valley or fishing hamlet. Norway was
urbanised later than many other European countries – largely
during the 20th century – and half of the population still lives in
rural areas. Of those who live in towns, many maintain strong
affective links with the home of their ancestors, as well as with
relatives who remain in the countryside. Even some of the most
urbane and sophisticated members of the Oslo bourgeoisie leave
the city at Christmas in order to visit a remote mountain valley
where their kin group originates. Norwegian identity, as it is

generally defined by Norwegians, is primarily a rural identity, not an urban one.

Foreigners sometimes complain that Norwegians are difficult to befriend; that they jealously guard their personal space and seem worried and slightly afraid when confronted with strangers. It has been claimed that most Norwegians rarely address strangers unless drunk or if for some reason or other they really have to. Perhaps such an assumed aspect of the Norwegian way of life could be related to their recent rural origins. In many rural areas, strangers were treated with suspicion, and every individual had only a small number of friends whom he or she knew intimately. Villages were, as noted, absent. The social situation typical of the city, implying a very high number of superficial acquaintances, may therefore seem alienating and difficult to handle for people with a rural background. A self-perception common among Norwegians conforms to this view: they do not regard themselves as a cosmopolitan and easy-going people, but rather as somewhat private and introverted. Lacking the mannerisms of sophisticated urbanites, they might argue they compensate through a sincere and trustworthy character – and this is a characterisation of Norwegians also commonly invoked by foreigners. The British expression "Norwegian charisma", used to describe people entirely devoid of grace and charm, confirms this image.

Nature and culture

The wild and varied Norwegian scenery and clean environment comprise a source of pride to many of the country's citizens, and it may be the most important component in the standard image of Norway presented to foreigners. Instead of drawing on grand cultural traditions or a proud military history, Norwegian patriots (and surely, visiting foreigners) may talk of their beautiful mountains, clean lakes and breathtaking fjords. A genuinely peculiar aspect of Norwegian identity, further, seems to consist in the social use of nature in the country. A Norwegian who lacks interest in nature and *friluftsliv* ("life out in the open") may well be accused of being a poor specimen by his fellow citizens. A great number of people own cottages (*hytter*) in some remote valley, forest or mountain area. and many spend the majority of holidays there – it has been estimated that over half of the population has easy access to a *hytte*. Rather than seeking contact with other people, or exploring foreign cities, they regard

Cross-country skiing is for the entire family.

the holiday as an opportunity to "get away from it all", which means spending it with the nuclear family in a remote place where they can fish, walk or ski. These cottages, although many are well furnished and equipped, are expected to signal an ideal of simplicity in lifestyle – an aspect of Norwegian self-definition to which I shall return below.

The origins of most Norwegians in rural, non-hierarchical environments are again apparent. For one thing, there is little to boast about as regards urban grandeur in the country. One need only compare the Royal Castle in Oslo with the rather more spectacular ones in Copenhagen and Stockholm to see the point. As the national anthem goes, "Hytter og hus, men ingen borge" ("Cottages and houses, but no castles"). Further, many Norwegians express that they do not feel at ease in the city. Many claim to live in the city *malgré eux* – in spite of themselves, and the ideal of living in a "small red house in the country" is widespread enough to have become a cliché. A TV journalist who had just completed a series of programmes about Oslo in the autumn of 1991, was asked what she valued the most about the capital. Not entirely unexpectedly, she answered *Nordmarka*, that is, the nature reserve just inside the city limits.[4]

Few Norwegians admit that they love the city. There is also a tendency that urban life is evaluated on the basis of standards originating in the country. If the city does not fulfil human needs in the same way as the rural settlement did, something must be wrong with the city. Since it is impossible to move the city to the mountain valley, one tries instead to move the valley to the city. Norwegians have slowly become an urban people to the extent that many of them live in towns and cities, but they have scarcely become an urban people in their own view. The rural connection and love of nature are very important aspects of the public self-definition of "what is typically Norwegian" (see also Witoszek, 1991).

Decentralisation

In his afore-cited book, Enzensberger points out that a peculiar characteristic of Norwegian society lies in the fact of 47 airports (actually, the number is 53) for a population of four million. Like many other commentators on Norwegian society, he sees the high value placed on a scattered settlement of the population (*spredt bosetting* in political rhetoric) as being typically Norwegian. If we compare Norway with say, France or Sweden, this notion is confirmed. A roadmap of France would indicate that virtually all main roads lead to Paris. Frenchman have accustomed themselves to seeing the main seats of finance, politics and higher learning located in the capital. As regards Sweden, that country, like Norway, had a very scattered population at the turn of the century. From the inception of the modern Swedish welfare state in the years after the First World War, there was an increasing awareness that it would have been extremely expensive to offer the same rights and benefits to people in remote Norrland as to people in the Stockholm area. Many of the erstwhile inhabitants of Norrland – the northernmost third of the country – have later moved to newly erected housing estates in central areas. The Norwegian picture differs starkly. Although there have been advocates for a greater centralisation of power and people in this country as well, their influence has been limited. In Norwegian politics, it is a widespread notion that people should be able to live in the place where they grew up, if at all possible. Subsidies, generous tax deductions and other economic benefits have been channeled into *Utkant-Norge* ("Peripheral Norway") to ensure this; expensive bridges and tunnels connect small islands with the mainland, and Norwegian agriculture is, along with Japanese and Swiss agriculture, the most heavily subsidised in the world. Language is decentralised to the extent that every valley has its own, semi-officialised dialect in which at least some of the inhabitants take great pride. Educational facilities up to University level are available in every county, and there are not only many airports, but also regional hospitals, libraries, post offices and administrative offices of various kinds in a very large number of localities. In 1990, the national library was moved from Oslo to a place called Brønnøysund, which – it has been noted by critics – is a remarkable place for not being within commuting distance from a single town. Small is still beautiful in Norway. The cost of all this, some have argued, is an overall decrease of welfare in the country. Besides, they claim, the decentralisation has come to a point where there remains nothing to decentralise: in other words, that the central institutions and urban areas have been neglected. Such criticisms seem to have had little effect yet, and few politicians would dare to omit the "districts" or *Utkant-Norge*, in their campaign speeches.

The priority given to peripheral areas in political life confirms the image of Norwegian identity as an essentially rural identity. It is further confirmed in the *nisselue* stereotype.

The unsophisticated, but practically minded farmer

The *nisselue*, the red woollen hat worn (particularly around Christmas) by the gnomes (*nisser*) featured in local folklore, has in recent years become an ambiguous symbol of Norwegian nationhood. "Pulling the *nisselue* down one's ears" refers to isola-

The *nisselue*, a red woollen hat, is a symbol of Norwegian nationhood.

tionist tendencies in Norwegian society, often invoked against, for example. those who oppose EC membership. The *nisselue*, frequently worn by people on skis, is also a reminder of the intimate relationship between Norwegian identity and rural life, and thus seems to present the typical Norwegian as an unsophisticated and clumsy peasant unable to move gracefully about in a complex and modern environment. Some Norwegians have tried to turn aspects of the *nisselue* stereotype into a laudable description of themselves, and tend to regard themselves as a *practical* and *earthy* people. The anti-EC movement has actually used the *nisselue* as their symbol. During the German occupation in 1940-45, the *nisselue* was a symbol of resistance, and was actually prohibited by the Germans. A symbol of earthiness and simplicity, the *nisselue* simultaneously signals independence and self-sufficiency.

To wear designer-made Italian clothes, to own a sleek but
impractical luxury car, and to relish the bouquets of fine wines
and champagnes would be considered emphatically un-Norwe-
gian. Despite the country's rise to wealth, a certain frugality and
simplicity are still considered proper in this society. There are
heavy taxes on "luxury goods", and wine and liquor can still only
be purchased in state monopoly stores at exorbitant prices. In
some parts of the country, puritanist Protestant sects which rail
against moral decay of every conceivable kind, remain powerful.
In these rural areas, one can sometimes travel for days without
coming across a wine/spirits monopoly outlet, since the politicians of the communities refuse to have one lest their inhabitants
should run astray.

Self-definitions of a typical Norwegian "personality" would
usually depict that personality as formal and slightly stiff, but
sincere to the point of naiveté. In a bid to defend Norwegians
against accusations that they are cold and dispassionate, Eduardo
Archetti (1984) has called attention to the institution of the Norwegian party where, it is true, people tend to bring their own
wine, but where a certain *joie-de-vivre* and lack of formality are
for once apparent.

The brown cheese

In 1990, the hosts of *Nitimen*, the most popular daily radio programme, which features light music and assorted small talk,[5]
invited its listeners to elect that object or cultural trait which was
most Norwegian. The programme had earlier designated the national bird (*fossekallen*, that is the dipper) and the national fish
(the cod). This time, a very large number of responses elicited a
variety of proposed "national totems", and the list suggests how
ordinary Norwegians perceive themselves as being distinctive
from say, Swedes or Englishmen. Among the suggestions were
the cheese slicer (a Norwegian invention), the Hardanger fiddle,
the Selbu mitten, Constitution Day (17 May) and the folk song
"*Kjerringa med Staven*". The winner of the competition was,
however, the *brown cheese*. Sometimes misleadingly called goat
cheese (only a minority of brown cheeses are made exclusively
from goat's milk; the classic G45 is 50-50 goat's and cow's
milk), the brown cheese could almost certainly be regarded as a
genuine Norwegian contribution to world cuisine. Perhaps more
importantly, the brown cheese epitomises central values in a
widespread Norwegian self-definition: Being a dairy product, it

is associated with the rural life; its unspectacular taste signifies frugality and simplicity in style; its widespread use in the bagged lunches typical of Norwegian society further expresses a spirit of common sense and a "no-frills" attitude. – Or maybe this interpretation is wrong. Whatever the case may be, the brown cheese did get the most votes.

National Identity in a Changing World

Characterisations of "national character" – such as those discussed above – tend to be stereotypical, and can be grossly misleading. After all, there are enormous regional and individual variations in a large society such as a nation-state. When Norwegian intellectuals talk about "Norwegian culture", they frequently exclude themselves from its compass. A common expression in many quarters is this: "Bah! That's typically Norwegian!". Besides, the anthropological literature on ethnicity has shown that ideas of cultural traits distinguishing ethnic groups (or nations) from each other are often oversimplified or simply mistaken. The "cultural traits" mentioned as unique by a group are often vaguely described or even shared with its neighbours. Besides, the presumed continuity in time of an ethnic group or nation can in several senses be regarded as mythical. It is obvious that the content of Norwegian nationhood and "national character" changes as the world changes; being a Norwegian in 1992 means something different from what it meant in 1952. I shall now sketch some ways in which the public discourse on Norwegian national identity may also be said to change, and in which ways changes in the external world may influence domestic reflection on the topic.

The social importance of "imagined communities"

Ideological constructions of national identity and uniqueness, misleading as they may be, are important for two main reasons: First, such designations fix a social identity and protect its boundaries. If Norwegians were convinced, for example, that they were the only herring-eating people in the world, this would confirm and strengthen their national identity. The very idea of cultural uniqueness serves to strengthen the boundaries against the external world. Second, cultural definitions of national identities may eventually become self-fulfilling prophecies. If one is consistently taught that one's culture is egalitarian, decentralist and concerned with formal justice, one will eventually define oneself as egalitarian, etc. A typical example concerns the Norwegian language. A traveller going from Bergen to Stockholm at the turn of the century – before Norway's secession from Sweden – would pass through valleys and towns where different dialects were spoken. However, he would scarcely be able to tell where the Norwegian dialects ended and the Swedish ones began. In 1992, it would have been possible to draw such a dividing line, corresponding with the national border. A nationalist ideology monitored through the state, the mass media and civil society has led to an increasing degree of cultural homogenisation. It has thus been argued that Norway became an integrated nation in the l960s, when national TV was introduced and virtually everybody – from Hammerfest to Lindesnes – began watching the same TV news at the same time every day.

The nation, seen as a collectivity of people defining themselves as "a people", came into being *after* nationalist ideology. To some extent, it was created through the implementation of nationalist ideology in the central agencies of the state and civil society.

Deconstructing national myths

A public concern with defining national identity, which has been very important in Norwegian intellectual life throughout this century, implies its own negation. As some "nation-builders" create a certain image of the history or the national identity of a country, others will – if they are allowed to – take the opportunity to tear it down; deconstructing, criticising, indicating in which ways the stories of their past and present have been misleading and ideological in character, aimed at presenting a certain, political opportune view of the past.

In Norway, as in many other countries, historians and creative writers have been instrumental in this creation of nationhood during the past two hundred years or so. Critical voices have throughout added their versions of Norwegian history to those explicitly or implicitly exhorting the virtues of nation-building. The national myth of the heroic resistance of the Norwegian people during the Second World War, largely created by historians and others writing on the period, could serve as an example. Several historians have in more recent times filled in this picture with new facts and interpretations of the period (for two recent contributions, see Dahl, 1991; Sørensen, 1991). They have argued that Norwegian Nazis, many of whom died on the Eastern Front for their fatherland, may be regarded as devoted patriots. Parallels between certain aspects of Nazi politics and social democratic politics have been revealed. It has also been shown that although many Norwegians actively resisted the German occupation from 1940 to 1945, very many did not.[6] In order to understand the controversial character of such facts and re-interpretations of history, one must understand the role of the Second World War in the contemporary national self-consciousness. A very great number of books have been published on the war, and many of them depict Norwegian resistance as heroic. This resistance highlights sacred aspects of Norwegian nationhood: it shows the willingness of Norwegians to sacrifice their lives for their country, the importance of patriotism in times of hardship, and the divine destiny of the area, as it were, as an independent country. It is not surprising, therefore, that re-interpretations offering alternative perspectives on Norwegian achievements during the war, can be controversial.

Other central nationalist ideas have also been tampered with recently. The transition from the heroic age of Norwegian nationhood (notably the Viking age) to the "four-hundred years' night" under Danish rule has been re-written by historians lacking the nationalist bias formerly widespread, and it has become possible to argue that there was no "necessary" continuity between the medieval Norwegian state and that Norwegian nationstate which was created in 1814, and which gained full independence in 1905. This presumed continuity, evident in the name of the new king (Haakon VII) which suggests that modern Norway was really the same country as the medieval kingdom, must be regarded as an ideological construction, neither more nor less. The king himself was originally a Danish prince, and spoke Danish till the day of his death.

In his book on the doctrine of national self-determination, the political scientist Øyvind Østerud (1984) reminds his readers that many "typical" aspects of Norwegian culture were really quite recent imports from the European continent at the time when they were discovered and fashioned as national symbols by the early nationalists. This holds good for "traditional" Norwegian handicrafts, musical instruments and folk costumes. Most of the regional *bunads*, an important type of national costume, were invented at the beginning of the 20th century; the patterns were profoundly inspired by costumes in Continental Europe. (See

Johansen, 1991, for a spirited attack on Norwegian myths about themselves.)

The very idea of Norwegian culture and society as a "natural" and constant entity evolving according to its internal laws for over a thousand years, is about to become untenable. Norwegian culture and society have developed through crucial, if sometimes sporadic, contact with continental Europe, and the changes have been dramatic. It can be argued that contemporary Norwegians have less in common with the Wergelands of the 19th century (Wergeland was a famous Norwegian poet and nationalist) than with contemporary Germans or Dutchmen.

The "tradition" on which nationalism and national identity feeds has been deconstructed; the great tradition of nationhood is increasingly being fragmented into several lesser histories which point out the ambiguities involved in interpreting the past, and which reveal nationalist versions of history as conglomerates of fact, myth and contestable interpretations. This does not mean that the Norwegian nation does not exist, but it reminds us that it is a cultural invention – and a fairly recent one at that. Since Norwegian history can be reinterpreted, the content of Norwegian identity can be changed. This, some have argued, is called for in our day and age, marked by two strong tendencies which apparently run counter to some currently held conceptions of Norwegian nationality. These tendencies are the emergence of a poly-ethnic Norwegian society, and the globalisation of culture. I shall first look into the challenges from minority ethnicity.

Are the Sami Norwegians?

Their numbers are few, but they are highly visible. Approximately 100,000 non-European immigrants and refugees and 40,000 Sami comprise a small percentage of the country's population, but in recent years they have increasingly demanded formal equal rights and an acknowledged minority status. A continuous reminder that nationalist ideology does not conform perfectly with social reality, ethnic minorities constitute a thorn in the flesh of many governments. Norway is no exception, and problems arising from the presence of minorities go to the naked core of nationalism: What is the actual content of the national identity? Who should be included in the nation and who should be excluded from it? And what kinds of demands should be placed on inhabitants who are not members of the nation?

The Sami, that sub-Arctic ethnic group who were formerly

known as the Lapps, are Norway's oldest ethnic minority.[7] In all probability, they have lived in what is now Norway for at least as long as ethnic Norwegians. Until the late 1950s, Sami identity had been strongly stigmatised. Many Sami living in ethnically mixed areas chose to undercommunicate their ethnic origins – that is, they pretended they were not Sami; and many indeed became Norwegians in a matter of a few generations. From the early 1960s, but particularly since 1980, the country has seen the growth of a powerful *ethnic revitalisation movement* investing pride and dignity into the formerly despised Sami identity; they have taken conscious measures to glorify and re-codify half-forgotten Sami customs and traditions, while simultaneously making certain that they receive their share of the national welfare. This ethnopolitical movement has enjoyed considerable success. The Sami language, threatened by extinction as late as the 1960s, has been revived, and it is now the main administrative language in those parts of Finnmark county which are defined as Sami core areas. In 1989, a Sami parliament with limited but real power, *Sametinget*, was officially inaugurated by the late Norwegian king, Olav V.

Only a generation ago, many Sami were about to become assimilated into the Norwegian ethnic group, while others were politically passive, poor, culturally stigmatised and largely uneducated. Their success has proven that it is possible for a well-organised aboriginal minority to reinvent and indeed strengthen its identity in the face of fast social and cultural change, and that there need be no contradiction between modernisation and ethnic identity. Although many Norwegians of Sami ancestry still reject Sami identity, the number of citizens who define themselves as Sami has increased. Today, the self-conscious members of this minority present themselves as a culturally self-conscious group whose identity has survived the process of modernisation. Only a minority engage in the reindeer herding with which the group is associated (and associates itself in its ethnic symbolism), but many thousands – many of them residents of cities – insist on their right to be non-Norwegians in an ethnic sense, and yet to benefit from the same rights as other Norwegian citizens. Many others, it should be added, have an uncertain and ambiguous identity, sometimes oscillating between Sami and Norwegian ethnic self-identification.

Non-European immigrants and Norwegian identity

The Sami's achievement of political, cultural and linguistic rights within the Norwegian nation-state also indicates that there need not be serious conflict between an ethnic majority and a minority living in the same country. However, the avoidance of conflict seems to require that the minority be granted cultural self-determination in respects defined as important by its leaders. This can entail demands for religious and linguistic rights which may not be accepted by the nation-state, which proclaims – as a virtue – the essential cultural homogeneity of its inhabitants. Indeed, if we look at the more recent immigrants to Norway (see Long's contribution to this book), it becomes evident that the rights successfully claimed by the Sami are not automatically granted by a national majority. During the election campaign of 1991, leading politicians in Oslo suggested that immigrant children should be deprived of the right to be taught in their mother-tongue in primary schools, and strong political lobbies have for years fought against the erection of a mosque in the city, although Muslim organisations were willing to fund it themselves.

The overtly anti-immigrant groups, some of which are openly racist, are small and politically marginal in the country. But suspicion, fear and myths, especially targeting Muslim immigrants, abound. Many Norwegians exaggerate their numbers if asked; many believe that Muslim women have an average of ten children each, and so on. In general, the very presence of Muslims in the country is seen as a threat against Norwegian identity by some zealous patriots, who deprecate that "mix of cultures" presumedly entailed by migration, and who would prefer that Norwegian society conformed firmly to nationalist doctrine, namely, that it should only contain people "of the same kind".

Two books on multicultural Norwegian society written from an anthropological perspective (Eriksen, 1991; Brox, 1991) have argued the need for a more finely nuanced debate on multiculturalism than that which has been typical so far. The public debate of the 1980s and early 1990s has polarised the Norwegian population in camps either violently for or violently against immigration. (As a matter of fact, regular immigrants have not been allowed to enter the country since 1975.) Instead, both books argue, one should see the non-European presence in the country as an empirical fact, if not as an unproblematic one. Issues which demand critical scrutiny include cultural conflicts, power relations and the future content of Norwegian national identity. In the 1990s, it is possible for a person to identify himself simultaneously as a Sami and a Norwegian. It is so far much less common for a person to identify him or herself as a Pakistani-born

Muslim and simultaneously as a Norwegian, even if the person in question is a Norwegian citizen. The idea of Norwegianness, as it is produced and reproduced in public discourse, seems incompatible with Islam. Since the new minorities must be considered permanent ones, I have suggested (Eriksen, 1991) that Norwegians should rethink their national ideology in order that ethnic minorities may be included as legitimate and "natural" members of Norwegian society.

Perhaps the future will see an increasing polarisation between Norwegians and immigrants; perhaps many of them later will leave, or perhaps many will be assimilated; that is, they will give up their language and their religion and become some kind of ethnic Norwegians. It is also conceivable that the Asian, African and South American immigrants and refugees will succeed along the same lines as the Sami; that they will be able to assert their minority identity while simultaneously becoming integrated into Norwegian civil society. Perhaps the future will even see an alliance between Norwegian cultural patriots and Muslim immigrants – against the onslaught of American mass culture? The outcome of the current situation of culture contact is uncertain.

The relationship between *isolation* and *contact with others*, or introverted and extroverted tendencies, is highly ambiguous in Norwegian history. The relative isolation of the society, which among other things entailed the absence of a powerful landed gentry, has had substantial effects on its ideology, social organization and self-definition. On the other hand, Norwegians are also proud of their large merchant fleet (which, it is sometimes claimed, can be traced back to the Viking age), and during the past century, Norwegians have been a very extrovert people; they are well travelled, have sent many Protestant missionaries to Africa and Madagascar, and are among the strongest supporters of the United Nations. Through migration, Norwegian society has come closer to the rest of the world in a different way; it has been confronted *at home* with customs and beliefs radically different from the endemic ones. In another sense, too, Norwegian society is much less sheltered from the rest of the world than it used to be. This concerns what we may call the *globalisation of culture*; the spread, through modern media of mass communication, of symbols, images and messages which know of no national or cultural boundaries, and which are virtually identical all over the world.

The globalisation of culture in Norway

Ours is the era of the jet plane and the satellite dish. The world has shrunk and some of its internal boundaries are vanishing. You may buy clothing from Marlboro Classics in Nairobi; you may watch *Dynasty* in Indonesia, and you may listen to Prince's latest CD in your hotel room in Rio. Travels which took weeks only two generations ago now take less than a working-day.

The Norwegian periphery, *Utkant-Norge*, is scarcely that picturesque, slightly anachronistic kind of place which tourist brochures try to depict it as – where time has stood still for a century, where the fisherman still patiently mends his nets on the wooden pier and the farmer's working-day follows the sun, where rustic and simple folk still worship nature and their Protestant God as if NATO and the European Community had yet to be invented. Surely these images are not difficult to come by, if one tries hard enough. But the picture is more complex. The representation of "average Norwegians" created by Marianne Gullestad (1984), who interprets everyday life in a Bergen working-class suburb, is probably more representative than the rather exoticising depictions of say, Hans Magnus Enzensberger. The inhabitants of the outlying districts are as much consumers of videos, pop songs and colourful weekly magazines as they are geographically marginal. Former groceries have been replaced by large shopping malls or by combined video shops and snackbars. MTV waves and hamburger outlets are present all along the Norwegian coastline. The farmers of Gudbrandsdalen travel to the Canary islands in July, just like everyone else; about forty per cent (my estimate) of the northern fishermen whistle Bob Dylan songs as they wait for their catch. Kjartan Fløgstad, one of the country's most highly esteemed novelists, describes the country as *Media Thule* and its inhabitants as *mediatullingar* in his book *Det sjuande klima* ("The Seventh Climate", Fløgstad 1987) – a pun meaning, literally, "media idiots", which refers to the presumedly immense power of the mass media over the Norwegian population. Norway is today a country whose inhabitants probably eat more hamburgers than fish balls, where Jackie Collins's novels are more widely read than Bjørnson's peasant tales, where well over half of the population can make themselves understood in slightly broken American English. The country is a more strongly integrated part of the global ecumene than many Norwegians prefer to think, but to be fair, it is a *local* part with a distinctive local flavour in which Norwegians take great pride. The impact of the current globalisation of culture is visible even in remote parts of Norway, where local shops may have American names and everybody wears jeans although the climate suggests otherwise. These processes of cultural change cause a great deal of worry. Some Norwegians fear the erosion of their cultural distinctiveness; some lament the appearance of Anglicisms in the local dialect; some worry about the standard-ising and alienating effects of mass culture, American style. When the local coffeehouse is replaced by an outlet of McDon-ald's, it is certainly an occasion for intense nostalgia. A sociol-ogist who has studied the "Americanisation" of Norway, Steinar Bryn, has argued that massive change of this kind took place during the 1980s, and that these changes were largely unnoticed by Norwegians. According to Bryn, Norwegians try to seem cosmopolitan and non-provincial through adopting aspects of American lifestyle and American words. Among the more curi-ous examples he cites as evidence is a hamburger joint in some remote parish called "McNoreg" (*Noreg* is New Norwegian for Norway).[8]

Many of the inhabitants of Norway, it has occasionally been suggested, are lacking in self-confidence on behalf of those very aspects of Norwegianness which they relish. Norwegian resist-ance against membership in the European Community – a movement unique in Europe – is simultaneously an expression of such a fear, and an indication of a strong and enduring cultural self-consciousness. Which other European country would in the early 1990s prefer to stay outside of that safe haven of abundance and protection that the EC offers? With that picture of Norwe-gian identity which has been drawn in this chapter in mind, it may be possible to understand – at least in part – why so many Norwegians (possibly more than half) stubbornly insist on standing alone, self-reliant, with as few commitments as possible towards unpredictable European partners.

National identity and cultural change

In the face of technological change and the fact that formerly discrete societies have become intertwined, it may seem that it will be difficult to maintain the idea of Norwegian culture as an egalitarian, rural "no-frills" culture. Since processes of cultural homogenisation erase cultural differences, and since increased geographical mobility creates a mismatch between territories and "cultures", one might expect the distinctiveness to vanish gradually. In one sense, this is doubtless happening. Like virtually every other ethnic group in the world, Norwegians nowadays watch Sylvester Stallone and Madonna on MTV; the pizza has become a local staple;[9] an Oslo flat may be furnished and decorated in the same way as a flat in Milan or Berlin. In terms of consumption and lifestyle, there is less and less to distinguish Norwegians from any other Western European people. However, a main argument in this chapter has been that social identities are created imaginatively in a specific political context, and that they have no imperative relationship to "objective" culture.

If we look at Norwegian *identity* - the current self-definitions – we will therefore find a picture of a highly distinctive people, notwithstanding "objective" cultural changes. Indeed, it could be argued that modern ethnicity, seen as cultural self-consciousness, is a result of an ongoing process of cultural homogenisation. As a general rule, it is when the carriers of an identity feel that it is threatened from the outside that it becomes most important to them. So for the Norwegian farmer of the 1840s, there was no reason to stress his social identity. He could take it for granted; probably he did not even reflect about who he was. To people living in modern, complex societies, the situation is quite different. Their way of life is different from that of their forebears, and resembles that of the neighbouring peoples, but the feeling of a continuity with the past may still remain important. They are now constantly brought into contact with people whom they define as different (foreigners, immigrants, etc.), and are thus brought to reflect on their identity. They must be able to explain why they describe themselves as Norwegians and not as Swedes, Pakistanis, etc. Furthermore, the shrinking of the world entailed by globalisation seems to lay pressure on their identity as distinctive: the old and familiar is replaced by the new and foreign, and threatens to erase one's uniqueness. In this way, the pressure from cultural complexity and globalisation is at the root of the modern identity crisis where ethnic identities are often seen as a solution in the face of the disappearance of boundaries. As Anglicisms enter the language, new shopping malls with enormous car parks replace the old family-run groceries, and the video machine replaces the storytelling grandmother, the individual may react by reaching towards that which seems constant and secure in a sea of accelerating change. The outcome is often the resurgence of ethnic or national identities which may have lain dormant for a period, and which now assert themselves with newly found vitality as a form of defence against perceived cultural change originating from the outside.

As with the ideological creation of national and ethnic groups, this resurgence of ethnic or national identities has no clear relationship to "objective" cultural changes or "objective" threats. It is only if a certain situation is *perceived* as threatening to one's identity that it inspires revitalisation. For example, it could plausibly be argued that the Norwegian way of life was transformed dramatically in the post-war decades, following massive US influence in the political, economic and cultural spheres. These changes, which entailed the introduction of television, the nearly universal use of private cars and consumerist ideology, were seen as threatening to the Norwegian identity only by a minority – and so Norwegian culture was allowed to change without its identity being seriously challenged. People felt just as Norwegian after the introduction of the TV as they did before. Since the 1970s and 1980s, on the other hand, the presence of a few thousand Muslims in the country has been perceived by many Norwegians as threatening to their identity, and they have taken measures to end immigration. The Muslims in Norway wield insignificant political and economic power, and they do not have any control of national mass media. Their presence is nevertheless perceived as threatening to some segments of the Norwegian population, who have responded through an intense glorification of certain symbols of Norwegianness.

Coda: Whither Norwegian Identity?

It is beyond doubt that a Norwegian identity will continue to be imagined by the overwhelming majority of the population for the foreseeable future, whatever the country's relationship to the European Community will be. This means that people living in the country, and counting it as their ancestral land, will continue to regard themselves as distinctive from others – as *Norwegians*. It does not, however, mean that the *content* of such an identity will remain constant. Although Norwegians – like any self-defined people or ethnic group – tend to think that there is a strong continuity with the past, it is a fact that being Norwegian in the 1990s means something different from what it meant in the 1950s. But what will it look like as we approach the coming milliennium? We do not know. But we may hazard the guess that Norwegian identity will remain proudly Norwegian.

In a comparison between the history curricula of the school

systems of the five Nordic countries, the historian Stein Tønnesson (1991) found that the Norwegian curriculum is the most nationalist in character. Whereas the Danes stress the intimate relationship between their national history and that of Europe, and the Swedes underscore the importance of "Norden"[10] as a cultural unit; while the Finns and Icelanders promote general humanistic and intellectual values instead of glorifying their national identity, the Norwegian school curriculum is markedly nationalist (Tønnesson, 1991). It presents Scandinavian, European and global history from a Norwegian vantage-point, and focusses extensively on the process of Norwegian nation-building. Can such an attitude be viable at a time when "internationalisation" is the big catchword everywhere – in business as well as in politics and intellectual life? Maybe so, but it should also follow from the foregoing that it cannot be predicted which social identities will be the most relevant ones for Norwegians in the future.

Acknowledgements

An earlier version of this chapter has been read and commented fruitfully upon by Anne Hambro Alnæs, Kjetil Folkestad, Anne Cohen Kiel, Iver B Neumann and Stein Tønnesson.

Notes

1   This is a common characteristic of most nationalisms, see Gellner (1983).
2   Linguists may regard the four Scandinavian languages – Danish, Swedish, Standard Norwegian and New Norwegian – as closely related dialects of the same language. With some initial effort, a speaker of one of the dialects (or languages, as they are defined politically) can easily understand the others. Icelandic and Faroese are more distinctive, although they are closely related to the others. Sami ("Lappish") and Finnish belong to a different language family, the Finno-Ugric languages.
3   About 20% of the population use New Norwegian, but 25% of national radio and TV broadcasts are expected to be in that language. There are virtually no problems of mutual intelligibility.
4   Oslo tries desperately to be a big, bustling and cosmopolitan city, although it fails to convince foreigners that it is. With friends like this TV journalist, the city will manage quite well without enemies.
5   P1 at 9 o'clock daily. In the summer, the same programme is called *Reiseradioen* ("The pocket radio"), alluding to Norwegian holiday habits whereby many people stay at some remote cottage or campsite.
6   An undercommunicated fact of recent Norwegian history consists in the healthy and vigorous relationship between Norwegian and German intellectual life, which was abruptly cut off after the Second World War. In the 1990s, few Norwegians are fluent in German.
7   There are also Sami in northern Finland and Sweden, as well as on the Russian Kola peninsula. The largest community is the Norwegian one.

8 In Lars Aarønæs's language column in the weekly newspaper *Dag og Tid*, inept Norwegians who try to give a cosmopolitan impression abound. One representative example is The Italian Pizza Company, which is located at Sinsen, North Oslo. – And of course, Norwegians, like many other peoples, are liable to call each other "provincial" when they disapprove of something.

9 See Lien (1988) for a highly readable study of changes in the culinary habits of rural Norwegians. The title of her work speaks for itself. It is called "From *boknafesk* to pizza"; *boknafesk* is a kind of dried and salted cod endemic to northern Norway.

10 *Norden* refers to the three Scandinavian countries as well as Finland, Iceland, the Faroe Islands, and sometimes Greenland. Since Finland has been a Swedish province and contains a Swedish-speaking minority, Norden is more important than Scandinavia to most Swedes. See Neumann (1991) for a comprehensive discussion of the idea of "Norden".

References

Andersen, Bent Rold. "Rationality and Irrationality of the Nordic Welfare State", *Daedalus*, vol. 113, no. 1 (Spring 1984). pp. 109-140.

Anderson, Benedict. *Imagined Communities*. London, 1983.

Archetti, Eduardo. "Om maktens ideologi – en krysskulturell analyse", in Arne Martin Klausen, (ed.), *Den norske væremåten*, pp. 45-60. Oslo, 1984.

Brox, Ottar. *"Jeg er ikke rasist, men..."*. Oslo, 1991.

Dahl, Hans Fredrik. "Those Equal Folk". *Daedalus*, vol. 113, no. 1. (1984): 93-108.

Dahl, Hans Fredrik. *Vidkun Quisling. En fører blir til.* Oslo, 1991.

Deichman-Sørensen. "Norge – en saga blott?" *Nyt Nordisk Forum*, no. 52, (1988): 22-33.

Enzensberger, Hans Magnus. *Norsk utakt*. Oslo, 1984.

Eriksen, Thomas Hylland. *Veien til et mer eksotisk Norge*. Oslo, 1991.

Fløgstad, Kjartan. *Det sjuande klima*. Oslo, 1987.

Gellner, Ernest. *Nations and Nationalism*. Oxford, 1987.

Gullestad, Marianne. *Kitchen-Table Society*. Oslo, 1984.

Haugan, Jørgen. *400-årsnatten. Norsk selvforståelse ved en korsvei.* Oslo, 1981.

Johansen, Anders. Sjelen som forretningsidé. *Nytt Norsk Tidsskrift*, no. 2, 1991.

Larsen, Tord. "Bønder i byen – på jakt etter den norske konfigurasjonen", in Arne Martin Klausen, (ed.), *Den norske væremåten*, pp. 15-34. Oslo, 1984.

Lévi-Strauss, Claude. *La pensée sauvage*. Paris, 1962.

Lien, Marianne. *Fra boknafisk til pizza*. Oslo: Occasional Papers in Social Anthropology, 18 (1988).

Neumann, Iver B. "Norden og den nye europeiske orden: Kulturfellesskap, oppdemning for stormaktspolitikk, regionsbygging". Forthcoming.

Østerud, Øyvind. *Nasjonenes selvbestemmelsesrett*, Oslo, 1984.

Sandemose, Aksel. 1953 [1933, 1937]. *En flyktning krysser sitt spor*. 1933. Reprint Oslo, 1953.

Sørensen, Øystein. *Solkors og solidaritet*. Oslo, 1991.

Tønnesson, Stein. "History and National Identity in Scandinavia: The Contemporary Debate". Trial lecture for the Dr. Philos. degree, University of Oslo, 25 October, 1991.

Witoszek, Nina. "Der Kultur møter Natur: Tilfellet Norge". *Samtiden*, no. 4, (1991): 119.

2

A National Identity in Person: The Making of a Modern Norwegian

Brit Berggreen

"A Social Democracy in a National Costume"

Two lines run through the modern history of Norway: the homespun, valley-bound and introspective, and the outward looking, which pursues a connection and a cultural relationship with the wider outside world. The balancing of these two trends and the confrontations between them, belong to the cultural lay-out of the country and its people. It split Norway into two equal parts in the 1972 referendum on whether or not to enter the European Common Market (EEC), the issue is current in the ongoing discussions on how to present Norway in the cultural program of the 1994 Winter Olympic games, and its omnipres-ence is felt as Norway once more faces the common market. The issue belongs to the history of modernization and may be traced back to the early 18th century. Then men, like the scholar and author Ludvig Holberg (1684–1754), were eager to maintain the importance of natural science, on behalf of the study of Latin and the classics. This was a time when Latin was the common lan-guage of the educated classes all over the western world.

It is common these days to talk about "culture building" and of nations as "imagined communities", or of the "construction of cultural heritages", and of the selective process of making a proper past for future use.[1] The popular belief that nations or cultures are natural entities is often dispelled through the study of how nations are shaped, and how a common history and heritage is created through hard work and power struggles. Even the creation of new personality types for the new nations belongs to the modern European experience. New ideals were introduced, sometimes hard to identify with, as "at the rebirth of Greece, the inhabitants were suddenly...taken in hand by rulers and hellen-izing poets and scholars...of the West, and introduced to a whole museum-load of forgotten marble relations" (Fermor 1983:104), or when, "at the end of the 19th century, the code of Hungarian norms of behaviour, and indeed the real aesthetic of the Hungarian character was born".[2] The Danish-Norwegian state was likewise concerned with the personality building of her citizens during the 1700s. Elements of this effect may be recognized through the nation building process of Norway after the union with Denmark was dissolved in 1814. How this was accomplished in Norway, and how a personality type was designed for this new nation state will be the topic of this presentation.

Norway has been called a social democracy in a national costume.[3] Thinking along the lines of Europeanness and Norwegianness, this is an indication of the victory of the latter: The archetypical Norwegian is rural, and the typical Norwegian accepts this national image. Even if the majority of Norwegians were spending their Sundays in front of the TV and their summer holidays in Spain or Greece, there is a feeling that they "ought" to be hiking in the forests or skiing in the valleys and mountain plateaus. Most Norwegians have a "*hytte*", a cabin where they can live out their longing for the great outdoors, or they have access to one. This could be seen as a sign of successful national image building, for the majority of Norwegians were not mountain hunters, herdsmen or even farmers when the national type found its shape.

Ironically, during the 1800s when the national rural image was being created, Norway's international involvements and achievements were already conspicuous through shipping, timber and fishing export. Rich and prominent foreigners came to Norway, however, to enjoy the mountainous scenery and to follow the valleys in search of "the national". The "national" meant the costumes and architecture and culinary ways of the peasants before "culture" had overtaken them. While these customs and artifacts were seen as old-fashioned and on the decline, an infatuation with the folklore made a selection of them fashionable through a renewed interest in peasant culture among the urbanizing and well-to-do classes. The interest of the trend-setters strengthened and encouraged the revival and re-invention of the peasant culture which may be seen all over Norway.

When elements of a past have been integrated into the proud history of a people, there must be a stirring of souls and sentiments creating a sense of sacred inviolability towards national symbols.

This may explain the strong reactions against the way textile designer and artist Ellinor Flor used elements from traditional rose painting and knitted patterns when she created her distinc-

tive modernistic textiles. It is as if blending the Norwegian valleys into New York high fashion or Parisian *haute couture* is to
desecrate the former. How did the Norwegians come to think of
their old peasant culture as being so inviolable?

A School Design and a Reader for the People

In cultural history 150 years is a short time span, a mere five
generations of people. The oldest of those living today have
known people who were born in the 1830s. The grandparents of
my generation, who were school children some hundred years
ago, might marvel at the reader their grandchildren used in elementary school with all the colours and pictures. Then they
would compare it with their own reader which might well have
been the renowned P.A. Jensen's Reader *(Jensens lesebok)* of
1863. But would there really be great differences in attitude and
contents? Earlier readers had been rooted in the 17th century
enlightenment tradition of "anonymous international moral and
informative literature for children".[4] They had been readers for
the educated classes. The 1863 reader was decreed by Parliament
and had a modern and "national" stamp, pioneering in breaking
away from the cultural bonds with Denmark which remained
strong long after Norway had entered the new union with Sweden in 1814. The new reader was for "the folk school and the folk
home" as well, this being a time when the educated elite was
neither national nor folk, whereas the peasantry was both.

We may see the new school system and the reader of the 1860s
as a building block for Norwegianness.[5] Jensen's reader was the
first Norwegian school book designed and publicly authorized to
introduce children from all regions and social classes to the same
literary texts of fiction, geography, history, religion and the sciences. In that sense it was democratic and egalitarian. It also
served as an introduction to contemporary Norwegian literature,
history and folklore. In that sense it was national, and a line
which later was to be continued. Sletvold has studied the history
of Norwegian schools for many years. He has stressed that "the
national line" introduced by Jensen is as marked as the pedagogical, and his concluding words are that the reader was and is
"a book about Norway".[6] Jensen's reader went together with the
revised and new comprehensive school system whose architect
was Hartvig Nissen (1815–74).[7]

Christopher Bruun (1839–1920), influential in the building of a Norwegian national identity. He was, however, a target for caricatures and ridiculing malice.

The Ideals of the Folk High School

Grundtvigianism has its name from the Danish theologian N.F.S. Grundtvig (1783-1872) who preached a "cheerful, popular and down to earth" protestantism where "the congregation and the people, the Christian and the national belong together." (Bull IV, 1:19) . In Denmark the so-called Folk High Schools, built on Grundvig's ideals, became important vehicles for the identity and culture building of the peasantry. In Norway their history became somewhat different. The schools did not gain the same kind of popularity in Norway, but the ideals they were built upon at an earlier stage were assimilated into the public school system.[8]

One name frequently mentioned in connection with Grundtvi-gianism is Christopher Bruun (1839-1920). His teachings were influential in building a Norwegian national identity for future generations. His series of lectures in 1879, called "Folkelige grundtanker" (Fundamental folk thoughts), are a manifesto for Norwegianness and high morale for the individuals. His lectures appeared in print in 1870, the last edition was published in 1920.

A close look at P. A. Jensen and Christopher Bruun may be sufficient to understand some of the premises for the develop-ment of a national character for modernizing Norway. Through the school ideology of equality, with the reader to go, and the ideals and world view suggested by Christopher Bruun, one can follow the tracks of what may be called the construction of a Norwegian.

Through Bruun, the track is pedagogically simple to follow. His vision of the Norwegian in the setting of their Fatherland is thoroughly described.

Norwegianness as a Cultural Construction

Strong national sentiments and enthusiasm for Norway were in the very marrow of Christopher Bruun's bones. His message was clear and simple: Norway is Best. He was a typical middle class man with a Latin school education and a peasant romantic out-look. He also had a strong belief in the peasantry for the building of Norway. His peasant romantic world view was used as a platform for what became the political party under Johan Sver-drup (*Venstre* "Left"), and was later the prescription for the "Norwegianness movement" (*norskdomsrørsla*). This developed as a reaction to the "magistrate culture" (*embetsmannskulturen*) and was used as a defence against the strong influences from abroad.[9]

Bruun became well-known as a language reformer, as an ad-herent of the New Norwegian language .[10] He was the leading figure within the association of peasant youth (*Noregs Bonde-ungdomslag*) in Kristiania (Oslo). His whole life was devoted to his ideals, and he felt as if he constantly was opposed by the educated, "the obstinacy" of politicians and "the tenacity" of the peasants. He was an easy target for caricatures and ridiculing malice. But when one sees him as Brand, the protagonist of Henrik Ibsen's drama (Ibsen allegedly used him as the model), there is nothing ridiculous about him. There is, however, much that frightens.

One might easily be led to believe that Bruun fought in vain
against an overwhelmingly superior force, as Bruun himself felt.
But he had been in step with contemporary thought and by the
end of his life, his views had penetrated influential men and
women in the country. His thoughts are easily recognizable as a
dominant ideology for Norwegianness and Norwegians which
has continued beyond the mid-20th century.

Bruun, a great rhetorician makes frequent use of dichotomies
to discuss and evaluate the Old Norse vs. the Classics, the Germanic vs. the Roman, the Educated vs. the Popular, the Heathen
vs. the Christian, the Female vs. the Male, etc. He lists hierarchies of merits and shortcomings – always to the advantage of his
domestic culture. A resumé of Bruun's cultural message should
stress the importance he puts on men and heroism. He addresses
young men, especially from the peasantry, the original pupils at
his folk high school.

He wanted them to "live poetry" and meet "the eagle of enthusiasm". For generations, young people had learnt to admire
the Graeco-Roman world of gods and heroes, and its literature.
But why should not the idols of their own stock have value? If
these idols were heathen, so were the Greek and Roman gods and
heroes. The young men of "Wotan's kin" should be brought to
"the sacred realm of Saga" and then be led through fairy tales and
folk songs, but above all through The Elder Edda (*Den eldre
Edda*). They should acquaint themselves with their legacy from
glorious heathen times where Sigurd, the dragon killer, and Olav
Tryggvason, the athletic king, were among the heroes.

Bruun aimed for a synthesis of the national heritage of the
peasantry and the cultivated educated elite, who had their cultural orientation towards the Graeco-Roman world of their
schooling. To become integral parts of the Norwegian national
culture, the educated classes must borrow the folkways and lore
from the peasantry as a basis for their education. A non-national
class could not create a really independent intellect. It was the
popular genius which must lay the foundation for future generations. Not only the Norwegian, but the whole Germanic tribe
could find itself, "know itself", through the old Norse writing.
"And it is not this Germanic tribe which is foremost of human-
kind", wrote Bruun, before ranking the countries of the world:
The Nordic countries come first, then Germany, Holland, England and North America. France is entered on his list with some
reservations, but "France is the land of the Franks, and the Franks
are Germanic by blood." Italy and Spain are clearly Latin/Roman

peoples, and without the influx of Germanic blood which they acquired during the Germanic migrations, they would hardly have "risen above the limpness they had fallen into at the end of antiquity, nor would they have had the strength to contribute to world history."

Bruun wanted men to be physically strong. Contemporary European civilization had had a tendency to look down on physical work for men who wished to pass as gentlemen. Thus, father and son, generation after generation, had "this frail, loosely built body", and "these thin, loose, weak muscles which we know all too well." This was against God's intention, for He did not want Man to be like this when He set him to govern over His creation: "It befits a man to endure a rain shower without immediately beginning to think of catching a cold." Bruun prescribes physical work and fresh air, and nothing is more likely to promote an understanding between "the educated and the uneducated."

Bruun praises Norway because "she has succeeded best in the world in killing the soil for the growth of Latin". His opinion is that even on a global basis, Latin is a totally useless language, except perhaps for the Italians. The new Europeans are well served through their modern languages, and the Latin schools, where the educated sent their sons, stand like a rootless tree, "without the right to exist, without the ability to survive". He criticizes the Catholic Church, the popes and the Catholic bishops who suppressed indigenous languages and made them fade away, "Latin put its foot on their necks." With a few exceptions, only in Iceland and Norway, work on popular literature persevered in the native languages.

The conclusion that follows is that Latin has caused great damage to Europe, especially within the Germanic tribes. The reason for "the darkness of the Middle Ages" was not, as has often been contended, "the raw and wild life of the Teutonic tribes". Great injustice has been made towards these "youthful peoples" in written history. This has been caused by the disdain of the arrogant Romans for everything that was not made by them (this is the cause of their judgement). The Teutons have here as elsewhere, innocently echoed them. In reality it was the Latin language which caused the crippling of other languages when it was allowed to take over the folk life. He admits, in a short reflective pause in his otherwise massive attack on the Papal church and the Latin language, a certain admiration for the heroes of ancient Rome, "I shall never cease loving those consuls, who dedicated themselves to die for their people."

When discussing girls' schools, there was no Latin teaching to attack. There, modern foreign languages, English, German and French were taught, which was as bad as teaching Latin: "Norway is a nation admiring the foreign", Bruun complained. Old Norse must substitute Latin (and the foreign languages). Indeed, the Norwegians have a sacred calling to read Old Norse instead of Latin. But the country's own language must also advance. The peasant language of the people must be elevated so that it can enter into the tongue of the educated Norwegian. Latin is the main barrier for a synthesis of the peasants' ways and the educated's culture. Not until the educated classes abandon their desire to speak in Latin phrases can the two classes meet on equal grounds. Latin is also a barrier between women and men. If only educated men would rid themselves of their Latin, women would be able to understand and assist them. As soon as Woman is brought up to understand Man, he will find her supportive of his Grand Deeds. Both sexes can be roused and inspired through knowledge of the old Teutonic and Norse heroes, but Bruun warned against women trying to become like men. They would make poor men. Women's task was to understand men, not to be men. Whenever he fights to save his fatherland, she will sacrifice both her own and her children's welfare for his sake. The division between woman and man can thus be erased through the removal of Latin and the whole foundation of higher education. Man shall meet woman as "brother meets sister" . A strong arm and a strong thought are the man's contributions to the woman. In return, the man receives the woman's understanding and companionship. The woman has the quality, according to Bruun, that when men begin to speak a language she can understand, she can disclose "thoughts which would rather be dressed in foreign words", and "lifeless, abstract descriptions".

Bruun's argument then was, above all, that Latin must be abolished, that Old Norse must be the substitute, and that the Norwegian language must be strengthened. The "new society", based on a mutual understanding between the male (and masculine) peasants and the more effeminate educated classes, is to have heartfelt Christianity as its framework and superstructure.

The (New) Norwegian Individual

Bruun's ideas had many supporters. Among them was the author Alexander Kielland who, through his novel *Gift* (Poison) from

1883, delivered a literary stab against the Latin school system. The confidence in women's ability to disclose any unstable figments of imagination in men is also mirrored through the character of Mrs. Wenche. She is "a Bruunian" and reads Snorri juxtaposed to her unsympathetic husband, "the Latinist". The female characters of Henrik Ibsen's plays are often characterized as well by "their feet firmly rooted in a reality that would far too easily slide away from the feet of the thinking man", as Bruun himself put it.

Bruun's cultural script is not connected with any particular occupation or profession or region, but may fit in anywhere. His background is urban, and the culture and personality type he designed might just as well be acted out in the towns as in the countryside. He is actually the great reconciler between social groups, urban and rural, and between women and men, and he harmonizes oppositions through compromise where he suggests a union between the educated class and the peasantry. His suggested platform for national development and well-being is the Nordic renaissance where the nation is to be built on a "homespun" and rural cultural heritage. He foresaw a rebirth in "the spirit of the fathers", and it was necessary to build the future on the peasants because, "so much of this remarkable inheritance got lost" in the towns.

How can one assess Bruun's influence? For one, there was the association of youths in the countryside where close to 500 assembly houses (ungdomshus), were erected from the 1870s onwards as "temples" for the promotion of Bruun's "Norwegianness" program. In addition, a cult developed around the polar explorer, sportsman and humanist, Fridtjof Nansen. The so-called Lysaker-circle gathered to keep up a state of preparedness for the fatherland. It all pointed towards 1905 and the dissolution of the union with Sweden.

The New Norwegian as The Norwegian.

In a description of the 1890s we may read how the Norwegians felt about themselves and the world outside. Every schoolboy and girl knew that the world outside was in progress, with Norway being in the front line. Even if this was similar to what every schoolchild in other countries learnt about their countries, it may be that Emil Smith (1936) was right in declaring Norway as unique in that almost the whole population shared the conviction that Norway was a forerunner. Many foreigners allegedly said

Fritjof Nansen posing in the artist Erik Werenskiold's study.

the same, "at least to us", Smith adds with some temperance.
What did the Norwegians have to make them so proud? They had
some names that loomed large: "The four great" (authors), Henrik Ibsen being among them. There was the composer Edvard
Grieg, there were the painters, and there was the internationally
renowned philologist, Sophus Bugge. In addition, there were the
archeological discoveries of the Gokstad Viking ship. In connection with this, there was the voyage made across the Atlantic
ocean in 1893 with a replica called "Viking" to demonstrate for
the world that Leiv Eriksson was the first European in the Amer-

The artist Erik Werenskiold used Fritjof Nansen as a model for the Viking king Olav Tryggvason in his illustrations for Snorre Sturlason's *Kongesagaer* (Sagas of the Kings).

icas. In the same year Fridtjof Nansen, after he had crossed the icecap of Greenland on skis, set out to reach the North pole on the arctic vessel "Fram". These are seen as proud achievements, even when measured by outside standards. Rather more doubtful is the praise Norwegians gave themselves on behalf of standards set by themselves: Norway had the best public school system (they said) and no illiteracy. There was no nobility and Latin was on its way out of the schools. The Norwegians were the true descendants of the Vikings, though now they were peace-loving. They thought themselves far from being snobs, but as straight-forward and easygoing. They were peasants but free, independent, proud and of pure breed (*ren rase*). The country was poor, but the most beautiful in the world and visited by prominent foreigners each year. Norway had the best agriculture, the climate considered, the highest civilization, latitude considered, and the largest merchant fleet, the population considered. The archetypal Norwegian was Fridtjof Nansen, almost a blueprint of the great viking hero King Olav Tryggvason, and used as a model for the king in the illustrated edition of Snorri.

After the passing of another generation, we meet The Norwegian again, reconstructed by Aslaug Nyrnes on the basis of the 1927 volume of the popular magazine, "*For By og Bygd*" ("For Town and Country"). This (New)Norwegian individual, as she calls him or her (det nynorske mennesket), adheres to the New-Norwegian language (*Nynorsk*), the alternative to the Danish-Norwegian which today has become bokmål.

The landscape of the (New)Norwegians is mountainous, grand and blooming, and surrounds an aristocratic peasant way of life. Rauland in Telemark serves as one ideal setting, but perhaps Våga in Gudbrandsdalen is even more The Norwegian Settlement. The city is synonymous with wretchedness (*styggedom*), and serves only to create a longing for a place far north, severe and cold and naked, fresh and windy, mountain valleys, mountain people. Even if Vestfold, near the Oslofjord, with its antique relics and sites from the Viking age, loomed large, the (New)Norwegian belonged to the mountains and valleys. In such surroundings they would devote themselves to activities beginning with "folk" or "popular" (-dance, -drama, -writing, and -language). Almost everything coming from the outside was seen as suspect and destructive.[12]

What is Going to Happen Now?

One should be careful not to be misled by Norway's doting on the domestic into believing that Norwegians have been isolated and introvert. On the contrary, through shipping, trade and emigration, Norway has had a cosmopolitan and outward-looking population. Maritime transportation was almost always easy and it carried Norwegians all over the world to settle, to write home, to return home and to receive kin and protégés abroad.

The traditional cultural orientation of Norway has been diverse. Through shipping and timber trade, Norway had strong connections with England and Holland. Through fish export she had ties with the Catholic countries in the south of Europe. Norwegian craftsmen belonged to the mainland European system of guilds (a period of wandering was a compulsory part of a craftsman's education until the late 1800s). Popular contacts were made across the Atlantic after mass emigration to America between 1860-1920. The educated classes had their ties with

German culture, a heritage from the union with Denmark. When the relationship with the Teutons and the references to the Germanic runs through Christopher Bruun's lecture, it was not only a "blood" relationship. Indeed German was the first foreign language of educated Norwegians until the 1950s, when attention was directed towards the Anglo-American language and culture.

In spite of this, or maybe because of this, there has been a long introverted tradition in Norway, supported by pride in the Germanic tribe and Norse accomplishments, and made into a whole instruction program on how to be and act as a good Norwegian. This program has undergone changes, but they have been gradual and organic. Strange as it may seem, the line of isolation and introversion has been strengthened through the modernization of the school system during the late decades. Nils Morten Udgaard (1992) writes along these lines in a forceful attack on the isolationistic line in Norwegian cultural orientation. He also reminds his readers that long cultural historical lines have once again become fields of fire: "While political activity has fallen into discredit and the military tensions are softened, traditions of culture and identity must become heavier". For many reasons there have been few thorough discussions on cultural orientation and cultural roots in Norway. They are bound to come, for in the whole of Europe there are now ongoing national culture building projects, and both Norway and other Nordic countries are discussing national identity issues again.[13]

The stigmatization of everything Germanic is a problem and blocks any debate. It may feel slightly sickening today to read Christopher Bruun in the light of later fascism. Any expression associated with the Germanic "tribe" has been muted, who can stand being a Germanic after Hitler's rule? The stigma that the Nazis put on whatever part of Germanic history they chose to cherish, and whatever symbols they chose for their flags and ensigns are tabooed. For many reasons, Norway has stuck to the self-image of the independent and innocent individual, almost grown out of Norwegian soil, rain and fresh air, with a national culture where nothing was inherited from "others". Maybe this is a strategy unconsciously applied to avoid the sensitive connections with the Teutons and the Germanic.

The Germanic stigma is not a problem for Norway alone. Germany has her own problems with Germanism, cultural legacy and identity. The new states of Europe are seeking the cultural roots of their new identities after the breakdown of communism. And Western Europe has begun to redefine its Europeanism:

The cradle of Europe has since the renaissance supposedly stood in Greece and Rome. Lately, within the EC, another source has begun to be stressed, the Celtic. The Celtic has in its turn a certain tendency to float along with the Germanic. A Continental and Northern Europe is seen as an alternative to the Byzantine and Latin-Mediterranean Europe as the origin of the European cultural heritage, and as the basis for creating new political and cultural identities today. [14]

Kristian Gerner (1992) who is quoted above refers to the intriguing observations of European mythology being changed from a Graeco-Latin to a Celtic-Germanic. Being outside the EC, Norway has not yet been integrated in this very captivating game of roots and origins and cultural heritage, except in asking again and again: What is typically Norwegian?

Notes

1 The literature on this topic is vast and demonstrates the similiarities in processes and strategies of creating nation states. (Gellner 1983, Anderson 1983 & Smith 1986.) Both monographs and general works give support to the notion of a "do it yourself kit" for nation builders, described in Löfgren 1989, Niedermüller 1989, Hofer 1991.
2 Péter Hanák, 1988, quoted from Niedermüller 1989:49f.
3 Lønnroth 1984.
4 Sletvold 1971:101.
5 Such processes are well known. Previously, Denmark had tried to create a barrier against Germany, whereas Norway in its turn demonstrated Norwegianness towards Denmark and Sweden. (Both Bulgaria and Greece have Turkey as their antagonist in culture building.)
6 Sletvold (1971:265) borrows these words from the editor of the dominant Norwegian reader from the 1890s to the 1950s, Nordal Rolfsen.
7 He was much influenced by the theologian and school reformer Johan Amos Comenius (1592–1670) who had decreed that there ought to be common schools for boys and girls of all social classes. The children should specialize later, when their abilities and interests became obvious, around the age of 10.
8 I would like to stress, however, the inspiration of Grundtvigianism on Hartvig Nissen, on P.A. Jensen (even if he refused to be called a "Grundtvigian"), and on other great popular educators as Eilert Sundt and Ole Vig. Eilert Sundt (1817–1875) is best known today through his studies of demographic and cultural aspects of Norwegian folk life during the 1860s and 70s. In the 1850s, Ole Vig made the blueprint which P.A. Jensen was to follow when he developed his reader. (Sletvold 1971:265)
9 Storaas 1985.
10 But, surprisingly, he went against the dissolution of the union with Sweden in 1905, and described his view in a pamphlet which was printed in Copenhagen, as no one in Norway would print it.
11 This catalogue of references may need a short explanation.

12 This may actually well be seen along the line of self-sufficiency that was advocated and encouraged by the Royal Society for the Welfare of Norway, established in 1809. Among its ambitions was also to encourage "homespun-ness", and prizes were awarded to young brides, who were wholly dressed in home-made attires, and to others who had distinguished themselves along the same line.

13 For example Löfgren (ed.) 1989, Linde Laursen & Nilsson (eds.) 1991, Feldbæk 1991, Hastrup 1992.

14 Gerner has references both to the grand Celtic historical exhibition in Venice 1991, and to the history textbook for EEC countries. He discusses the substituting of the Celts for the ancient Greeks as the cultural aborigines of Europe. This particular textbook has created much stir in Greece, and protests have been delivered to the EEC commission.

References

Anderson, Benedict. *Imagined communities: Reflections on the origin and spread of nationalism.* London, 1983.

Berggreen, Brit. *Da Kulturen kom til Norge.* Oslo, 1989.

Berggreen, Brit. "Kvinner selv ...": Kvinners nasjonalerfaring. In: Linde Laursen & Nilsen (eds.), 1991.

Bruun, Christopher. *Folkelige grundtanker.* 1878. Reprint. Bergen, 1920.

Bull, Francis. Norges litteratur fra februarrevolusjonen til første verdenskrig. *Norsk litteraturhistorie IV.* Oslo, 1960.

Christiansen, Palle Ove. "Peasant adaptation to bourgeois culture?" *Ethnologia Scandinavica* (1978): 98–152.

Feldbæk, Ole, (ed.) *Dansk identittetshistorie 1-2.* København, 1991.

Fermor, Patrick Leigh. *Roumeli: Travels in Northern Greece.* 1966. Reprint. London, 1983.

Frykman, Jonas. "Social mobility and national character." *Ethnologia Europaea* 19 (1989):33–46.

Gellner, Ernest. *Nations and Nationalism.* Oxford, 1983.

Gerner, Kristian. Nygamla identiteter i Centraleuropa. *Tvärsnitt 4 (1991), 12–23.*

Graubard, Stephen R., (ed.). *Norden – The Passion for Equality.* Oslo, 1986.

Hastrup, Kirsten, (ed.). *Den nordiske verden I–II.* København, 1992.

Herzfeld, Michael. *Ours Once More: Folklore, Ideology and the Making of Modern Greece.* New York, 1986.

Herzfeld, Michael. "Within and without: The category of 'female' in the etnography of modern Greece." *Gender and power in rural Greece,* edited by Jill Dubish, 1986.

Hofer, Tàmas. Construction of the 'Folk Cultural Heritage' in Hungary and rival versions of national identity. *Ethnologia Europaea* 21, 2 (1991):145–180.

Laursen, Anders Linde & Jan Olof Nilsson, (eds.). *Nationella identiteter i Norden – ett fullbordad projekt?* With summary in English. Nordisk Råd.

Löfgren, Orvar. The nationalization of culture." *Ethnologia Europaea* 19, 1 (1989): 5–24.

Lönnroth, Lars. "The intellectual civil servant". In Graubard (ed.). *Norden – The Passion for Equality,* Oslo, 1986.

Niedermüller, Peter. "National culture: Symbols and reality." *Ethnologia -Europaea* 19, 1 (1989): 47–56.

Nyrnes, Aslaug. *Det Ny(norske) mennesket. En litterær analyse av familiebladet For By og Bygd.* Oslo, 1985.

Sletvold, Sverre. *Norske lesebøker 1777–1969.* Trondheim, 1987.

Smith, Anthony D. *The Ethnic Origins of Nations.* Oxford, 1986.
Smith, Emil. *Disse fjerne år: Tids- og miljøskildringer fra Norge i tiden omkring århundreskiftet og frem til verdenskrigen.* Oslo, 1936.
Storaas, Randi. *Å velja fortid – å skapa framtid.* Bergen, 1985.
Udgaard, Nils Morten. "Norge på vei bort fra Europa." *Aftenposten* 18. januar 1992.
Weber, Eugen. *Peasants into Frenchmen: The modernization of Rural France.* Stanford, 1976.

3

Confessions of an Angry Commuter: Or Learning How to Communicate the Non-Communicating Way

Anne Cohen Kiel

Upon arriving in Norway, I was anxious to try out the Norwegian repertoire I had acquired in my crash course, which included the greeting *"God dag"*. I had unpacked my bags at the student village and proceeded to take the train to the University campus. It was a beautiful summer day as I stood alone on the station platform. An elderly lady arrived and I smiled at her, nodded and produced a *"God dag"*. Startled, the woman took a step in my direction, looked me over from top to toe and replied, *"Jeg kjenner Dem ikke"* (I don't know you), and then she turned away. At that point, I knew I had broken some hidden code, but I had no idea as to what it was. It would take me a number of years to find a suitable answer.

Theoretical Perspectives on Cross Cultural Communication

Communication is broadly defined as the exchange of ideas or knowledge by some form of transaction, verbal and/or non-verbal. The purpose of communication is to convey meaning or a message. If communication is to succeed to the extent where one reaches an understanding, a common code or a common experience is presumed (Dahl/Haberg:1986). This common code can be seen in terms of patterns of culture which we acquire during the process of socialization within a society.

A particular social group's patterns of culture present themselves in the common sense knowledge of the individual who lives his everyday life in and among that particular group. Alfred Schutz (1975) defines patterns of culture as patterns which describe all of the special considerations, institutions and systems of orientation and leadership (such as customs, laws, values, norms, etc.), which characterize, if not constitute, any society at any given point of time in its history.

The actor in a social world examines the world around himself and classifies it from his own terms/conditions (i.e. with the norms and values he has learned through interacting with members of his society). Patterns of culture are knowledge of reliable or dependable "recipes" for interpreting the social world's handling of things and people in order to find the best result in any situation with the minimum of exertion to avoid unwanted results (Schutz 1975). It is knowledge which we do not question and are often not aware of until we meet new patterns that do not correspond to our own. These patterns of culture or codes are often invalid in a new cultural setting.

An example of a cultural "recipe" is simply how one is taught to hold a fork and knife. In the United States, it is considered "correct" behavior to cut food with the fork in the one hand, and to switch the fork to the other hand before eating the food. In Norway, it is "correct" to eat and cut food with the fork in the same hand.

In this article, I am interested in the individual separated from his/her society. One comes to a new country with the cultural patterns that one has been socialized into. One interprets events, actions, from these patterns which can be, and often are, conflicting with the native patterns of culture.

In many respects it would be useful if the foreigner could "set aside" his previous socialization and begin again to learn cultural patterns and codes at a primary level. This cannot actually be done because we are unaware of so much of what we have learned. There is a need to look for another way to describe the process by which the foreigner goes through his adjustment to the new country. This process is called cross-cultural understanding and learning. Relevant to the process of cross-cultural understanding and learning, is *sociocentrism*. [1]

Anyone who comes to a new country, and thereby a new culture, is *sociocentric*: that is, formed by his own society and thereby *centered* on that particular society. It is the process which allows the newcomer to *decenter* himself from his own *sociocentric* point of view which is of interest. It is this process which can be useful in understanding the tensions and frustrations which, when eased, lead to some form of understanding and knowledge concerning the country in question.

The foreigner who is not a member of the Norwegian social group has little or no knowledge of necessary recipes for interpretation. He has no frame of reference from the past as do members of the Norwegian society. He can only interact from the present and in the future. Norwegians acquire this frame of reference implicitly through the process of being handed down knowledge from one generation to the next, i.e. through the process of socialization.

The foreigner's frame of reference from the past based on his socialization is necessarily precarious and can even be invalid for use in the sojourn country. If the foreigner uses the patterns of culture from his own culture to interact with Norwegians, he is bound to receive confusing and conflicting results.

To exemplify this, one can talk of degrees of indirectness or directness when dealing with conflicts. In Norway, in comparison with many other cultures, conflicts are dealt with in a certain form of indirectness. There is an expression for this, "to pack it in cotton" (å pakke det inn i bomull). An example of this is the foreigner who comes to work each day late and is greeted by his Norwegian boss who says things with a smile like, "Did you sleep well last night?", "Did the tram-car break down again?", "Did you have trouble with your alarm clock again?", "It was nice that you could come today!" Then one day, the foreigner is fired from his position because he was late almost everyday. The foreigner responds with an exclamation, "But my boss never told me it was a problem!"[2]

One can say that the foreigner tries to "translate" actions into his own cultural frame of reference, if indeed his culture has an equivalent, or at least a similar, reference point. It is within this translation that communication between the foreigner and the native often is weakened or broken down... often without either side noticing, or at least realizing, why. The foreigner, at this point, has not *decentered* himself from his own cultural frame of reference. The foreigner is not usually aware of what the problem is, at least not at first. On the contrary, while interacting with and observing members of Norwegian society, the foreigner finds that individuals are not always responding as expected.

The realization that things in the new surroundings are completely different than one expected from one's own country, is often the first area of tension for the foreigner. Suddenly his own ways of interpreting the world lose their validity. The new culture loses its novelty and is seen instead as a labyrinth (Schutz), a labyrinth which manifests itself firstly in terms of culture shock.

Culture shock refers to the idea that entering a new culture is potentially a confusing and disorienting experience (Bochner/ Furnham 1989:12). However, one must also consider culture shock on an individual level. Persons used to traveling and living abroad, as well as individuals who are more flexible than others, may not experience culture shock in its extreme. There can be a wide spectrum from flexibility to rigidity. I do, however, argue that all foreigners are affected by culture shock whether to a minute extent or to a much larger extent. Most importantly, culture shock should be viewed as a vital part of the cultural learning process, instead of something negative.

One important point involving cross-cultural interaction is that both sides (e.g. in a meeting between a foreigner and a Norwegian), try to use the specific social forms they have command of. What happens is that Norwegians are in the position of power since they have an unquestionable knowledge of the Norwegian culture. The foreigner suffers because he is unable to rely on the norms and values which he has the most control over (those which he inherited through socialization in his homeland). He is thus forced into a powerless situation. Interactions become a relationship of power between the "majority" and the "minority" (Grønhaug:1975). The inability to communicate effectively is a very frustrating and trying situation.

As the foreigner gains more and more insight into the patterns of culture of the country in question (through *decentering* and *centering*), interactions with members of that society become more and more comprehensible. With this new insight, the negotiating of certain social situations become less problematic, and the intensity of individual experiences of culture shock dwindles away. It is important to keep in mind, however, that although individual experiences of culture shock may occur less frequently, even the most "integrated" foreigner can face new situations which start up the process of *decentering* and *centering* again.

In reality, the foreigner is *modifying* patterns established during early socialization. It is within the process of *decentering* that one can gain insight into the patterns of Norwegian culture. And it is at that point that one can modify the existing patterns from the patterns based on Norwegian culture. The trouble arises with how to interpret the new patterns within one's existing patterns of behavior. How close one can come to interpreting the Norwegian way of life depends very much on one's ability to *decenter*.

If the foreigner does not make an effort to *decenter* himself from his own society, *sociocentric* interpretations create a basis for building stereotypes about Norwegians that do not necessarily mirror the Norwegian reality. One goes from the state of *sociocentrism* to *ethnocentrism* with all its negative aspects like prejudice, racism, etc.

Public transportation is an interesting point of departure for observing everyday behavior of people in any culture, i.e. patterns of culture. What I would like to do in the rest of the article is to "confess" to my own theories and answers to why Norwegians behave in the way they do. I will take you through my personal journey in the last ten years from *sociocentrism*, and the processes of *decentering* and *centering,* to an increasing understanding of communicating in the non-communicating way of Norwegian urbanites (and perhaps more specifically Osloites).

Eye Contact

I have lived at my present address for three years. During these years I have taken the same tram-car to work nearly every day. I have seen the same people over and over again from my neighborhood and yet we do not even nod in recognition to each other! On the contrary, we see each other and then quickly avoid eye contact. It took two years before my next door neighbor gave me eye contact, and even longer before he spoke with me, when we took the same tram home together in the afternoon. By observation, I can tell you where my neighbors get off the tram-cars on their way to work and what their probable professions are. In fact, there is one person in particular who takes the same tram-car with me daily who has become part of a family joke. This particular man gets off at the Veterinary college. We often see him from our kitchen window, in the neighborhood store, or during one of our afternoon strolls. Inadvertently, someone cries out, there goes Annie's veterinarian!

One day, I came on the tram-car at the station near my work and sat down where there was an empty seat. The man next to me turned and said, "You are not Norwegian, where do you come from?" Now I should mention here that I do not look "foreign". I am a small caucasian female. I was quite startled and asked the passenger (who was clearly a foreigner both from his appearance and his language skills), how he possibly could know that I was a foreigner. He said that I had given him eye contact and smiled at him, something which, according to him, Norwegians do not do. There is a very interesting point here. My *own* cultural actions are unconscious to me. Had someone asked me if I had looked at the man or smiled to him, I would have answered no.

In Norway, the avoidance of eye contact or the avoidance of nodding in recognition to neighbors or strangers one sees everyday is in some sense the direct opposite of what would be expected in other cultures. Nodding to strangers, "striking up a conversation" with strangers, "chatting" with the person sitting next to you or whom you are standing in queue with, is quite common even in larger cities in other countries. The foreigner can perceive this avoidance strategy as a product of racism, rudeness, coldness or another negative statement, coming from Norwegians.

One anthropologist has said that in Norway, avoidance is a typical strategy both *before* a certain amount of alikeness is established and *when* alikeness can no longer be maintained (Gullestad 1988:117).[3] Having something in common, perceiving each other as alike, seems to be of great importance in face-to-face interaction. Without some common factor, a "symbolic fence" can be erected which makes the persons in question "unavailable" to each other (Gullestad 1988, Haugen 1978).[4] The concept of alikeness is closely related to egalitarianism. Many researchers have written on the subject of egalitarianism/ alikeness as an important symbol for the Norwegian identity (Archetti in Clausen,1984, Berggreen, 1989, Gullestad, 1989, Eriksen in this book).

The Law of Jante (*Janteloven*)

1. You shall not believe that you are something.
2. You shall not believe that you are just as good as us.
3. You shall not believe that you are cleverer than we are.
4. You shall not imagine that you are better than we are.
5. You shall not believe that you know more than we do.
6. You shall not believe that you are more than we are.
7. You shall not believe that you amount to anything.
8. You shall not laugh at us.
9. You shall not believe that someone cares about you.
10. You shall not believe that you can teach us something.
    (From Sandemose, 1962)

Norwegians themselves refer to the "Law of Jante" which was the law of a village in a novel by Sandemose, a famous Norwegian author. It says, among other things, that you must not think that you *are* something, nor, more importantly, that you are better than someone else. The value of egalitarianism/alikeness, however, does not necessarily mean factual equality. Berggreen (1989) changes the first part of the Law of Jante from "You shall not believe you are something", to "You shall not let others see that you believe you are something(:160)."[5]

For the foreigner, this means learning how to be modest in all endeavors and to avoid holding a banner up which says, "I am somebody important". It should be mentioned here that society is changing rapidly. During the past ten years I have noted that people are beginning to talk more openly about their endeavors, although those who talk are still looked upon with a certain amount of scepticism. I will return to some possible consequences of alikeness/egalitarianism later.

Politeness and Rudeness

On one particular day, I was sitting on the tram-car with my husband and our daughter. There had been a public transportation strike from 12.00 a.m. to 6:00 p.m., a very rare occurrence in Oslo. This was the first tram-car out of the city in the direction of our apartment. The tram-car was packed like a can of sardines, all the seats were taken and most people were standing. The tram-car had closed its doors in the center of the city when no more people could get on. Everybody was quiet, looking at some hidden point on the horizon, or looking down in their newspapers. There were a few couples who were discreetly whispering to each other.

Just after passing the first station, the tram-car came to a jolting stop. From the back of the tram-car, there was a high pitched noise, sounding like some type of alarm. The tram-cars are quite long, about fifty feet. We were sitting only ten feet from the back of it. Some boys all the way at the back, most likely from Pakistan or India, started to laugh. One of the boys said in perfect Norwegian that the emergency brake was pulled partially down and he asked if the other people on the tram could pass this information to the driver. At the moment the boy had first started talking, people looked up and turned towards him, but immediately looked down at the floor or outside the window as soon as it became clear that he was directing their attention towards himself on purpose. Nobody "passed" the information further to the driver. A little louder, the boy repeated the fact that the brake had been pulled slightly down and requested again that the driver be informed. Nobody looked up, although many looked uncomfortable. It took more than five minutes before the driver finally got the information. I am still unsure as to whether she actually got the information from a passenger or from going through all the possibilities as to why the tram had stopped so abruptly.

This is of course an extreme situation, but it is quite fascinating. The entire experience from the strike to the emergency stop would, in many cultures, produce a feeling of community, a feeling of solidarity among tram-car riders. The incident would cause a commotion and give a reason to talk with fellow passengers even in a metropolis like New York City.

There are a great many older people, senior citizens, who use the public transportation system. When an older person comes on to the tram and all the seats are taken, it is quite seldom that somebody gives up his place so that the older person can sit down. The people who are sitting on the seats designated for the elderly and handicapped don't even move. What is of particular interest is that the people sitting are aware that an elderly person has come on to the bus, tram, or whatever; they look at the person and then quickly turn away, either to stare into the distance, out the window, or at the newspaper they have at hand.

More often than not when somebody does get up, it has been observed (both by foreigners and by Norwegians), that it is a foreigner who gives up his/her seat for an elderly person. It has also been observed that it is foreigners who are most willing to offer help to mothers who cannot get their prams on to busses and trams by themselves. My father, a native New Yorker, was particularly bothered by what he insisted was the Norwegians' rude refusal to make room for fellow passengers.

The public transportation network (*Oslo Sporveier*) has even had a comprehensive campaign to try to get people to give up their seats to the elderly: Posters were placed in all the tram-cars where there is usually advertising. In bold black print with large lettering, the message said, "Here comes an elderly man... Shall I pretend that I do not seem him?"

Another, but closely related issue is the rather infrequent use of the expression "excuse me" (*unnskyld* or *forlatelse*). I used to say that I could count on my fingers the number of times people said "excuse me" (*unnskyld* or *forlatelse*) when they bumped in to me, both on public transportation and in the city. I have now lived in Norway ten years and it is time to admit that I must also include my toes when counting. I have been stepped on, pushed over, I have been hit by innumerable briefcases, backpacks without hearing an "excuse me" (*unnskyld* or *forlatelse*). I have even had a cup of coffee spilled down the front of me without an

"Der står en gammel mann.

Skal jeg late som jeg ikke ser ham?"

 AS Oslo Sporveier

This and similar posters were displayed in tram-cars during a campaign for senior citizens. (The official retirement age in Norway is 67, hence 67+ in the poster). The text reads: "Here comes an old man, shall I pretend I don't see him?"

apology! Not long before we purchased a car, I wrote a letter which I never sent to the newspaper. It started like this: "Today I am going out to buy a car despite my belief in public transportation to combat environmental pollution. I have been pushed over on the tram-car for the last time! To hell with Oslo commuters!"

What I have noted as of particular interest is that in cars, drivers communicate with each other continuously. For awhile, I stopped using public transportation because, despite the half hour

Public transport: tram-car in Oslo.

long queue to come into the center of the city, drivers smiled,
waved me into a queue, blinked their lights if mine weren't on,
etc. In other words there was what I ethnocentrically would call
"civil communication" between strangers. It is as if the physical
shield of the car allows the driver to make contact with other
drivers. Some call this phenomenon "the fellowship of the road"
(*landeveiens felleskap*).

One micro-study by a student of Norwegian as a foreign language suggested that Norwegians were more polite than the foreigners, at least Norwegians were no less polite than the foreigners (Parks 1986).[6] This is of interest because it seems
contradictory to how many foreigners regard, and more specifically how I have regarded, Norwegians based on observations
and interactions with them. The data is quite useful in analyzing
the actions of Norwegians in relation to their own notions as to
how they should act. There seems to be an implicit conflict
between what the Norwegians *say* is important in their social
arena, and how they actually *interact* in their day to day life.

Many Norwegians when asked directly about the resulting
conflict between values and corresponding behavior, responded
with a sort of resigned sigh or a nervous laughter. Quite a few
said something to the effect that Norwegians are so afraid to
attract attention to themselves that even in a potentially danger-

ous situation, they clam up. It would appear that many Norwegians "know" they are not responding at a time they could, or at a time that might seem appropriate. Why don't Norwegians act out their notions? What implicit barriers in the social structure prevent Norwegians from acting? What possible sanction can occur which causes many Norwegians to turn their heads when an older person approaches and obviously needs help, or looks down when an acquaintance is approaching on the street or even standing in line in front of them? Why do many Norwegians look away when someone has fallen, or do not excuse themselves or apologize in an accidental situation when their *own* culture implies that they should help?

"An evening on Karl Johan", painted by the artist Edvard Munch in 1892, depicting an evening scene on Oslo's main street.

Norwegian notions about what is right and wrong, polite and impolite in everyday situations are generally in agreement with the notions of many of the foreigners who have reacted against the general Norwegian behavior. There would appear to be a contradiction between the values which Norwegians are socialized with and socialized into, and how Norwegians actually behave in particular situations. In the quest to be viewed as the same, one might say that Norwegians prefer to be private and faceless in a crowd. Saying that you are something is a worse "offence" than not helping someone in need.

If one sees what the Norwegians say is the fear to draw attention to oneself, or the fear of doing something embarrassing in public (losing control), in connection with the need to be explicitly alike, one can perhaps begin to understand why Norwegians don't respond to situations that they themselves might feel they should respond to according to their own ideational values (and the values which individuals from other societies either respond to, or say they would respond to). It implies that the importance of remaining anonymous and thereby remaining alike has stronger sanctioning powers than one's value system of what is right and what is wrong.

There is another issue at stake here, one that perhaps might pacify the Norwegians who argue either that what the foreigners observe is not true, or that their own milieu does not practise such behaviors. It may offer an explanation as to why Norwegians might not react to situations in the way that many foreigners feel that they should: the concept of personal space and boundaries.

Personal Space and Boundaries

Perhaps one reason why Norwegians don't approach the older person and give up their seats, is that they do not wish to invade the older person's space. What, for example, if the older person were to be offended?

Personal space is something which individuals do not think about but which individuals indirectly understand. I define personal space as the physical and abstract distance which individuals have between themselves . One might say that each person has an "aura" around him which is defined in terms of culture and of an acceptable amount of space between people, and also in terms of individual preference.

In other words, when defining personal space, there is room for both the cultural specific element and the individual's own preference. In some societies it is common to kiss each other on the cheek when meeting an acquaintance or a friend; in some societies hugging is a common behavior; in still other societies, little contact is expected. In each society there is room for a certain amount of leeway which is acceptable before behavior is considered abnormal.

Norwegians seem to have a deep respect for individual space. They respect others' personal space and they do not wish their own privacy or space to be invaded. Here, I mean not only physical space between people, but also space in a more abstract form. Looking at the examples of taking the same tram-car each day with my neighbors or an older person getting on to the tram-car or bus, one can speak of personal space. The same goes with the situation of a person who falls in the street. Respecting people's privacy includes not running over to the person who has fallen.

Making contact with a person will also mean an invasion of your personal space, and will also imply that you will have a responsibility to make that contact everyday. This brings us back to the issue of unavailability before a certain amount of alikeness is established. It is as if one does not wish to allow the other person to step over a hidden boundary line. A number of Norwegians have connected this form of distancing to personal property and its importance in Norway. Every summer, it is possible to read in the newspapers about feuds that have started between neighbouring summer cabins when someone builds a lavatory or road too close to the other's land.

Even in medieval Norway, trespassing was a "mortal" offence. In the poem *"Draumkvedet"* (a dream told in verse), which is over 500 years old, a man walking through hell discovers the groups of sinners who have been sent there. Together with those who had cursed their mother and father and who had married their cousins, the wanderer found people whose sin was to have moved boundary markers, " . . . God have mercy on the poor souls who have moved the boundary stones (*grensestein*) in the woods. . .!" (Liestøl 15:1964)

Even why people pretend not to notice others on the tram-cars has been explained to me through the importance of personal space/property, "If I sit on the seat, it is *my* seat. Why should I share it?"

When asked at a dinner party recently about foreigners' views of Norwegians, I recited many of the above incidents and ideas. One Norwegian man, quite offended by what I had said, retorted that Norwegians have an unspoken rule that it is O. K. not to say "excuse me" on the tram-cars and therefore it is not rude behavior. I think he has made the point quite clearly. Unspoken rules are very important in Norway. Unspoken rules are the last rules learned (if ever) by the foreign population.

If I now return to the story on my first day in Norway, what did I do wrong? I broke an unspoken rule. I hopped over the "symbolic fence" and made myself available to a stranger. I probably also frightened the poor woman because she thought she should recognize me, and when she didn't, she became worried about her memory !

Returning to my observations, it is not a question of whether Norwegians are polite or not, or what is right or wrong in the interpretations, it is a matter of different realities based upon experiences and cultural backgrounds. In other words, the issue at stake here is cultural competence: It is one thing to speak the same language and an entirely different thing to speak the same culture.

Notes

1   The concepts which I am introducing here come originally from the work of Jean Piaget, perhaps one of the greatest contributors to theories of understanding intellectual development. While there has been critique that Piaget's stages are in many respects cultural specific, his concepts are still useful. I therefore feel that it is unnecessary to go into a debate around the critique in this article as it has no relevance to the borrowing of his concepts.
2   A similar version of this story is found in *Jobb? En vei å gå – Et opplegg for fremmedspråklige* by Sindre Sulutvedt.
3   This is my own translation from Norwegian and my own emphasis.
4   Inger Haugen speaks of the Management of Reachability in an article with the same title (1987). I choose to translate the word as availability, since this seems to fit better with the contexts in which I use the concept.
·5   This is my own translation from Norwegian.
6   The study involved both Norwegians and foreign students who answered a questionaire about how they would respond in certain situations.

Acknowledgements: I am grateful for the suggestions and comments I have received from Arne Kiel, Cinnamon Rogers, Astrid Torud, Thomas Hylland Eriksen, Ellen Røst and Lars Vold.

References

Berggreen, Brit. *Da Kulturen kom til Norge.* Oslo, 1989.
Bochner, Stephen., and Furnham, Adrian. *Culture Shock: Psychological reactions to unfamiliar environments.* Reprint. London, 1989.
Dahl, Øyvind., and Haberg, Kjell. *Møte mellom kulturer: Tverrkulturell kommunikasjon.* Oslo, 1986.
Gullestad, Marianne. *Kultur og hverdagsliv,* Det Blå Bibliotek. Oslot, 1989.
Grønhaug, Reidar. "Transaction and Signification". Unpublished paper: University of Bergen, Norway, 1975.
Grønhaug, Reidar. "Fremmedarbeiderne i Norge", *Sosial forum/Sosialarbeid.* n. 9 (1975).
Haberg, Kjell., and Lillebø, Arild., *Made in Norway.* Oslo, 1988.
Haugen, Inger. "Om forvaltning av utilgjengelighet: Et perspektiv på studiet av boligmiljø og samværsform." *Tidsskrift for samfunnsforskning,* nr. 5-6, 1978.
Kiel, Anne Cohen. *It is One Thing to speak the Same Language, It is Another to Speak the Same Culture.* Hovedfagsoppgave ved Universitetet i Oslo, 1990.
Parks, Catherine. "Kommunikative Kompetanse." *NOA* nr. 3, Universitetet i Oslo, 1986.

Piaget, Jean et. al. *The Child's Construction of Reality.* London, 1955.
Sandemose, Aksel. *En Flyktning krysser sitt spor.* 1953. Reprint. Oslo, 1980.
Schutz, Alfred. "Den Fremmede: et socialpsykologisk essay" i *Hverdagslivets Sociologi.* Hans Reitzel, KBH, 1975.
Sulutvedt, Sindre. Jobb? *En vei å gå – Et opplegg for fremmedspråklige.* Arbeidshefte. Oslo, 1991.

4

Regional Politics - Regional Policies

Richard Malinowski

Introduction

The hurricane that hit the coast of northwestern Norway on New Years Day 1992, with ensuing widespread damage to roads, rail and power supply facilities, and of course to thousands of buildings, was a reminder. It reminded us all, nationwide, how inclement and how inhospitable the conditions are in the outlying regions of this spectacularly beautiful country. The extremely difficult terrain and climatic conditions have been fought for generations. This struggle continues today.

Simply stated, Norwegian Regional Policies (RP), called *"distriktspolitikk"*, consist of a considerable array of goals, measures and incentives, formed and administered by the central authorities. The main aims are to counter the disadvantages of the natural conditions, to give the regional population a standard of living as close to the rest of the country as possible, and to retain the existing settlement patterns of Norway. The first regional political measures were introduced as early as the end of the last century. These have gradually been developed to become more all-embracing, and today cover all aspects of daily life.

Regional Policies have become an integrated part of ongoing central government in the post-war era, found both explicitly and implicitly in nearly everything that is decided. Most of the ideological background for RP comes from the social democratic ideals of egalitarianism. Despite the natural barriers and conditions, the inhabitants of the outlying regions should ideally have the same quality of life as those living in the central areas. This can be illustrated through one of the fundamental goals of central government in the 1950's and 1960's. The main yardstick for measuring the size of government subsidies to the primary sector was that the average agricultural wage should be the same as the average industrial wage. Central government compensated for the difference in many different ways, both directly and indirectly.

The author has lived in Norway for over twenty years and is only just now beginning to appreciate the whole philosophy of Regional Policies. In a small country like Norway there is a greater sense of solidarity between the urban and regional population, a solidarity that is only now beginning to be eroded. Everyone has a farmer or fisherman in the family, or so it seems. To many living in the central areas, the sums of money given in annual subsidies to the fishing industry or to agriculture were, and to some extent still are, deemed generous but acceptable. This also applies to the amount of public money being used to subsidize transportation and investments in infrastructure in the regions.

Looking at this phenomenon as an outsider, Norwegian Regional Policies seem to be more than a legitimate response to hardship. They seem to be part of a feeling of collective national responsibility towards those living in the regions.

It ought to be noted, however, that not all of the resources that are allocated to the regions through public channels and budgets are a result of regional policies. Some of the resources are needed to cover the ordinary running costs and maintenance of infrastructure and service. The distinction between the two in this complicated field is not easy to define. The motivation for the spending of public money in the regions of Norway is a combination of these factors.

Has the Solidarity Disappeared?

The social democratic egalitarian ideals that are fundamental to so much of Norwegian society in health, education, the welfare state, between the sexes and between the regions, are easier to accept and practise in times of growth and prosperity than in a period of decline. In the former situation one is mostly concerned with relative standards and the distribution of wealth. In other words one can afford to be generous, in the way I mentioned earlier. However, in times of depression attitudes change and it becomes more a case of the survival of the fittest.

This situation is especially relevant when one looks at Regional Policies. The fundamental differences of interest that exist between the outlying regions of Norway and the central areas become veiled in times of prosperity and growth. In the post-war era, right up until the early 1980's there was sustained growth. The situation can be characterized using the old Labour Party

(Arbeiderparti) slogan: *By og Land, hand i hand.* (Urban and Rural, hand in hand.)

When the depression started to take hold in the mid to late 1980's the old humorous twist to the slogan, with its serious undertones, suddenly became topical again: *By og Land, mann mot mann* (Urban and Rural, man against man.)

The solidarity that existed between the regions has not disappeared, but it is wearing thin. There are three main reasons for this:

– The larger urban areas have experienced serious economic difficulties since the mid 1980's. The redistribution of local income tax from the central (supposedly wealthy) local authorities to the periferal local authorities, a Regional Policies measure, has been an excessive financial burden. To cite one example, about 900 million NOK is taken from the Oslo municipality annually and redistributed. This has led to reduced service levels and other austerity measures in the capital, unpopular in any situation.

– In our post-industrial society innovation is a crucial economic pre-requisite. Recent studies have shown that over 80% of Norwegian innovation is generated in central, southeastern Norway. However, due to Regional Policy grants, subsidies and benefits to newly established industry, a large share of the industrial activity is located in "regional" Norway. Many now feel that this is no longer acceptable due to the high, and steadily rising, unemployment in the central areas. Oslo now has the highest unemployment rate in the country. The general attitude is now that a greater part of production ought to take place where it was created.

– The positive regional policies are supplemented by certain restrictive measures to curb the growth in rapidly growing, often centrally located, urban areas. The most commonly used of these is *Etableringsloven*, introduced in 1977. This requires entrepreneurs to apply for a central government concession to put up buildings for commercial or industrial use. This can be refused on regional political grounds.

In times of depression these measures have often been reluctantly enforced, sometimes hindering development when development of any kind, anywhere, would be welcome. In the last few years "etableringsloven" has not been used much in practice. However, there are examples of unfortunate, restrictive intervention during the transition period from growth to recession. Due to the inability of government policies to adapt rapidly

enough to changing conditions, *etableringsloven* was used to
stop a centralization process, which in effect had already
stopped.

In addition to these national reasons for the erosion of solidarity between urban and rural Norway, international ones are
emerging. The "generous" subsidies to the primary sector by the
Norwegian government have been attacked by GATT. Although
the Norwegian government strongly disagrees, GATT has accused Norway of allowing certain products to be exported at
unreasonably low prices due to regional subsidies. USA has even
gone as far as to introduce penalty duties on certain fish products,
because the Norwegians were found guilty of exporting at
"dumping prices".

The new agreement between the EFTA-countries and the European Community (EC), and the possibility that Norway applies
to join the EC have highlighted the differences between central,
urban Norway and the rural, regional areas. On the whole, the net
benefits from European cooperation will be greater in the urban
areas than in the regions. Hence there is more support for European Community membership there. There is already a growing
gap between the prosperous metropolitan regions of Europe and
the poorer areas. Increased European cooperation will increase
hostility between regional Norway and the central, southeastern
parts of the country.

The Reasons for Regional Politics

In order to understand the reasons for, and the evolution of
Norwegian Regional Policies, one has to look briefly at their
historical development. In large part today's policies and ideology stem from the 1945-60 period. Up to the Second World War,
a number of measures were introduced, but these did not form a
comprehensive policy. It was in the immediate post-war period
that a broader, more comprehensive policy began to take shape.

Initially, the reasons behind Regional Policies were almost
exclusively economic in nature. The main single factor that led to
the establishment of Regional Policies was the flight of people
from the outlying regions of Norway with a large primary sector
and a relatively small industrial sector. The rapid urbanization of
the industrial regions to the southeast of the country led to considerable movement of the population to these areas from the
north.

At this time the regional problems formed a relatively uniform

picture. The regions of the north and west, with a large proportion of the labour force in the primary sector, became less populated. Rationalization in the fishing industry and agriculture led
to a decrease in the number of jobs. With few or no alternative
possibilities for employment, people were forced to leave. It was
the younger people, with the least tenacious roots in the community, who were the most mobile and who emigrated.

The south-east of the country on the other hand experienced
rapid economic growth and a rapid expansion of the industrial
sector.

This is a situation that began in the 1950's and continued into
the 1960's. Those in central government were looking for the
solution to two main problems: the migration of people from the
regions to south-east Norway, and the imbalance of economic
growth between the regions. The solution appeared to be quite
obvious: Industriliazation of the regions.

At this time the economic development of the regions was at
the same time a contribution to the economic growth of the
whole nation. Investment in the regions was also a national investment.

Not Just a Question of Economics

In addition to the primary economic basis for RP, there have
always been two other fundamental political ideals. Firstly, as
previously mentioned, the social democratic egalitarian ideals.
The regions were to have equal employment opportunities,
service levels and quality of life as the central areas of Norway.
Secondly, there were agrarian ideals tended by *Senterpartiet*
(traditionally known to be an agrarian party), aiming to retain a
feasible basis for the primary sector in the regions.

During the period of continuing economic growth and industrialization these ancillary parts of Regional Policies supplemented the economic policies. However, with the approach of the
post-industrial era in Norway in the 1970's these ancillary goals
took over as the main aims, at least politically, of Regional
Policies. The main thrust of Regional Policies was no longer the
creation of new industry, it was the relocation of central wealth
to the regions. With reduced national economic growth this reallocation required considerable governmental intervention and
stimulation which became, after a while, coupled with restrictive
measures to curb the growth in central Norway and in particular
in and around Oslo.

The Post-Industrial Era

The successes that Regional Policies experienced in the 1950's and 1960's ultimately came to be a contributing factor to the exacerbated regional problems in the 1980's. A continuing reduction of industrial employment and increased competition from the European Community and southeast Asian countries resulted in the closure of many "cornerstone" enterprises in the regions. The steel industry and iron ore mining are examples of industries particularly hard hit. Thousands of jobs have been lost in places like Mo i Rana and Sulitjelma. In the aluminium producing centres of Sunndal and Årdal, a long lasting recession had the same effect as the closures further north. The economic life of the whole community was based on these plants. The closures, with little or no alternative employment for the work force, have had catastrophic and deep rooted consequences. Both economically and symbolically these centres of what was considerable economic growth in the regions, now take on a different meaning and role in regional Norway.

To counter these new problems central government has been willing to introduce a variety of measures to try to help the regions. These range from direct grants, subsidies and loans, to the establishment of development agencies and even to direct tax relief both for individuals and companies.

During the 1980's Regional Policies seem to have lost their way, or got lost, as a comprehensive and consistent policy. The changes in Regional Policies have for the most part been introduced as mere additions of new measures to old ones. Each new problem has been countered with a new measure. There were, in effect, only marginal changes taking place, while the problems were increasing in dimension and consequence:

> "The policies that once started as policies for the modernization of poorly industrialized regions, have today turned into a general policy for the creation of economic, social and culturally feasible regions" (Nilsson).

However the problems were more serious than the central government anticipated. Even the usually reliable fishing industry had to drastically reduce catches in order to preserve threatened fish stocks. This affected both the fishermen and the dependent land-based processing industry. The considerable problems in the regions in both the primary and industrial sector increased throughout the 1980's. The Regional Policies designed by the central government to tackle these problems became less strategic and structured, and increasingly inadequate.

Today's general economic recession has added to Norway's regional problems, as it is once again the regions that are worst affected. At the same time there is increasing competition for central government funding in almost every field of government activity. The metropolitan areas have started to present their own problems of urban poverty and deprivation. A deep seated animosity between the central areas and the regions of Norway is becoming more apparent. This can be quite significant in the near future.

The Future of Regional Policies in Norway

In order to accommodate a worsening economic situation Regional Policies measures are now being used for an increasing geographic area of Norway. An example of this is the designation of Moelv as an area where regional policy measures can be applied. Moelv is the home of a large, but virtually bankrupt manufacturer of prefabricated houses. It lies in the heart of the most properous area of southeastern Norway. The only similarity to the regions is that the community is dependent to a large extent on one "cornerstone" factory. This means that Regional Policies measures are now used in the outlying regions, in old, established industrial areas, in the regions where fishing and agriculture are still dominant, and in the areas where people (especially the young) are emigrating.

However, much of Norway RP's stem from the need to give direct financial aid to ailing communities. This has to change in a world where both the European Community and GATT are playing an increasingly important role.

The fact that Denmark is already a member of the European Community and that Sweden has applied for membership, means that Finland and Norway will probably also apply for membership. (Norway's application will probably be forwarded in 1992 so that membership can be granted at the same time to all the Nordic countries.) This means that Norway must take into account the regional policies of, and the current development in, the European Community. Regionalization is the key word here, because the development of the European Community is more based on city-region development and inter-regional development than on national issues. The European Community has special programmes for the stimulation of growth in underdeveloped regions, for the redevelopment of antiquated industrial regions, for regional cooperation across national boundaries and for the building of infrastructure. The regional areas of Norway must prepare themselves for this new challenge, and adopt new measures. For example, many European Community regions have established lobby offices in Brussels, manned by a full-time staff.

Norway's adaptation, whether as part of a European Community/EFTA agreement or as a full member of the European Community, will create tremendous regional political challenges. This is because the ideology and problems at the root of European Community regional problems are fundamentally different from those in Norway.

In Norway, the essence of regional problems is the isolated areas based on primary industries facing continued population loss and a threat to their very existence. In the European Community this type of problem is virtually unknown. Here it is the densely populated regions with a weak economic base and widespread poverty that are the main problem.

Even in the most outlying areas of Norway, Regional Policies have ensured a relatively high standard of living as compared to the poorest regions of the European Community. When using European Community criteria in defining those in need of assistance, Norway's regions score relatively highly. This is because the European Community criteria are based on a poverty index measured as per capita production rates, and the local unemployment rates. Using these criteria all Norwegian regions will be excluded from the assistance funds. It is only in the agricultural sector that some areas of Norway will be eligible for modest grants.

These strict rules concerning economic help to the regions imposed by GATT and the European Community imply that the Norwegian government and those living in the regions must rethink regional policies. These have to be more forward thinking and progressive. Measures will have to be used to invest in the future, in infrastructure, in innovative Norwegian products, developed and produced in the regions, and on international cooperation.

One main advantage that Norway's underdeveloped regions have is that they are the cleanest, purest, most unspoilt parts of Europe. These environmental qualities will increase in value in the years to come in this otherwise overcrowded and polluted part of the world. These advantages can form a considerable economic base for the future development of the regions.

The Instruments of Regional Politics.

After giving a relatively summary overview of the significance of and the changes in regional policies in Norway, I would like to examine some of the instruments of Regional Policies. To do this we ought to define what is meant by Regional Policies, and in order to understand the functioning of today's Regional Policies we need to look at their history.

Most people in Norway refer to Regional Policies as "distrikts-utbygging", literally the building of the regions. The term "distriktsutbygging" is in fact relatively new, dating from the late 1960's, and came into use after the creation of the most important agency in the administration of regional policies "*Distriktenes Utbyggingsfond* (DU)" – The Regional Development Fund (RDF). It is usually used to describe government contributions, both on the national and local level, in areas that have special employment problems that lead to high unemployment and emigration rates. The aim is both to create a basis for increased and varied employment of a lasting nature and to even out the differences between the regions.

The aid can be given in many forms. It can cover the cost of planning and feasibilty studies. It can cover the costs of moving and re-establishing a business in one of the regions, or it can be used as a grant, loan or loan guarantee when all other sources of financial help and the companies' own resources are fully exploited. "*Distriktsutbygging*" also covers some of the costs of improving infrastructure and/or service in the regions.

How Did Norway's Regional Policies Begin?

At the beginning of 20th century, it was generally accepted that the development of industries was not a public task. Up to that time there had been a number of state initiatives in agriculture and fishing with the setting up of various funds to support primary industry in northern Norway. These often developed into more permanent features such as nationally owned banks, and were supplemented in the 1920's with certain tax relief features for export businesses.

In 1928 the Norwegian crown (NOK) was finally tied to the international Gold Standard. This increased debts by three or four fold and especially affected small primary industry and regional Norway. This came at the same time as the general, worldwide depression of the late 1920's.

The acceptance of public intervention came at about the same time and in the wake of Roosevelt's "New Deal". Ironically, some of the thinking behind the new measures and plans were also influenced by the communist 5-year plans of the Soviet Union. This is when the the famous Labour Party slogan "everyone in work" (*arbeid for alle*) was created under Prime Minister Nygaardsvold.

The concrete result of this new thinking was "The Fund for New Industry etc." in 1936, to develop industries and tourism. Later that year The Norwegian Bank of Industry, part state and part private ownership, was established. In addition to this a crisis package for northern Norway was established, together with the principle that the state was to be responsible for the development of hydro-electric power and for its delivery to every corner of the country.

However, perhaps the most important creation of the pre-war period was the "Income Tax Redistribution Fund" of 1936. This was designed to level out local authority income-tax over the whole country on the Robin Hood principle of taking from the rich and giving to the poor.

These measures remained intact until after the war. The Nazi scorched earth policy left a tremendous rebuilding task in northern Norway in 1945. The policies for rebuilding and other temporary programmes were included and developed further in the Program for Northern Norway of 1951. The stated aims of the programme were the increase of productivity and employment opportunities, and it included many new features in addition to loans, grants and subsidies. These included the building of infrastructure and vocational retraining.

The Programme for Northern Norway functioned, as intended, for ten years when the RDF was established.

What is the Regional Development Fund?

The Fund was created by Parliament in 1961 by amalgamating the funds and staff of The Programme for Northern Norway (NNP) and The Fund for the Relief of Unemployment. This was the first fully national agency created to initiate and support regional development. Furthermore it was, for the first time, no longer a programme limited in time.

The RDF continued the policies of the Northern Norway Program as a governmental agency, with the board being appointed by and responsible to Parliament. RDF administers most of the grants, loans and subsidies from the state to the regions.

What Sort of Measures does the Regional Development Fund have at its Disposal?

The most important measures in use since 1961, and the supplementary measures introduced in the intervening years, are as follows:

- Loans
- Loan Guarantees
- Investment Grants
- Relocation Grants (from 1965)
- Grants for Vocational Training (from 1965)
- Planning and Feasibility Grants
- New Enterprise Grants (1965 – 1974)

The RDF is restricted both in geographical terms and in regard to the type of venture it can support. For example, since 1971 the regions have been divided into three main groups where the level of grants available is limited to 15%, 25% and 40% respectively. Most of the measures began as aid to industrial development, but the scope has been widened during the 1970's and 1980's to include both the service and tourist industry.

In addition there are also various tax relief measures and transport subsidies to overcome the difficulties that distance, terrain and the spread settlement pattern in the regions impose. These subsidies can be as high as 70% depending on the product and location.

The RDF also administers the restrictive procedures in the central, urban areas. The RDF staff reviews applications for new industrial or commercial projects, while the Board makes the decisions.

The RDF functioned well in the period from 1961 to 1979, but migration from the regions began to increase in the 1980's. The percentage of the national population in RDF areas was 38% in 1970, and this declined to 36% in 1990.

Recent Regional Development Fund Innovations

The main thrust of RDF activity has changed slightly during the last few years. There is now less emphasis on the administration of financial help, though this is still the main activity. RDF has now created an advisory service for those looking for new sites, it assists in establishing contacts between firms and the state, county and local authorities, and it has established tailor made programmes for special sectors. These include applied information technology and marine biotechnology.

Another example of RDF's innovative programmes is the Program for Women created in 1985. This program is specially designed to give women better career opportunities by both helping them to establish themselves in male dominated branches, and to assist the development of female dominated branches in the regions. There are four types of assistance:
– Firms that want to engage women.
– Women establishing their own firms.
– Projects aimed at giving women a leading role in the local community.
– Firms that create day-care facilities for the children of women workers.

The results have been encouraging. However, this program has also uncovered various barriers that have to be overcome. Day-care facilities are a particular area of concern.

It is expected that the next government White Paper on regional policies will include a special section on women's employment in the regions.

Conclusion

The Parliament and the Central Government have been committed to trying to stem the tide of urbanization and centralization in Norway for the past forty years or so. Many purists argue that by concentrating on industrial (i.e. manufacturing) development in the early years regional policies in fact increased urbanization, firstly by directing what growth there was in the regions to the larger settlements such as Hammerfest, Tromsø and Bodø; secondly, with the decline of the industrial sector in the post-industrial era, by driving people south to the large urban centres. These arguments are for the most part correct, but they do have the advantage of hindsight. It is not possible for anyone to say what Norway would have been like without the vast sums of money, the incentives and the programmes that collectively make up the regional policies. For this reason it is also impossible and inappropriate to use the terms "success" and "failure".

The only thing that is certain is that the Regional Policies will have to change, and quite radically too, in order to take account of the changing political and economic conditions in Norway and Europe.

In response to this, the government has established the SND. This is a new body combining nearly all of the established institutions (Regional Development Fund, State Banks etc.) that give support to business and industry. The SND was established in 1993. The aim is to derive greater efficiency from the total grants and subsidies given to business and industry.

References

Bugjerde, Audun. *Norsk Distriktsutbygging, Eit oversyn.* Oslo, 1981.
Carlsen, Reidar and Bugjerde, Audun. *Bruddstykker av Norsk Distriktsutbygging.* Oslo, 1981.
Distriktenes Utbyggingsfond, Årsmelding/Statistikk 1990.
Halvorsen, Knut and Mønnesland, Jan. Regionale virkninger av alternative tilpasninger til EF's indre marked. *Regionale Trender,* 2/1991.
Nilsson, Jan-Evert. 90-talets regionalpolitik – populära løsninger eller malinriktade ergärder. *Nord Revy* nr 4, 1991.
Olsen, Alf. EF og Regionalpolitikken, 1991. Distriktenes Utbyggingsfond.
Torstensen, Joel, Metcalf, Michael and Rasmussen, Tor. *Urbanisation and Community Building in Modern Norway.* Urbana Press, 1985.

5

The Norwegian Welfare State: From Post-War Consensus to Future Conflicts?

Kåre Hagen and Jon M. Hippe

Introduction

In all western, industrialized countries, the future of the welfare state has been questioned. Although the Norwegian economy has fared better than most others, and has literally been oiled by huge state revenues from the exploitation of oil and gas in the North Sea, the 1980's saw rising unemployment and a halt in the expansion of the welfare sector. The era of "full employment welfare capitalism" had come to an end. For the last decade a revival of neo-liberal economic thought has challenged the dominance of the state both over the individual and over the economy as a whole. The post-war 'Keynesian formula", in which the state by macro-economic demand management and by a comprehensive development of public welfare schemes mixed state intervention with a free-market economy, is no longer working.

The object of this chapter is to give a broad overview of the main principles on which the post-war welfare state in Norway was founded, and the challenges it now faces. In the following section, three major traits of the Norwegian welfare state are emphasized: Its universality, its income related cash benefits and last, the profound role of the state as a producer of social services. The third section is a historical review, arguing that the development of the Norwegian welfare state is best understood as an evolution through four distinct phases: The establishment of selective, public welfare policies in the last decades of the nineteenth century; the ideological breakthrough of modern state interventionism in the wake of the great depression in the 1930-ies; the post-war expansion and, for the last decade, a period of stagnation in, and a possible reorientation of, the public initiative in the welfare area

Section four discusses the assertion of a specific "Scandinavian welfare model". An important feature of the Nordic countries is how social and educational policies have been embedded in a comprehensive policy for full employment: More than in other advanced societies, the institutional arrangements for production and redistribution of wealth have been developed as a division of labour between the democratic institutions and legislation on the one hand, and organized interests and corporate arrangements on the other. In the last section, we point to the most pressing challenges to the Norwegian welfare state. Demographic trends will shift the needs of the population towards more services, needs that can only be met by a combination of economic growth and wage restraint on behalf of the population. This may give rise to conflicts between contributors and beneficiaries of welfare goods, and these tensions may erode the political consensus that until now has characterized the Norwegian welfare state. Also an increased demand for occupational social benefits, combined with a more selective approach in the public system, may herald a new social division of welfare. At the same time, challenges follow from closer European integration and an expected intensified international competition in the wake of the implementation of an internal market in the European Economic Area (EØS). The future of the Norwegian welfare state depends on how the political system responds to these challenges: By reinforcing its universalist and redistributive traits, or are we to witness a farewell to solidarity?

A System of Citizens' Rights

All modern societies have developed comprehensive systems of social insurance, protection and education. They are all, regardless of the definition chosen, welfare states. However, these welfare societies differ considerably both in terms of what are considered a state social policy responsibility, and in how state policies intervene, by stimulating and regulating the institutions of the family, markets and voluntary organizations. In short, welfare states differ in how the relationship between the central political authority (the state) and the private sector welfare arenas has developed and how it is structured.

By international comparisons, the Norwegian welfare state differs from the welfare systems found in other advanced (non-Nordic) countries. The post-war policy has been built on three basic principles, or pillars. The first is the universal insurance of every citizen against all major cases of income loss and sickness. Individual social rights to (old age and disability) pensions, unemployment, sickness and maternity benefits as well as free access to medical care, are derived not from the position of the individual in the labour market nor from one's family status. Rather, they form an intrinsic part of the political citizenship. All social rights are compiled in the National Insurance Scheme (*Folketrygden*), inaugurated in 1966 and later completed by the inclusion of unemployment and sickness cash benefits in the 1970's. The social expenditures are financed through a proportional employer contribution and general taxation levied on income from work. Unlike the systems found in other countries, there is no formal link between an individual's contribution and the rights accumulated.

The political aim of this administratively unified, tax financed scheme has been to provide for every member of the society a basic guarantee for income and health throughout a person's life, and thereby, render all kinds of means and needs tested allowances as well as private for-profit insurance superfluous. The basic idea, shared by all parties and across social classes, has been that access to social security, health and education should encompass all, irrespective of social status, economic position and – important in sparsely populated Norway, of region.

The principle of universality regulates eligibility, and should not be confused with the second major principle, namely how benefits are calculated. The second pillar is that all cash benefits granted in the universalist schemes should be proportional (and close) to a person's (former) income from work. The argument is that involuntary interruption of paid work, be it temporary or permanent, should not imply any substantial decline in the standard of living for any individual or social class. The implications of this "equal standard guarantee" are twofold: The first is that stigmatizing and resource demanding means and needs testing is made redundant (Lødemel 1990), the second is that middle and high-income groups are included in the public schemes. In addition, and politically significant, it has dried up the demand for (additional) occupational and individual social insurance. Hence, the public system marginalized alternative, private sector sources of social insurance by "copying" wage differentials created by the market in the calculation of cash benefits. This illustrates well how Norwegian social policy accepted inequalities of income in the labour market, but at the same time how it has tried to control these inequalities within a public system of social insurance.

The old age and disability pensions are calculated by the same formula, in which the beneficiary's income and employment record is taken into account. Yearly income from work is transformed into "pension points" (recorded by the National Insurance Institution, *Rikstrygdeverket*), which in turn enters the formula for the calculation of the pension. Those who have never had income from work (i.e. housewives, handicapped) have the right to a basic pension and a supplement to compensate for the lack of an economic career. This guaranteed minimum pension equals about 40 percent of an average production worker wage. Sickness cash benefits and maternity allowances equal full wage continuation for twelve and nine months respectively, whereas unemployment benefits are approximately 65 percent of former wages, and paid for 80 weeks.

The combination of universal coverage and income-proportional benefits is the very core of the Norwegian system of income insurance. The third pillar however, is the public sector responsibility for financing and production of all major social services. Health services, care for children and the elderly and care rehabilitation and training for the disabled are provided, in general, by the counties (hospitals, secondary education) and the municipalities (primary health care and education, care services). Private sector, non-profit organizations play an important role in implementing public policies in the field of rehabilitation and in the care of children and the elderly. This voluntary "third sector" operates however, in close collaboration with public authorities, and is funded mainly by public transfers. It should therefore be conceived of, in practice, as an integrated part of the public sector (Kuhnle and Selle 1990, Lorentzen 1990). As we shall return to later, in recent years these voluntary agencies have enjoyed increased interest, and many have argued for a more independent role for a private, non-profit, sector (NOU 1990:90).

The scope for commercial, for-profit provision of social services is both legally restricted (as for health) and not subsidized, as in most other countries, by generous tax concessions. The result is that, on the one hand, alternatives to public services have become virtually non-existent, and on the other, that all demand for social services is channelled towards the state and the municipalities. The economic recession in the 1980's hit local government, and, in combination with an austere expenditure policy from central government, an unmet need for services arose dramatically during the 80's. This demand is reflected both in growing queues for health care and care for the elderly, whereas a black market for childminders relieves the most pressed double-working families with small children.

It is, above all, the combined application of these three principles that constitute the cornerstones of the Norwegian welfare state. The principle of universality, the idea of income proportional benefits and the near public monopoly in the provision of social services have, however, been increasingly questioned for the last decade. But before turning to the challenges facing the Norwegian welfare state, a brief look at how it evolved historically is useful.

Historical Developments

The first traces of "public social policy" are found as far back as the 12th century. By law the king obliged all farmers, for a specified number of days, to provide housing and food for paupers passing by. Since the 15th century, the organization of "health services" (at that time, the regulation of the economic activity of doctors), was a prerogative of the king. And one of the first initiatives the new-born Norwegian state took in 1814, was to provide widows of military officers and clergymen with income insurance (Seip 1984, Øverbye 1990). However, it was not until the second half of the 19th century that modern social policies emerged. The development since the first poverty law of 1845 can, roughly, be split into four distinct phases.

The first is the spread of modern social insurance in the period 1884–1920. Public policy in these years is recognized by a dual approach. The first was to develop a more comprehensive system of help for poor people without family or other sources of income. Although British liberal "pauper management" ideology never gained any widespread adherence among the Norwegian bourgeoisie, the provision of help was accompanied by moral condemnation and loss of citizens' rights for the claimants.

The anti-poverty measures were administered at the local level, and in some regions they were developed by local authorities into systems of communal old age pensions (Hatland 1987). In contrast, the second group of welfare policies was developed at the national level, namely obligatory social insurance for the most risk-prone segments of the working class.

Inspired by the German Chancellor Bismarck's pioneering social legislation, the dominant political party in the years from the introduction of a parliamentary system (in 1884) and the First World War, "The Left" (*Venstre*), was a driving force in the introduction of, at that time, progressive social legislation. By its leaning on state paternalism, it made the working class an object of social legislation, and in fact, brought Norway from being a laggard in Europe, to develop one of the most advanced systems of social protection at the outbreak of the First World War (Kuhnle 1983, 1986).

Norway managed to avoid being pulled into the First World War, and as an exporter of food (fish) and transport services (shipping), Norwegian economy boomed during the war. But the 1920's were years of economic crisis, growing social tensions and political instability. The working class had grown in numbers during industrialization, and manifested itself as a well organized and ideologically radical political force. However, in terms of social policy the period 1920-35 was one of stagnation. Important social programs adopted were postponed, among them a national old age pension scheme (from 1923). The argument for freezing the development of welfare programs in these years was financial: The nation "could not afford", the various governments argued, to implement expensive programs agreed upon in the boom years.

The social policy stalemate was broken in 1935, when the Labour Party (*Arbeiderpartiet*) entered government after a "crisis accord" with the Agrarian Party (*Senterpartiet*). The major breakthrough was one of intent rather than of extensive legislation. The social democrats abandoned their revolutionary programme in the late 1920's, and embraced the "bourgeoisie" institution of democracy. On the other side, the conservatives were weakened by the political chaos in the 20's and, of course, by the deep economic depression. This produced a new political climate and a broad political consensus on the first welfare state pillar, namely the responsibility of the state for all its citizens, i.e. universalism.

The unanimous popular resistance to the Nazi occupation of Norway 1940-45, reinforced the political consensus from the late 30's. In their exile in Sweden and England, the government and other members of the national elite drew up ambitious plans for the construction of a comprehensive welfare state as soon as peace came. Thus, the Joint Programme (*"Partienes Fellesprogram"*) adopted by all political parties from the communists to the conservatives right after the war embraced the idea of (a Keynesian inspired) active economic policy, full employment as the primary goal, and a comprehensive, public system of social and health insurance.

The three decades after the end of the war was the golden age of the Norwegian welfare state. Whereas the principle of universal insurance was accepted by all parties, the question of flat rate or income proportional benefits gave rise to a debate within the social democratic movement: Should the further expansion of the income insurance system be towards income proportional occupational benefits in addition to flat rate public benefits, or, should the public benefits become income proportional? (Pedersen 1990, Hippe and Pedersen 1991). The Labour Party was ambivalent, and hesitant to implement an expensive reform benefiting mainly the middle classes. On the other hand, both in the field·of sickness cash benefits (1956) and old age and disability pensions (1958) agreements were made between the Federation of Trade Unions (LO) and the employers' organization (NAF).

The growth in occupational systems helped to trigger off a political process which led to the establishment of statutory income proportional schemes. This was due to the fact that the occupational schemes left a significant part of the labour force, and hence, voters, without supplementary pensions and sickness benefits. Prior to the 1961 election both the Liberal Party (*Venstre*) and the Labour Party signalled commitment to extended coverage by supplementary pensions to wage earners outside the LO-NAF agreement and to the self employed. After the government crisis in 1963, the Labor Party announced plans to establish a statutory pension scheme aiming at 2/3 of prior income. The opposition, fearing electoral defeat, supported the proposal and thereby created a broad political consensus for a radical new pension policy. Thus, a public income proportional pension system was put into effect in 1967. In the case of sickness cash benefits, an occupational system continued and was expanded in 1978. As was the case for pensions, the sickness insurance reform was also based on a broad political support in Parliament.

By these reforms, the debate over the income maintenance system was laid to rest. Political priorities were given to the third major objective, the expansion of social services. The desirability of using the public sector as the major measure for this expansion was never questioned, not even by traditional conservative forces usually emphasizing the role of the family and voluntary agencies in the provision of care. Instead, they frequently criticized the government for not being sufficiently aware of inadequate levels of services in the rural districts. Thus, from the late 1960's and during the 1970's, Norway experienced a dramatic rise in the level of publicly provided health care and social services for the elderly, children and the disabled. And, as this expansion of labour intensive services took off from a situation of full employment among men, a sharp rise in female employment followed as a consequence (Hagen 1992). Hence, at the beginning of the 1980's the third pillar was established. But at that time, anti-welfare, anti-state sentiments had already begun to enjoy increased support, and the 1981 election for Parliament produced the first single party conservative government since the 1920's.

SOCIAL REFORMS 1840-1990

THE FIRST PHASE: The establishment of modern welfare policies:
1845: First poor law
1894: Accident insurance for manual workers
1894: First law on worker protection
1900: Law enabling the battle against TB.
1906: State contribution to unemployment insurance
1908: Accident insurance for fishermen
1909: Sickness insurance for manual workers
1911: Accident insurance for sailors
1915: Laws on the protection of children's interests
1915: Working day restricted to 10 hours.
1919: Working day restricted to 8 hours.

THE SECOND PHASE: Stagnation 1919-1935

THE THIRD PHASE: The breakthrough of universal insurance
1935: Sickness insurance for fishermen
1936: Disability pension for blind and handicapped.
1936: Means tested old age pension
1938: Unemployment insurance for all industrial workers

THE FOURTH PHASE: Post war expansion
1946: Child allowance from second child
1946: State bank for housing
1948: Old age pension for sailors
1949: Unemployment insurance for agricultural workers
1950: Old age pension for blue collar workers in the state
1951: Old age pension for lumbermen
1953: Sickness insurance for all wage earners
1956: Paid maternity leave
1957: Old age pension for all
1958: Single mother allowance

1959: Income proportional unemployment benefits for all
1960: Extended disability pension and paid rehabilitation
1964: Modernization of the poor law.
1964: Widows' pension
1966: Income related old age pension for all
1974: Law regulating day care
1977: Employment law
1978: Wage continuation during sickness

THE FIFTH PHASE: Stagnation and cutbacks
1991: Reduced old age and disability pensions
1993? Waiting days in sickness cash benefits

A Social Democratic Regime?

The Norwegian welfare society is, together with those societies in Sweden, Denmark and Finland, frequenty conceived of as belonging to a specific welfare model or regime, – the so-called Scandinavian model. The pillars we have identified: universalism, income related benefits and state provision of services, have beyond doubt, been more profound characteristics of the Nordic countries than of other welfare societies. A fourth pillar not discussed in this chapter is, of course, full employment. In addition, the financing of the Scandinavian welfare edifice relies more on a comparatively high local government tax, high rates of value added taxes (VAT), and not the least, progressive state taxation of personal income.

The combination of full employment, universalist social insurance and progressive taxation of personal income developed in the Scandinavian countries after the second world war is the core of the "Scandinavian model". As a "regime", it is probably the most ambitious (and successful) attempt to combine a market economy with democratic institutions and a policy for redistribution and equal opportunity for all (Esping-Andersen, 1990).

Some claim that the "Scandinavian welfare model" reflects a Nordic passion for equality (Graubard 1987), others point to the political leverage of a well organized and united social democratic left (Korpi 1982, Esping-Andersen 1985). The primary role frequently attributed to the social democratic movement is, however, questioned by Baldwin (1991). His argument is that the decisive factor was the strength of the peasant dominated, political centre. Universalism in social policy was, Baldwin argues, a demand from agrarian groups, and not a socialist invention. Yet others (Kuhnle 1983, Brox 1988, Senghaas 1984) emphasize that the social structure in the Nordic countries was, and has always been, egalitarian. Hence, sociological factors facilitated the development of a specific type of welfare policy, – the classless universalism based on an extension of equality of rights from the political to the social sphere.

Social policy developments in the last couple of decades in Europe have probably moderated the Scandinavian exeptionalism. Other countries have gradually approached a system of complete inclusion of all groups in basic income insurance, whereas systems of (additional) occupational social benefits have emerged more clearly in, at least, Denmark and Norway. The progressive tax system has been eased off in Scandinavia in an attempt to stimulate demand, but the ruling social democratic governments in Norway and Sweden were unable to hinder unemployment from rising dramatically in the late 1980's.

Thus, the most profound Scandinavian trait still clearly found is the third pillar, the public service sector. As mentioned, the expansion of public responsibility in these areas in the late 60's and the 70's induced a considerable rise in the labour market participation of women. As Esping-Andersen (1990) and Kolberg (1992) have emphasized, this expansion of the welfare state was a driving force in the post-industrialization of the Nordic societies. High levels of female part-time work and consequently, two-income families became, and still are, a Nordic phenomenon.

Future Prospects: Five Challenges

A highly developed welfare state has been built during three decades of social reforms. The establishment in 1978 of a national sickness benefit paying full wages without waiting days represented the apex of this development. Since the early 1980's, welfare state expansion has been replaced by stagnation and cut backs, due to both structural economic problems as well as new political priorities. The future of the Norwegian welfare state is uncertain. There are good reasons to ask whether we are now experiencing a temporary halt, or witnessing a turning point for the Norwegian welfare state model. Among the political parties, in the trade union movement as well as in the employers' organization, doubts have been raised as to the very future of the health and social security systems.

Five major challenges can be identified as core areas of debate. First, population changes give rise to excessive costs and structural changes in the welfare systems. Second, financial difficulties can undermine the "solidarity contract" between generations. Third, the expansion of private welfare arrangements causes a new social division of welfare. And fourth, increased international economic integration creates new conditions for national welfare policies. In this situation, the future of the Scandinavian model depends heavily on how we deal with the last challenge: To establish a new political base for a solidarity welfare state.

The demographics of social security

Like other European countries, Norway has to cope with two demographic trends (ILO 1989): The number of very old people is growing, and there is a drop in the birth rate. The result is a significant change in the population structure, and the proportion of older people in the work force is increasing.

A fascinating aspect of this development is the fact that the unfavorable effect of an aging population on the social security system has been statistically perceivable and predictable since the 1950's. Even so, it seems to come as a surprise to policy makers, and it is likely to create social, political and economic tension in the Norwegian society. The aging of the population is bound to have repercussions on all aspects of family, social and economic life.

Social security payments linked to old-age, survivor benefits as well as early retirement and disability pensions are particularly sensitive to changes in the demographic structure of the population. A growing number of older people, with accumulated pension rights, puts severe pressure on the old-age pension system. At the same time, many workers leave the labour market prior to the general pensionable age. The lack of a public, non-medicalized early retirement scheme, has triggered a substantial pressure on the (medicalized) disability pension. By 1992 more than 200, 000 persons have left the labour market as disability pensioners. This is of course closely related to the general labor market development. Further growth in unemployment will dramatically increase the number of invalided pensioners in the next two decades (NOU 1990:19, Bowitz 1991).

An increased number of old, and, in particular, of very old people, will have major impacts on the demand for medical care. More than 40 percent of the total health expenditure is services for persons above 65 years of age (ILO 1989). The national health care system must not only adjust to this fact, but also to the problems of financing the necessary increase in health expenditure. The changes in the health care needs that accompany advancing age will undoubtedly mean that manpower and investment must be channelled to old age related treatment in hospitals and not to long term institutional care. The pressure on the institutions depends heavily on the ability to tailor an effective outpatient sector in order to let people live as long as possible in their homes. The need for structural changes in the health sector may enforce already existing tensions between well organized professional groups. Treatment and care of old people seem to give less prestige than working with younger and economically active people.

Improved methods of diagnosis and treatment have opened up possibilities unknown to us only a decade or two ago. The number of older people in hospitals is rising. The upside of this development is that technically advanced surgery and other forms of modern treatment may render more people independent of institutional care. On the other hand, the enhanced possibilities of keeping each of us alive for an even longer time will nourish the ongoing debate on who and what should be given the highest priorities within scarce and limited resources.

Taken together, this implies an expansion of time spent on care in the Norwegian society. The important question is how to meet the growing demand for care and treatment. In essence, policy makers have three different options: They can (try to) repeat the development from the 1970's, and stimulate a massive entry of women into the institutions of the welfare sector. This implies a rise in public employment, higher public expenditures (on wages) and therefore, more of the private sector income being paid in taxes. Another option, and for the time being popular among conservative political parties, is to stimulate the so called "third sector". The popular slogan of voluntary community care will however, be extremely hard to implement. There is no large army of women or men ready to take part in unpaid care for elderly people outside their own family. A third strategy is to shift more responsibility on to the families and rely on unpaid domestic work. This would in effect stimulate a market for social services. For two-income families used to a high level of living standard, the prospects (for women) of going back to the family to look after other members is not very attractive. Another important aspect is the effect on the quality of life for older people in changing the dependency from public to informal care.

The aging of the population is an international phenomenon. The fact that social and health services are a public responsibility in the Norwegian welfare state does, however, contribute to the political conflicts to a larger extent than in other countries.

How to Foot the Bill?

The Norwegian welfare state is based on a solidarity contract between generations. Those gainfully employed today contribute from their income enough to ensure that pensions can be paid, that elderly can have a decent standard of living, that the sick can be treated, and that those temporarily out of work because of unemployment or sickness can be guaranteed an income.

A system of this kind can succeed only if there is a sufficient number of contributors who produce enough to provide for the needs of the others. The relationship between the providers and recipients is to a large extent dependent on crucial conditions as high employment and economic growth. It appears that some of these conditions have been undermined. Reduced economic growth and demographic developments have sharpened conflicts in the Norwegian society. A post-World War II peak in unemployment makes this picture even bleaker.

In sum this can make it difficult to increase or even maintain disposable income for wage earners without lowering social security standards. There are several methods for dealing with this situation:

The first is simply to curb public expenditure and thereby reduce the future financial pressure on those in paid work. In 1989 a broad coalition in the Norwegian Parliament agreed to cut substantially in the future the compensation level of old-age and disability pensions (from 1992). There is also reason to believe that proposals to reduce compensation level or to introduce waiting days in the sickness benefit scheme will be put forward during the next few years.

An alternative way to ease financial troubles is to restructure the system of social security. One of the recent proposals (popular in the insurance business) is to change the pension system from a pay-as-you-go to a system based on funds. This is supposed to reduce the uncertainties of future ability to finance pensions and at the same time contribute to increased savings. Since these funds do not exist today, and we have to finance the current pension expenditures, such a change of financing struct-

4

Old age existence in the countryside might in many ways be preferable to spending one's last years in an institution.

Hospital corridor.

ure will result in one generation having to pay for both their own and their parents' generation's pensions.

A more optimistic strategy is to increase the level of employment and thereby change the proportion of dependents compared to providers. This could be done by fighting unemployment, increasing female employment, and providing the older part of the population of working age with employment options. Employment among older workers is, however, rapidly declining. At present, Norway has one of the highest participation rates for people above 60 years of age, but it is an open question whether it is possible for a single country like Norway to go against an international trend of a rising exit from the work force of older workers.

A more flexible pension system, stimulating (part time) work after the age of 67, would contribute to ease the financial difficulties of the pension system. There are also reasons to believe that a growing number of people in fact want to keep up their professional life in the years to come.

The political discussion on the future financial problems of social security has a tendency to conclude that there is little to do but curb rights and cut expenditures. However, one has to bear in mind that the level of public social expenditures in Norway (related to the Gross Domestic Product) is lower than in many other European countries. During the next decade we will even experience a temporary halt in the aging of the population. This gives the political authorities some breathing space, and a unique chance of preparing for the future. The changes in the economic policies in the late 1980's have demonstrated that it is possible for a government in a democratic country to drastically change the economic course.

A Renaissance for Occupational Welfare

It is traditionally assumed that the inclusiveness of public social security programs in the Scandinavian countries has marginalized occupational and commercial welfare arrangements. Among others, Gøsta Esping-Andersen and Walter Korpi argue strongly in favor of this hypothesis: "The traditional boundaries of the welfare state have been trespassed to a greater extent than is typical, and public responsibilities have marginalized and even superseded private provision" (1987). This marginalization of market provision is looked upon as one of the major tools of distributional policies.

The thesis that inclusive statutory welfare arrangements have an equalizing effect on the welfare distribution among wage earners seems to be confirmed by data of indirect labor costs from 1954 to 1988 (Hippe and Pedersen 1991). In this period the growth in statutory schemes almost eradicated the former welfare division between white and blue collar workers.

Recent developments in Norway indicate however that we are past the high tide of public dominance in the provision of welfare. In the 1980's profit-based welfare provisions have expanded despite comparatively high standards in statutory social security schemes. The most striking feature in this development is the growing role played by occupational social insurance compared to the market for individual pension savings. From 1970 to 1990, the number of employees covered by occupational pensions doubled, from around half a million to more than a million. This means that about 60 percent of all employed are members of an occupational pension scheme.

The combination of public pensions, occupational supplements and tax-rules for pensioners secures high compensation rates for those covered by occupational pension schemes. Even for high income groups, members of private occupational schemes often receive close to full wage continuation when they retire.

The recent cut backs in compensation levels in the public social insurance will probably provide further impetus for the development of occupational schemes. Occupational pensions are but one out of several employment related welfare rights. A representative survey in 1990, among private companies with more than 10 employees, shows that many private employers offer a wide range of welfare benefits to their employees (Hippe and Pedersen 1992). Together with pensions, employer financed life insurance and supplementary sickness benefits for the highest paid employees figured among the more widespread benefits.

Early retirement schemes, extended maternity leave, child care facilities, and health insurance schemes were relatively rare among private companies. For instance, only two percent of the companies organized child care facilities for their employees. These were, however, mostly large companies counting for one percent of the work force. Similarly, early retirement schemes are almost exclusively found in large companies. The tendency among large companies to provide opportunities of exit from the labor market prior to the general retirement age at 67 is a fairly recent phenomenon. Often these schemes serve as management instruments for rationalization and flexibility without leaving a real choice to elderly employees (Hippe and Pedersen 1991).

These types of occupational welfare have been established outside the framework of centralized wage negotiations, either unilaterally by employers or through bargaining at the company level. The range of occupational welfare schemes offered by private companies is, however, systematically related to firm size, industry, composition of the work force (educational background and sex), wage level, and union density (Hippe & Pedersen 1992). These differences at the company level in turn translate themselves into systematic differences between different categories of wage earners.

There is also a long tradition for occupational welfare within the public sector. All central and local government employees are covered by supplementary occupational pensions (Hippe & Pedersen 1988, Øverbye 1990). Female state employees also enjoy extended maternity leave and have a right to shorter working hours if they are nursing.

The expansion of occupational welfare schemes and political attempts to restrict public welfare expenditure seem to be common features in the western world. The Norwegian case is, however, interesting, as it is a frequently found opinion that the Norwegian welfare state model, not only sustains a higher degree of social equality than others, but also is supposed to be more resistant to public welfare cut backs.

International pressures: A small country in big markets

A third class of challenges are those raised by increased global competition, and in particular, by Norway's future relationship to the European Community. As a small country, with one of the most export dependent economies among industrialized countries, the conditions for economic growth are largely determined beyond the reach of national policies. On the other hand, successful welfare policies rely on an active intervention in the play of market forces.

This may pose a dilemma: Most observers seem to agree that a closer Norwegian integration into the Common Market (either by membership in the European Community or inclusion in the European Economic Area) enhance the prospects of national economic growth, both by better access for Norwegian exporters to a larger market, and by imports of products at lower prices. On the other hand, supranational decision making (and especially majority voting) may deprive the nation state of just those means it needs to pursue welfare objectives, – like regulation of labour markets, social security and not the least, taxation policies.

Thus, the question of national sovereignty, for example the right to maintain higher national standards on health, workers' protection and social security, enters welfare policy through the back door. The fear among the sceptics (that is, the alliance between the radical left and the agrarian centre) is that integrating Norway into the common European market may enhance economic growth, but at the same time suggest a loss of policy measures to distribute the additional national income according to welfare objectives. Others, like the ruling social democratic government draw the opposite conclusion: They argue that the major challenges to the national ability to maintain a comprehensive welfare state are that market forces have become increasingly transnational, and that this economic interdependence renders traditional policy measures ineffective. Therefore, the only strategy to maintain a comprehensive, full-employment welfare state in Norway (as in other countries) is to participate in the development of a supranational, pan-European and coordinated welfare policy (a "Social Dimension").

Both sides on the EC-membership issue point to a crucial fact, namely that as the specific type of welfare model developed in Norway (and Scandinavia) relies so heavily on public institutions, the Welfare State and the Nation State have been intimately interlaced. This implies that the Scandinavian welfare state model, compared to more market or occupationally based welfare systems, is more vulnerable to supranational legislation restricting the competence of the nation state: A supranational harmonization of taxes towards an European average, could imply a loss of state revenue for the high-taxing Nordic countries, and hence make it difficult to maintain present social standards. Second, social protection is an important cost factor because it adds to the cost of labour. The opening up of an internal European labour market may induce a process of so-called "social dumping": Scandinavian products are expensive due to high social and employment standards, and they may therefore lose in the competition with products from southern parts of Europe, where labour is cheaper and social standards lower. This may therefore enforce or sharpen a trade-off between jobs and social standards to which there is only one solution, and that is to lower social standards to improve competitiveness. Another form of benefit erosion is the possibility of immigrant workers willing to accept lower social standards. Closely linked to the issue of dumping, is the fear that capital and new investments will flow out of Norway to regions in which labour and social laws are more lax, labour more flexible and investment returns higher. The assumed increased volatility of investments increases the power of capital, and may provide an efficient leverage when bargaining wages and social benefits. A last consequence is that traditional Norwegian means of promoting high employment through regional and industrial subsidies will have to be abandoned.

Farewell to Solidarity – From Consensus to Conflict?

Compared to almost all other welfare societies, Norwegian welfare policy has been based on a broad political consensus since the 1930's. Post-war conflicts have been over policy means and pace of expansion, not over goals of principle. This post war consensus should, we think, not be attributed to a special Norwegian character or affinity for social equality, but to a favourable coincidence of historical factors: The class compromise as response to the great depression of the 1930's facilitated by the labour movement's acceptance of democratic institutions, the continued presence of a political centre, the alliances built during Nazi occupation, and not the least, the post-war economic boom. In short, the political will of expansion coincided with the economic means to do so.

Although opinion surveys still report a considerable popular support in favour of a comprehensive, public welfare state, there is no doubt that the factors which historically underpinned consensus are weakened. New generations enter into the electorate and the labour market and a high level of social security is taken for granted. Taxes are unpopular, and one of the weaknesses of the Norwegian welfare state is its "diffuseness". As an effect of its distributional goals, the link between individual contributions (taxes) and benefits is necessarily broken. Therefore, the universalist welfare state of the Nordic type is probably more vulnerable to populist tax-protest than welfare states in which the relationship between contributions and rights are made explicit. On the other hand, the universalist nature of the Scandinavian model gives every citizen a share in the system, and this may induce loyalty through dependence. In addition, the large numbers of welfare state employees is a considerable army in the defence of the present system.

At the ideological level this contradiction between, on the one hand, a scepticism as to whether the welfare state can fulfil its built-in promises, and, on the other hand, the dependency of all groups of the population on its income, health and social care guarantees, is found in competing visions of the future: The conservatives have proposed to restrict the public provision of income insurance to a basic minimum given to all, leaving supplementary benefits to the responsibility of the individual. This of course, would create a demand for private social insurance welcomed by business interests. On the other side of the political spectrum, the social democratic left has shown a considerable interest in using occupational benefits as an arena of exercising bargaining power and providing the rank-and-file with concrete benefits in the areas where the welfare state is being dismantled. Filling the space left open by welfare state retrenchments may therefore be a most likely response from the political left and in fact, strengthen the labour movement. This, however, is no desirable consequence from the point of view of business and conservatives. The Norwegian welfare state, based on its pillars of universality, income proportional benefits and public services, might therefore survive the way it always has survived, as a compromise.

References

Baldwin, Peter. *The Politics of Social Solidarity. Class Bases of the European Welfare State 1875-1975.* Cambridge, 1990.
Bowinz, Einar. "Will restrictive demand policy improve public sector balances?", Discussion Papers, Central Bureau of Statistics. Oslo, 1991.
Brox, Ottar. *Ta vare på Norge,* Universitetsforlaget. Oslo, 1988.
Esping Andersen, Gøsta. *Politics Against Markets. The Social Democratic Road to Power.* New Jersy, 1985.
Esping Andersen, Gøsta og Walter Korpi. "From Poor Relief to Institutional Welfare States: The Development of Scandinavian Social Policy." In *The Scandinavian Model.* Erikson (ed.). M.E. Sharpe. New York, 1987.
Esping Andersen, Gøsta. *The Three Worlds of Welfare Capitalism.* Cambridge, 1990.
Graubard, Stephen R., (ed.). Norden: *The Passion for Equality.* Oslo, 1986.
Hagen, Kåre. Nasjonalstat, velferdsstat og Europeisk integrasjon. *FAFO-rapport.* Oslo, 1991.
Hagen, Kåre. "Welfare State Employees. Where did they come from?" In Kolberg, J.E. (ed.) *The Welfare State as Employer.* New York, 1992.
Hatland, Aksel. Oslo-Trygden. Fra nasjonal modell til fortidslevning. *INAS-rapport.* 87:10. Oslo, 1987.
Hippe, Jon M. and Axel Pedersen. For lang og tro tjeneste. Pensjoner i arbeidsmarkedet. *FAFO-rapport.* Oslo, 1988.
Hippe, Jon M. and Axel Pedersen. "Tilleggspensjoner-offentlig eller privat ansvar?" in Hatland A. (ed.) *Trygd som fortjent?* Oslo, 1991.
Hippe , Jon M. and Axel Pedersen. 1991b. *The Labour Movement, Social Policy and Occupational Welfare in Norway.* Paper presented at the XIIth World

Congress in Sociology. Madrid, July 1990

Hippe, Jon M. and Axel Pedersen. Arbeidsplassen som velferdsarena. Arbeidsmarkedsbasert velferd i historisk, komparativt og fordelingspolitisk perspektiv. *FAFO-rapport.* Oslo, 1992.

ILO. From Pyramid to Pillar. Population Change and a Social Security in Europe, 1989.

Kuhnle, Stein. *Velferdsstatens utvikling. Norge i Komparativt perspektiv.* Oslo, 1983.

Kuhnle, Stein. "Norway", in Flora P. (ed.) *Growth to Limits.* Volume 1. Berlin, 1986.

Kuhnle, Stein and Per Selle. *Frivillig organisert velferd-Alternativ til offentlig?* Bergen, 1990.

Lødemel, Ivar. *The Quest for Institutional Welfare and the Problem of the Residuum.* PhD. Thesis, LSE. London, 1990.

NOU 1990:19. Uføretrygd, Norges Offentlige Utredninger. Oslo, 1990.

Kolberg, Jon Eivind, (ed.). *The Welfare State as Employer.* New York, 1992.

Korpi, Walter. *Den demokratiska klasskampen.* Stockholm, 1981.

Lorentzen, Håkon, (ed.). *Privat eller offentlig velferd?* Oslo, 1984.

Pedersen, Axel. Fagbevegelsen og folketrygden. *FAFO-rapport.* Oslo, 1990.

Senghaas, Dieter. *The European Experience.* Dover, 1984.

Seip, Anne Lise. *Sosialhjelpstaten blir til.* Oslo, 1984.

Øverbye, Einar. God tjenestepensjon eller høy lønn. *INAS.rapport* 1990:1. Oslo, 1990.

6

Norwegian Political Economy

Lars Mjøset

Norway is an open economy on the north-western fringe of Europe. A very poor and backward society in the early modern period, Norway experienced considerable economic transformation since the mid-19th century. Despite heavy dependence on the international economy, Norway avoided vicious circles of underdevelopment, and became one of the world's richest countries (per capita) in the postwar period. In the first part of this introduction to the political economy of Norway, we shall apply a long-term perspective, studying the country's successful process of modernisation, which culminated in the Golden Age of the 1950s and 1960s. We then turn to a study of the politics of economic policies in a medium-term perspective, surveying some of the problems which have made life unpleasant for Norway's economic policy makers in the 1972-92 period.

What is Political Economy?

The essence of political economy is not contained in its two words. While a study of the interaction between politics and economic structures may be one part of political economy, its essence is the study of both economics and politics as embedded in social relations. The term *institutional economics* can be used interchangeably with *political economy*. Institutional economics holds that the pure market is not interesting. Rather, one must study the institutions which make economic development a mix between market and non-market principles. Institutional economics thus provides typologies of various institutional aspects of modern national economies, of national development patterns and of international structures.

Political economy is sceptical towards the models of liberal economics, which have the isolated «economic man» as the only acting unit and the market as the main mechanism of social integration. In a classic of institutional economics, *The Great*

Transformation, written during World War II, Karl Polanyi (1944) connected this view to liberalism as a political project. According to his definition, liberalism tried to treat the three main factors of economic life — land, labour and capital — as commodities. Liberal policies towards labouring human beings, for instance, required that wages should fluctuate according to the state of the market. Even if it turned out that the wage that would clear the market was below what was required to ensure the survival of a human being, the liberal idea was that the worker had to work at that wage, or become voluntarily unemployed.

Treating labour as a commodity implies that human beings are seen as things: silent and passive. But human beings are capable of acting and of collaborating. Thus labouring people would mobilize to secure political and economic rights. In Polanyi's terms, this mobilization implied the «self-protection» of labour. Its result was that the wage would no longer be determined by market forces, but by collective bargaining. He also held that human beings took action to protect the other factors of production, land and capital, from the «ravages» of the market. As for land, he mentioned both agricultural protection and environmental concerns. As for capital, he held that a money market unguarded by central bank intervention would immediately break down, and productive investments would be lost due to fluctuations in the value of money.

The totality of these processes of collective mobilization and formation of institutions relating to the factors of production implied nothing less than the «self-protection of society». The term «decommodification» denotes the same phenomenon (Esping-Andersen 1985, 1990). Polanyi traced many tendencies towards the breakdown of liberalism in the interwar period. He believed that they would become even stronger in the postwar period. The development of the postwar Norwegian welfare state supports this view.

Norway is a country of about four million inhabitants. It is sometimes argued that small economies form a separate group since such countries are particularly strongly exposed to external challenges because of their economic openness (Katzenstein 1985). But no country, small or large, is insulated from external pressures. All economies face a combination of external and internal pressures. Only exceptionally, have countries been so strong that they can simply ignore external challenges, be they economic, political or military ones. Taking this into account, it is more relevant to distinguish between great powers and all other states. For most countries, international trends, like internal developments, imply both opportunities and pressure.

To conceptualize international opportunities, we shall use a simple periodization of the techno-economic paradigms generated by industrialism (Perez 1985, Freeman 1987, Maddison 1986). The late 18th century industrial revolution was related to textiles, while a much deeper industrial revolution followed as railway-networks spread around Europe and the new world in the mid-19th century. The third paradigm was related to the new chemical and electrical lines of production at the turn of the century. The fourth paradigm was based on the mass production/mass consumption complex (sometimes also called the «Fordist» complex, since Ford pioneered mass production of cars). Presently, a fifth such paradigm, based on microelectronics, defines many of the challenges encountered by industrial countries.

Analysing Norway's political economy, we must combine such external features with the internal forces behind development, emphasizing both pressures and opportunities. Doing this, a historical perspective is decisive. In this respect, political economy has a lot in common with economic history.

A Historical Perspective — from Liberal to Organized Capitalism in Norway.

The name Norway — the way to the north — is related to trade routes stretching along the country's long Atlantic coastline. (For surveys of Norwegian economic history, see Hodne 1975, Milward & Saul 1973, Ch. 8.) Norway traditionally exported two major staples, fish and timber, drawn from the resources available to the Norwegians along their coastline and in their forests. Ships sailed from around Europe to fetch these staples, and the Norwegians were also a seafaring people, so they soon developed their own shipping sector. Thus, fish, timber and shipping are the three keys to the economic structure of Norway in the 19th century. These export trades flourished in a setting which was otherwise marked by small-scale traditionalist agriculture.

The institutional framework, however, was less backward. Like the 16 colonies which in the late 18th century broke loose from England to form the United States, Norway lacked an indigenous aristocracy and consisted largely of ethnically homogenous self-owning farmers. Thus, when Norway established its own constitution in 1814, the inspiration came from the American revolution, as well as from the French one. This constitution was maintained even when Norway was under Sweden 1814-1905. It granted voting rights to a relatively large share of the population. During the union with Sweden, Norwegian home rule was exercised by a quite autonomous state apparatus imbued with an ideology of modernization (Sejersted 1979). The capitalist bourgeoisie linked to forestry, mining, fisheries, and shipping, had strong ties to both bureaucrats and petty bourgeoisie, and like the latter, much of their activity took place scattered around in rural regions or in small coastal towns.

The impulses from the first and second technological revolutions reached Norway at about the same time — the 1850s — as both a textile sector emerged and the first railway lines were built. From this time onwards, Norway succeeded in establishing a tradition for manufacturing industries which interacted with local demand (Senghaas 1985). Small workshops began to produce industrial inputs for railways and sawmills, shipyards developed their shipbuilding skills (Bergh, et al. 1980).

The second half of the 19th century were the high years of liberal capitalism in Norway. In the early 20th century this liberal constellation was shattered. At the global level, the third techno-economic paradigm entailed the development of electrical and chemical industries. As a consequence of new electricity-generating technologies, Norwegian waterfalls could be used to produce cheap energy, which became an attractive resource in modern energy-intensive chemical production processes (fertilizers, aluminium, steel, chemicals, pulp and paper). This influenced the location of Norwegian heavy industry, with plants close to the great waterfalls.

The political and economic elites which had dominated the liberal phase were unable to exploit the new options. The new ventures therefore became heavily dependent on foreign capital. But nationalist petty bourgeois forces succeeded in passing laws to secure some control for Norwegian authorities over natural resources such as forests and waterfalls (Lange 1977). Still, linkages between the heavy industries and the rest of the economy were weak: output was exported and input — apart from energy and labour — imported. These heavy industries formed an "enclave", which would be crucial to the development of the Norwegian economy in the 20th century. In addition, the shipping sector adjusted itself and remained a main sector of the Norwegian economy. This sector shares some of the same fea-

tures as the enclave. In the late 1960s, another energy-source —
oil — was discovered on the continental shelf west of Norway
and became part of the export enclave.

Norway's peculiar bureaucratic state lost some of its independence as parliamentary government was introduced in 1884.
In the period leading to full independence from Sweden in 1905,
nationalist mobilization dominated politics, but with the boom
which coincided with World War I (in which Norway was neutral), the cleavage between labour and capital grew increasingly
important. These two major classes of industrialism also organ-
ised in comprehensive federations: LO and NAF. The 1920s and
1930s were years of great economic instability and open class
struggles. The state was a fighting ground for different groups.
The two major 19th century parties, the Liberals and Conservatives were unable to fuse into one non-socialist party. In the
interwar period, parties relating to special interests split from the
Liberals: an Agrarian Party (1920) and a Christian Party (1933)
supported by teetotalist and lay protestant countercultures. The
non-socialist side in Norwegian politics thus became fragmented
into four parties (Rokkan 1966).

In the early 1930s, workers faced downward pressure on wages and high levels of unemployment. Farmers experienced
falling prices and increasing real debts (Ramsøy 1987). These
classes became the pillars of a new political constellation evolving in the mid-1930s: a political alliance between the labour
movement and rural groups (farmers and fishermen), paved the
way for a Labour government, with initial parliamentary support
from the Agrarian Party, in 1935. The Labour Party adopted a
reformist (or social democratic) strategy which, through legislation and political control, aimed at creating a welfare state based
on equal citizens' rights for all (Castles 1978). Subsidies served
to bolster the support of small farmers and agricultural labourers
for Labour's policies. Simultaneously, a class compromise between labour and capital (administered by their respective federations) was consolidated at the industrial level: the 'Main Agreement' of 1935 established a general framework for collective
bargaining. The Norwegian trade union federation (LO) experienced a strong increase in membership with union density increasing from 18 to 34 percent between 1930 and 1936. The links
between the Labour Party and LO grew increasingly close. The
Labour Party, relating both to the labour/capital compromise and
the worker/farmer-alliance (Esping-Andersen 1985, Korpi 1983),
stayed in office for nearly thirty years (1935-65). The only in-

terruption was a national coalition government which held office about five months in 1945 after the end of the war.

A Social Democratic Golden Age — 1945-73.

These historical developments established the elements crucial in Norway's development in the postwar period: an export economy based on the enclave, a socio-economic compromise betweeen the centralized organizations of the two main classes of industrial capitalism (labour and capital), and political-institutional patterns in which Labour played a crucial role, striking bargains with the various parties on the right and in the center.

The basic structure of Norwegian postwar politics consisted of a homogeneous social democratic left facing a fragmented non-socialist bloc. The existence of a small Communist Party and a more important independent neutralist Socialist Party (SF, since 1961, later reformed as SV, The Socialist Left Party), left of Labour, did not alter this structure.

The social democratic strategy involved greater public activism. Civil servants largely shared the Keynesian convictions of the social democrats, according to which the state would conduct counter-cyclical policies and generally influence the economy via its budgetary policies and other legislation. Economists became the most important profession in the planning apparatus of the postwar administrations. Consensus was also bolstered by the memory of wartime Nazi-occupation. In comparison with the interwar period, the state apparatus became more autonomous, more like the position it had prior to 1884.

Norway's successful postwar development depended on a number of international conditions. During the first half of the 20th century, the U.S. had become the technological and political great power of the western world. The outburst of a cold war in which the U.S. decided to contain Communism in Eastern Europe from 1946/7, motivated U.S. foreign policy makers to support the reconstruction of Western Europe. This region thus became marked by pervasive economic and cultural contacts with the U.S. In fact, a Western European Golden Age of economic development emerged from the interplay between local conditions and U.S. supplies of new technologies, new methods of work organization and the consumption norms associated with the «American way of life».

Norway benefited from such U.S. transfers, and also from the general West European climate of higher growth 1950-73. The

Bretton Woods monetary system secured a stable system of exchange rates. Furthermore Norway occupied an important strategic position in the cold war system. Its border towards the former USSR in the far North is close to the Kola peninsula, where the USSR built up its largest concentration of marine forces. Norway has been a member of the NATO alliance since its founding in 1949.

Given the internal and external conditions just outlined, a specific Norwegian model of economic policies emerged in the postwar Golden Age. It was decisively influenced by the social democrats and the economists. Conservative and centrist forces had only a moderating influence. The Conservatives had other visions, and if they had dominated in the late 1940s, the institutional patterns of Norway's political economy would have looked different. But Labour also ceded to secure broad consensus. Their original visions of direct planning were soon modified into a more eclectic reformist view, favouring a mixed economy. The terms of the class compromise were thus specified: The labour movement influenced social development via its position in democratic politics, while business elites would decide on investments and work organisation.

The routines of the economic policy model combined two major considerations: accumulation and legitimation. Accumulation of capital would support long term structural change, and secure the economic well-being of the country. But the activism of social democrats also had to be legitimated. Redistributive politics would reward the broad alliance supporting the party. While accepting the mixed economy, with little direct state ownership of industry, Labour wanted to cushion the inequalities created by the market, working towards the goal of social equality. Pursuing this goal, social democrats could rely on a historical tradition, since earlier important features of Norwegian social development — the absence of an indigenous aristocracy, a historically weak bourgeoisie, strong state, united labour movement, small-scale owner-occupier farming — had already bolstered equality as a basic norm.

The social democratic strategy had three major components. First, to ensure a steady flow of export incomes, enclave activities were promoted. One particular advantage which the state could provide was low energy prices. In matters relating to such industrial policies, Labour could rely on support from the Conservative party.

These capital-intensive activities of the enclave, however,

created few jobs. To maintain support from the working class, it was crucial that the government's economic policy ensured a growth of jobs in secondary and tertiary sectors. Thus, the second element of the government's strategy was incomes policies which would create industrial employment in lighter manufacturing industries. This policy was based on the 'Scandinavian model of inflation' (Aukrust 1966), mainly formalizing the postwar labour/capital-compromise. The model concluded that 'responsible' wage growth was determined by the growth of world market prices and productivity growth in the exposed sector of the economy. The exposed sector would be the wage-leader, and the cost-competitiveness of this sector — which included the crucial export enclave — would remain roughly constant. For the economy as such, this secured steady growth in per capita consumption along with growth of productivity.

Such incomes policies presupposed effective collective organisation by workers. This shows that wages depended on collective bargaining; they were not determined on a decentralized basis as a model of liberal capitalism would require. Labour was decommodified, as Polanyi predicted.

The consumption side of the American way of life was soon fully absorbed. Modernization set its mark on working life and on lifestyles outside work. A sector of small engineering industries producing durable consumer goods (some of which emerged already in the late 1930s), developed through linkages to this mass consumption model. They were influenced by American technologies and production methods in the early postwar period. Waves of industrial rationalizations were based on American ideas, with taylorization in the form of decomposition of the labour process as well as time-motion studies, and widespread application of scientific knowledge. Due to the specific geographic and economic structure of Norway, mass production according to assembly line principles played no important role. But the smaller manufacturing firms became quite successful producers of various consumer durables during the 1960s when trade was significantly liberalised. The administrative strata in companies — involved in planning, designing, advertising and development — ballooned. Real wages grew steadily, and mass consumption spread in train with mass production.

The process of industrial restructuring implied a centralizing pressure pulling labour out of agriculture. This leads us to the third aspect of the model. Concern for the parliamentary alliance with farmers made it necessary for Labour to moderate this pressure. Consequently a system of regional policies was established to channel long term investments into agriculture and peripheral regions. Also, security considerations in the far North influenced such policies. There were several large scale regional support schemes, starting with the 'Northern Norway Plan' of 1952. Clearly, as Polanyi implied, land was sheltered from the pressure of market forces. However, the other aspect of land-protection, environmental concerns, was not central on Labour's political agenda at that time. Norway benefited from a non-pollutive source of energy (water power). But the large-scale plants of the enclave (paper/pulp, other chemical industries) proved to be heavy polluters, and there was also pollution from both modern agriculture and the transport sector, as in most other Western countries.

The routines to channel funds into long term investment purposes implied a pattern of fiscal and monetary policies that might be termed 'credit socialism'. It clearly implied, as Polanyi emphasized, that money (or capital) was not a commodity. The price of capital (interest rate) was not determined by market forces. A credit-based, government-directed financial system (Zysman 1983) was established, building on earlier institutions. The private financial sector played a subordinate role, as both the volume of credit and the rate of interest were determined by the state. The rate of interest was kept very low, which meant that credit had to be rationed. Among the few tasks left for private financial institutions was partly to administer this rationing.

State banks were crucial to the system. State banks for farmers and fishermen had existed since the early 20th century, and new ones were added, in particular the state banks for housing (1947), agriculture (1948), education (1947) and regional industrial development (1960) and also a similar institution supporting local government.

The system thus established extended further than just regional policies, as investments were channelled into sectors of priority for other reasons as well: the establishment of a proper infrastructure for a modern industrial society, and the improvement of social welfare. The credits supplied by state banks were largely financed by public sector budget surpluses. Thus, the most important instrument in regulating the ups and downs of the economy was credit policy, not fiscal policy. For example, the state would finance inventories in the export enclave when prices slumped, or the housing bank would stimulate construction if demand slackened.

The main rationale of this economic policy model was to supply the economic foundations for the Norwegian welfare state. Building on earlier collective action to secure full democracy, the labour movement now worked through democratic institutions to secure not only political, but also *social* citizenship for all Norwegians. In the case of liberal capitalism, workers had neither political, nor social rights. In the 19th century, the ordinary family fully depended on incomes from work. Illness, disability or unemployment of the breadwinner(s) had disastrous consequences for the family's standard of living. The welfare state, established during the Golden Age period, implied a system which protects all citizens from such disasters. It covers those who are not in the labour market (not yet, like students, or never, like housewives), and those who retreat from the labour market (temporarily, as in the cases of sickness or unemployment, or permanently, like the aged or disabled).

The welfare state is discussed in another chapter of this book, so we shall just deal with its relations to the Golden Age economic policy model. While the reallocation of employment from agriculture to other sectors in the Golden Age made Norway a wage-earners' society, the welfare state maintains the purchasing power of those who are not wage earners. The welfare state is related to the Keynesian approach to macroeconomic management. If, for instance, the government succeeded in maintaining full employment, it would not be necessary to spend large amounts on unemployment benefits. Labour market policies emphasized training and geographical mobility, also preventing unemployment. Similarly, housing policies not only secured cheap and reliable housing for many people, but the funds for construction could be given out countercyclically, counteracting trends towards economic depression. This extended welfare system contributed to two of the protective concerns analysed by Polanyi: protection of labour and of capital. The welfare state bolstered the legitimacy of social democracy in broad groups of the population, not only among blue collar, but also white collar workers (the number of which increased), not only among wage-earners, but also among many people outside the labour market.

The Golden Age period saw major improvements in the standard of living. There was full employment, working hours were reduced, and the electrification of the country was completed. Housing standards rose, and the number of private cars (per capita) trebled between 1960 and 1974. The home became larger, but family members spent less time there. The home was industrialized, but lost its earlier importance as a place of production, becoming a place of consumption only. It was equipped with consumer durables contributing to efficient production: for instance, the fully automatic washing machine (available from the mid-60s) made it possible for households themselves to do their own washing, which many had previously sent out to the laundry, or had help with. Television (from 1960) made it possible to «produce» at the domestic level entertainment services which people formerly had to go to the cinema or the theatre to experience (Gershuny 1983). When housework is done more efficiently, the housewife can go out to work, either part time or full time. Larger sections of the population went to work. The participation of women in working life increased especially from 1970 and onwards. Higher levels of education also led to women wanting to work. A larger share of these women went to work in the public sector. This seems to be a peculiarly Nordic pattern: women employed in the welfare state supply many of the services (e.g. caring for the sick and old) which in continental Western European countries are largely done by women in the home and in England or the U.S. by women working in the private sector (Esping-Andersen 1990).

Many aspects of Norway's social transformation implied an «americanization»: But this trend was not total. Most importantly, politics were not americanized. The U.S. is a country without a social democracy. In Norway, in contrast, the social democrats could cash in most of the political gains from the spread of the mass production/mass consumption complex. Given the Norwegian tradition for equality, Norway in fact was able to generalize the mass consumption model more broadly than in the U.S. itself, particularly since Norway's income distribution was less skewed than the U.S. one.

The late 1960s and early 1970s represented the culmination of a virtuous circle influenced by the Norwegian economic policy model. But the process of structural change also led to cumulative problems. Despite regional policies, large numbers of people left sparsely populated areas to live in urban areas as agriculture became more productive. Norwegian authorities signed several treaties implying liberalisation of trade: The European Free Trade Agreement (EFTA) from 1959, and the rounds of tariff liberalisation under GATT, the General Agreement on Tariffs and Trade, in the 1960s. As a result, openness increased and more sectors became exposed to international competition. The distinction between sheltered and exposed sectors was increasingly blurred. In the late 1960s, the first signs of crisis in smaller, labour-intensive manufacturing industries were visible. Finally, there was also growing attention to the problems of pollution, caused by both the enclave, agriculture, the transport sector and modern mass consumption.

End of the Golden Age. A Defensive Social Democracy is Challenged by Neo-Liberal Forces 1973-92.

In the early 1970s, both internal and external developments destabilized the Norwegian Golden Age model. Two triggering forces may be identified: In regard to internal developments, a heated debate broke out in the early 1970s on whether to follow Norway's major trading partner, Britain, into the European Community. The pro-EC bloc brought together the two main elements of the post-war labour/capital-compromise: the Conservative Party as representative of business elites and Labour as representative of the working class. However, the farmers and most parts of the rural population were against, as were large parts of the urban intelligentia and some parts of the labour movement. Still, it came as a surprise to many when Norway — as the result of a referendum in September 1972 — became the first and so far only European state to reject EC-membership. The anti-EC victory was taken as a proof of the continued strength of the grass-roots, counter-cultural movements in Norwegian politics. The EC-controversy may be seen as a struggle between those who wanted to halt modernization and those who wanted to continue it.

As for external events, the OPEC oil shock dramatically increased the price of oil — a key input in the postwar mass production/mass consumption model — in 1973-4. This triggered off the deepest world economic recession since the interwar period, marking the start of a troubled period in which both world trade and production grew at a much weaker pace than in the Golden Age. The deeper roots of the recession were linked to the fact that the U.S. dominance of the Western world had been reduced. The Bretton Woods monetary system had broken down, being followed by periods of monetary instability. The technology gap between the U.S. and its major allies (Japan and Western Europe, especially Germany) had been closed, so competition on the technological research frontier was much fiercer than before.

The crisis was marked by inflation, contrary to the deflationist 1930s crisis.

Both sets of changes created problems for Labour. Their approach to macro-economic management depended on high international growth, and the EC controversy split the party. But there were also cracks in the non-socialist coalition. Labour remained the largest party and was in office when the economic crisis broke.

In the following, we provide a brief summary of economic policy adjustments in the period 1973-92. The analysis must necessarily be rather stylised, and in order to provide a *plot* to guide us, we shall focus on the struggle between defensive social democrats and offensive neo-liberals through four phases.

Before the story is told this way, however, beware of Golden Age myths. As many crucial external conditions changed, the earlier model of economic policy would have had to change in some way. However, in a political economy perspective, there is not one technically defined solution to such adjustment problems. The specific adjustments made depended on a number of internal factors, such as the strategies of the political parties, and the attitudes in certain sectors of the administration. It is the direction of the change, and the irreversible consequences that are important.

The 1974-78 phase

The challenge to Labour was not only to manage the economic crisis, but also to regain political credibility among large groups of anti-EC voters. Both concerns made them go for very expansive policies.

In two respects, the government did not stick to earlier routines: Responding to strong wage pressure, incomes policies allowed wages to grow at a much faster rate than the rule established by the Scandinavian inflation model. Centralized incomes policy settlements with governmental participation, combined with price and profit controls and generous tax policies, ensured that the real disposable income of households/employees grew at a record average of five percent a year between 1974 and 1977. Furthermore, fiscal policies were very expansionary, while the rule required them to be tight. Parts of this spending were subsidies to the agricultural sector as a result of a broadly supported parliamentary decision to equalize earnings in manufacturing and farming. Farmers' income levels shot up, doubling in the 1974-

77-period. Reforms in social policy (shorter working hours and retirement age) also benefited households. Partly as a result of these reforms, the public sector — particularly local government — expanded strongly throughout these years. The female labour market participation rate increased.

In other respects, however, the routines of the Golden Age model were maintained. The government continued to keep the rate of interest at a low level. Inflation, however, was now much higher than earlier. As a consequence, the real rate of interest turned negative, especially after tax. This made credit policies much more expansive than expected. This interacted with the generous fiscal and incomes policies, creating a veritable boom in consumption and the largest current account deficit in the whole OECD area. By the end of 1978, total foreign debt reached a record 47 per cent of GDP. There were also defensive, «backdoor» measures to shore up export sectors such a shipping, shipyards and fisheries that were affected by the slump.

A major reason why this did not create much trouble for Norway was the lucky incident of an oil adventure. It was mentioned above that oil was not very different from earlier Norwegian export staples, but the timing of Norwegian oil exploitation was surely perfect: Just as the oil price exploded in international markets, Norway's first barrels of North Sea oil were ready for export. Although exports were far too small to eliminate the current account deficit, expected future incomes made it unproblematic to run such a deficit.

Furthermore, in 1975 and 1976, it was still expected that the world economy would return to its «normal» growth pace after the recession. Only in 1977 and 1978, was it slowly recognised that growth was on a permanently lower trajectory. By then, the elections of 1977 proved that the political situation had normalised, with support for Labour back at its earlier level. But this was of little relief for Labour, since they now faced a sluggish world economy, with fiercer competition and monetary instabilities. Since their only experience was to manage the Norwegian economy in good times, they were now driven back into a defensive position.

The 1978-81 phase

The Labour government responded with a fumbling revision of economic policies. To save the system of credit allocation, it would have been necessary to adjust the real rate of interest upwards (increasing the nominal rate relative to the inflation rate) and to reform the tax structure. It was politically impossible for Labour to increase the interest rate enough, and a much too moderate tax reform was delayed as long as to the 1981 budget. While more constructive reforms of economic policies were barred, the measures taken pointed towards increasing direct regulations. The two most prominent examples were housing and the financial sector. In both cases, we encounter the effects of economic actors (households and firms) who have adjusted their economic behavior to the higher level of inflation.

In the housing sector, state controls and financing had kept the price of cooperative flats (allocated according to fixed rules of seniority, length of time in the queue, etc.) far below the market price. Compared with owners of private houses and flats, members of housing cooperatives found themselves unable to reap the wealth effects of inflation and increases in the real price of houses. A number of ingenious techniques were developed to evade the regulations. This undermined Labour's policy goal of a regulated, low-price market for urban housing and the government attempted to ban the various irregular transactions. The Conservative Party was able to capitalize on the pressure for abolition of price controls, and this was probably one of the factors behind Labour's setback in the 1981 elections.

In financial markets, the effects of a higher rate of interest was to increase the liquidity of the state banks. The growing impact of the state banks was not really the result of a conscious policy, but by the end of the 1970s, these banks squeezed the private banking sector. Booming demand for credit overburdened the old system of credit rationing and spurred the growth of grey credit markets. Other economic policies were tight. In incomes policies, a wage freeze without compensation for inflation, was implemented.

The increasing number of direct regulations in a situation of increasingly tight policies weakened support for Labour. Regulations were attacked both by business interests and by non-socialist politicians. In fact, many leading social democrats were discouraged and started to support proposals for deregulation of the credit system. 1977 and 1978 were the take-off years of a blue wave in Norwegian politics (Mjøset 1989). Old ideas about the strength of the market mechanism, and about state interventionism creating inefficiencies, were used to support a program of deregulation. Such views spread in the Conservative Party, which was also increasingly challenged by the Progress Party, a right-wing populist tax-revolt party, formed in 1973.

The 1982-85 phase

In late 1981, the non-socialist parties won the elections. The Conservative party was in office alone in 1981-83, and in 1983-86, there was a centre/right coalition. Such a government had also been in office in 1965-71, but in that period, centre views (the Agrarian, Christian and Liberal parties) dominated over right-wing views. Taken together, centre views were not very different from social democratic ones, so there was consensus on Keynesian approaches to economic management, and on welfare state extension. But 10-15 years later, Keynesian techniques were discredited, and international neo-liberalism (Thatcher in England since 1979, and Reagan in the U.S. since 1981) had become a major source of inspiration. At the domestic level, the problems which the social democrats had run into provided opportunities for the new right-wing governments in 1981-85 to search for a wholly new economic policy model, one which accorded to their neo-liberal convictions. Right-wing views now dominated over centre views.

At the most general level, the right wanted to restore the dominance of the market. In order to curb inflation, improve competitiveness and to spur economic growth, it was deemed necessary to reduce growth in public spending, cut taxes for high-income households and the business sector, and to deregulate markets, especially in the strongly regulated areas of credit and housing.

The government took steps to make the stock market more vigorous. This produced a stock exchange boom in the first half of the eighties. Deregulation of major segments of the housing market soon brought down the number of flats under price control, and made home-ownership changes a very profitable activity. Since the rules concerning tax deductibility of interest payments had not been changed, demand for loans to such purposes soared. Private banks willingly responded to such demand, since they had easy access to liquidity. The government, however, had deregulated credit controls but kept the central bank's interest rate on loans to private banks quite low. Lending from state banks was restrained. In the 1984-5-period, policies were procyclical and expansionary. This policy was facilitated by the high oil-related tax-incomes following the 1980 «second oil-shock». The general result was a negative savings rate and another consumption boom.

The Conservative government clearly succeeded in strengthening the private banks and in giving new life to the stock market and the financial community. Employment in the financial sector and other business services increased. Invigoration of the stock market led to a number of mergers both within and between the financial and industrial sectors. The major achievement of these years, in fact, was the rise of a speculation economy in which it became far more profitable to engage in asset-stripping, or in home-ownership changes, than to create new real assets in the industrial sector. Later developments made it eminently clear that numerous misinvestments were made during these yuppie-years. There was no improvement in cost competitiveness despite several devaluations. There was only slow growth in manu- facturing output. The share of manufacturing in total employment continued to decline. Full employment was attained in 1986, but with a large deficit on the current account.

The 1986-92 phase

The deficit was caused by the oil price slump in 1985, which created severe adjustment problems. The centre/right government encountered various problems and frictions, and left office in May 1986. A minority Labour government took over. As in 1977/78, the challenge to Labour was to tidy up after a period of economic destabilization. While earlier, the problems had followed from Labour's Keynesian attempt to bridge the gap to a new upturn which turned out to be much less vigorous than expected, the problems now stemmed from the attempts by the right to deregulate institutions which had been crucial to Norway's political economy.

Due to strong speculations against the Norwegian krone (NOK), the government devalued the currency (by 12 percent) in May 1986. Given increasing financial deregulation at the international level, the government decided to avoid such a soft currency policy for the future and opted for a fixed exchange rate commitment. Following this hard currency decision, the government proceeded to complete the external deregulation of the Norwegian credit market, allowing free capital movements.

Fiscal policies were tightened. In 1988, there was a reform of personal income taxes, which reduced the advantage of credit-financed consumption and investments for high and medium income groups. The government also managed to persuade the LO to accept a very moderate income settlement in April 1988, which was generalized by law to include all other areas, effectively barring any possibility for the non-LO organizations to reach better terms. Two such confederations, one for the craft organizations (YS, founded in 1977) and one for academics (AF, founded in 1976), had grown since the mid-1970s, gradually challenging the position of LO. (By 1986, the distribution of organized wage earners was 62 percent in LO, 12 in YS, and 11 in AF; cf. Mjøset 1989) Finally, a strict monetary policy prevented the nominal rate of interest to decline along with inflation.

This shock therapy led to declining real incomes, and an increasing real rate of interest. Due to comprehensive changes in the tax system (reducing the value of the deductibility of interest payments from taxable income) many households were forced to use a much larger proportion of real income to service debts than what they had earlier foreseen. Most households decided to decrease their level of indebtedness, or at least not increase it. This had two consequences. First, expansionary fiscal and income policies were now less efficient than earlier as a means to increase total demand and the level of economic activity, since households would use the additional income mainly for savings in order to reduce debts. Second, and as a consequence, households were generally unwilling to make new investments in housing. Demand for housing declined, and so did prices, with a drop in prices of around one third in a few years. This reduced the wealth of households, leaving them even more exposed than before, and strengthening the tendency towards recession.

As the recession widened, many firms ran into difficulties, a fact which, among other things, led to reduced demand and prices of business property. This led to collapse for many property investors. In the end, the losses were carried over to the banks. During 1988, the banks first realized that they were trapped. Although they were rescued by a safety fund accumulated by the banks, problems aggravated. By the autumn of 1991 it was obvious that the whole financial sector was on the verge of collapse, and the government had to rescue the three largest commercial banks by means of large cash-injections. One of these banks is now formally owned by the state.

The intention behind the 1988 wage law was that wage-moderation would create latitude for the government to pursue full employment policies. But other economic policies were quite austere and interacted with new household strategies determined by the high real rate of interest, financial instability and tax reforms. Thus, unemployment increased. During the 1975 recession unemployment (yearly average) had barely risen above 2 percent of the labour force, following the 1980-2 recession it reached 3.3 in 1983, but in 1989 it passed 4 percent, and by the end of 1991, the monthly level passed the 5 percent mark. While until the late 1980s, Norway's labour market performance had been recognized as very good in a European comparison, with full employment and high rates of labour market participation throughout the first decade of recession (Therborn 1986), this recognition now began to falter.

Besides unemployment and financial instability, stagnating manufacturing production is a main problem. The government has tried to respond to this challenge with various reforms. The need for a supply side oriented tax reform, broadening the tax base and reducing tax rates, was finally generally accepted, but timing was bad, as the reform made credit-financed investments more costly at a time when the economy was in deep recession. A new energy law was aimed at achieving a more efficient allocation of resources, but it does not reduce the large difference in energy prices between the enclave and other domestic users of energy. This means that one of the oldest elements of the Norwegian model, the priority given to the enclave, still dominates industrial policy. Following the recent round of negotiations in GATT, the government has also argued for reductions in the transfers to agriculture, and some (very) minor policy changes in that direction have been announced.

It is possible that the priority of the enclave was once a consistent part of an investment programme that secured high growth in national income through exploitation of Norwegian natural resources. But today, a resource such as hydro-electric energy can easily be exported at a price which is higher than that paid by the enclave. If Norwegian authorities and private investors had been willing to take the chance of more wideranging industrial restructuring, more energy could have been exported, while new growth could have been based on investment opportunities in other areas, probably based more on knowledge than on resource rents.

Conclusion

During the sequence of economic policy adjustments between 1973 and 1992, a main element of the Norwegian Golden Age model, the regulation of financial markets, has been completely dismantled. Other elements of the earlier Norwegian model were reintroduced by Labour in the late 1980s. Incomes policies are still important: the wage laws of 1988-9 tried to reach back to the main track of the Scandinavian inflation model. But there are more legitimation problems, both towards white collar groups (since the non-LO-confederations, YS and AF, had to be forced into the agreement) and towards LO-members themselves (since full employment is not restored). Furthermore, the late 1980s and early 1990s have seen strong Keynesian countercyclical policies. However, the crisis of the financial system undermines the employment-creating effects of such fiscal policies. The welfare state is in no way dismantled, but the pressure on it is much greater since the Norwegian welfare state was connected to an economic policy model which promised full employment: it was not designed to finance mass unemployment.

The deregulation of the credit market during the 1980s did not lead to higher efficiency, but — as the banking crisis of the early 1990s proved — to a more unstable economy and a misallocation of resources without precedent in modern Norwegian history. In fact, this supports a main point in Polanyi's account, namely that the credit market is not just like any other market. The market for credit is inherently unstable and has to be regulated. It is ironic that the neo-liberal attack on Norwegian credit socialism ended by the early 1990s with the state taking over or bailing out the three largest banks. The neo-liberal solution has proved a disaster, but social democrats are too much on the defensive, governing from a minority position in the parliament and bogged down in problems of unemployment and manufacturing decline. It is therefore doubtful that the state will use its renewed dominance in the financial system to pursue an activist policy. In a situation in which capital controls are deregulated and the old system of credit socialism cannot be recreated, the only way the state can influence the allocation of credits and investment is via its own funds, and its ownership or control of banks and large firms. Social security funds have recently been used to buy shares. There is a growing attention to the close informal relations between leading government members and the top managers of large state-owned (e.g. Statoil, Hydro) and private (e.g. Uni-Storebrand) firms. This could be the start of an informal system of regulation in order to secure reliable shareowners, willing to take risk and stick firmly to serious business ventures. Whether such a scenario of «Norway, Inc.» could really function as state activism in disguise, remains to be seen. Such an informal system seems vulnerable to changes both in economic and political business cycles. (In fact, after this essay was written, this approach to industrial policy received a major blow with the crisis in the summer of 1992 of Norway's largest insurance company: Uni-Storebrand attempted to position itself in the anticipation of the single European market, but its bid to take over a large Swedish insurance company failed.)

Norway's development must be judged successful in a long-term perspective, but the medium-term adjustments throughout the last decades have not led to a new coherent economic policy model. It is a historical fact that none of the successful developers in Western Europe have seen a reversal of their position in the world economy so far, so obviously more is needed than 20 years of cumulative problems of economic management to degrade a country like Norway to a more peripheral position. In the longer term, however, the inability of decision makers and interest groups to arrive at a new coherent model of economic management may be a threat to Norway's success.

A Note on the New EC-Controversy

Presently, Norway not only has problems of economic management, but is also experiencing a political polarisation which is a reprise of the EC-debate of the early 1970s.

Any description of the situation as it stands today risks to be outdated when this book leaves the printers. While this essay was finished in March 1992, the following notes have been updated as of November 1992. (See also Mjøset 1992.)

Already in 1989-90, the new EC-controversy brought down a brief non-socialist coalition government (1989-90), as the centre and the right could not agree. Remembering only too clearly the setbacks for the party in the mid-70s, Labour tried to postpone its decision on EC-membership as long as possible. Only after a broad arrangement (EEA — The European Economic Area) had been negotiated between the EFTA-countries (Austria, Finland, Iceland, Norway, Sweden and Switzerland) and the EC, and also considering the conclusions from thorough discussions among party members, the party made its final decision in November 1992. As expected, a new application for full Norwegian membership was favoured by a majority at the Party Congress. But a significant minority within the party (above all concentrated in the Northern areas of the country) remains unconvinced.

While the Norwegian Labour Party has been hesitating, its social democratic sister parties in Sweden and Finland have been central in deciding on full applications for membership. In the early 1970s, these countries were not candidates for EC-membership, mainly because of their emphasis on full neutrality in security matters. But with the ending of the Cold War, they were quick to apply. Another EFTA-country, Austria, applied even earlier. Thus, even if an EEA-treaty will be in place from January 1, 1993, many argue that it will be just a temporary stage on the way to full EC-membership for all EFTA-members.

Even if Norway reaches agreement with the EC on the terms of membership, however, the final decision will be by referendum, as in 1972. At the moment, yes and no factions are mobilizing and it seems obvious that the EC-issue will dominate Norwegian politics in the coming years. The possibility of staying on with an EEA-treaty is however a new feature compared with the early 1970s. Such a treaty, put roughly, will give Norwegian business full integration into the EC's single market, but Norway would remain outside the EC's monetary and political union. Thus, in the EC-controversy of the early 1990s, there is a third option between yes or no. It is too early to say whether this is enough to prevent full polarisation between the yes and no camps. While the broadly popular «No to EC»-movement has been relaunched and presently has more members than any of the Norwegian political parties, the EEA-question has created certain difficulties for the movement's unity.

External events also make the situation difficult to interpret. In the summer of 1992, a referendum in the only present Nordic member of EC, Denmark, voted against ratification of the EC Maastricht-treaty, thereby blocking full Danish support for the EC's monetary and political union. Presently, Danish politicians are trying to convince the EC that certain amendments must be added to the treaty. It is not clear whether they will succeed, and if they succeed, it is not clear whether new members can also choose to subscribe to these amendments. Thus, for the new Nordic applicants, it is quite unclear what kind of EC they are applying for membership in! It could be a loose collaborative system between basically sovereign states, or it could be a full-fledged federal state.

References

Aukrust, O. «Inflation in the Open Economy», in L. B. Krause & W. Salant, editors. *Worldwide inflation,* Washington D.C. 1977.
Bergh, T., T. J. Hanisch, E. Lange & H. Ø. Pharo. *Growth and Development. The Norwegian Experience 1830-1980.* Oslo: Norwegian Institute for International Affairs, 1980.
Castles, F. C. *The Social Democratic Image of Society.* London, 1978.

Esping-Andersen, G. *Politics Against Markets. The Social Democratic Road to Power.* Princeton, 1985.
Esping-Andersen, G. *The Three Worlds of Welfare Capitalism.* Cambridge, 1990.
Fagerberg, J., Å. Cappelen, L. Mjøset & R. Skarstein. «The Decline of Social-Democratic State Capitalism in Norway». *New Left Review,* No. 181 (1990).
Fagerberg, J., Å. Cappelen, & L. Mjøset. «Structural change and economic policy: the Norwegian model under pressure.» *Norwegian Journal of Geography,* Vol. 46 (1992).
Freeman, C. *Technology Policy and Economic Performance,* London, 1987.
Gershuny, J. *Social Innovation and the Division of Labour.* Oxford, 1983.
Hodne, F. *An Economic History of Norway.* Trondheim, 1974.
Katzenstein, P. *Small States in World Markets.* Ithaca, 1985.
Korpi, W. *The Democratic Class Struggle.* London, 1983.
Lange, E. «The Concession Laws of 1906-09 and Norwegian Industrial Development.» *Scandinavian Journal of History,* Vol. 2, No. 4 (1977).
Maddison, A. *Phases of Capitalist Growth.* Oxford, 1986.
Milward, A. & S. B. Saul, *The Economic Development of Continental Europe 1780-1870,* London,1973.
Mjøset, L. «Nordic economic policies in the 1970s and 1980s.» *International Organization,* Vol. 21 (1987).
Mjøset, L. «Norway's Full-Employment Oil Economy — Flexible Adjustment or Paralysing Rigidities?» *Scandinavian Political Studies,* Vol. 12, No. 4 (1989).
Mjøset, L. *Kontroverser i norsk sosiologi.* [Controversies within Norwegian sociology.] Oslo 1991.
Mjøset, L. «The Nordic Model Never Existed, but Does it Have a Future?», *Scandinavian Studies,* Vol. 64, No. 4 (1992).
Polanyi, K. *The Great Transformation,* (1944), Boston 1956.
Perez, C. «Microelectronics, Long Waves and World Structural Change: New Perspectives for Developing Countries», *World Development,* Vol. 13, No. 3 (1985).
Ramsøy, N. Rogoff. «From Necessity to Choice: Social Change in Norway 1930—1980», in R. Erikson, et. al., *The Scandinavian Model: Welfare States and Welfare Research.* Armonk 1987.
Rokkan, S. «Numerical democracy and corporate pluralism», in R. Dahl, editor, *Political oppositions in Western democracies.* New Haven, 1966.
Sejersted, F. «Democracy and 'the rule of law'. Some historical experiences of contradictions in the striving for good government». *Social Science Information,* Vol. 18, No. 6 (1979).
Senghaas, D. *The European Experience.* Leamington Spa, 1985.
Therborn, G. *Why some peoples are more unemployed than others.* London, 1986.
Zysman, J. *Governments, Markets, and Growth.* Ithaca, 1983.

[*] This chapter partly relies on work done jointly with Ådne Cappelen and Jan Fagerberg, cf. Mjøset 1986, Fagerberg, et al. 1990, 1992. These works also contain a wider selection of relevant references. Some of the historical and theoretical aspects of the first part of this chapter are more thoroughly discussed in Mjøset 1991, Chs. 4 and 5, but this work is only available in Norwegian.

7

Norwegian Social Democracy and Political Governance[1]

Erik Oddvar Eriksen

Introduction

The Norwegian Labour Party (*Det Norske Arbeiderparti* – DNA) was founded in 1887. It came to power by the aid of *Bondepartiet* (The Agrarian Party) in 1935, and has been the most influential political party since then. With the exception of a three-week period, it was in government all the years from 1945 to 1965. However, the party had an unstable youth and seems to be heading for a less heroic period of old age. An editor of a large newspaper had this comment to its 1991 election campaign: "The Labour Party has not been dethroned, but is no longer a real election machine and far from a real 'movement'. Even the rhetoric has dissolved."

DNA's early period was full of radicalism and fights between different factions. A fight over whether to join the communist international organization Komintern resulted in a split of the party in the 1920's and the establishment of the Norwegian Communist Party. The foundations for a more responsible, parliamentary political party were thus established, even though DNA ever since, has had a critical left wing. A part of this opposition broke loose in 1961 to form The People's Socialist Party (*Sosialistisk Folkeparti,* to become *Sosialistisk Venstreparti* in 1973), following a debate on NATO membership, and a similar splinter resulted from the issue of EC-membership in 1971. The result was a stronger alternative on the left and an increasingly moderate DNA.

In the 1970's and 1980's DNA faced new challenges to its economic policy and new values and norms created other problems for the party. The support decreased from 43.1 percent in 1965 to 34.3 percent in 1989. Even though this in itself is not enough to challenge the leaders of the party, there is a widespread feeling that the party has moved to the right. Previously, the party adhered to the concept of socialism, but it is now explicitly (from 1987) a social democratic party. This change did not follow any fundamental debate. Disagreements within the party are today not so much about ideological issues, but are concentrated on unemployment policies and social security (Nyhamar 1990). The left wing, especially the youth organization, demands stricter measures.

The background to the new schism is to be found in the 1980's, the decade of the market. Keynesianism and macroeconomic planning were heavily opposed, the traditional ways of governing did not give the wanted results and demands for tax cuts were increasingly heard. Because the DNA had no alternative recipe for economic management, they, like many of their European sister parties, were forced into accepting market solutions. One may say that the golden days of social democracy ended in the late 1970's. When the social democratic parties were in government in the 1980's, they were forced to govern like any conservative party would have done.

This chapter will discuss whether the principles of governance practised by the DNA actually are the same as the neo-liberalists', and to what extent they are different.

Principles of Governance

Governance is a process through which one is looking for ways to reach specific goals. Formally, governance implies social control – i.e. the question of efficient sanctions – and rational means-end calculation. Concepts of political governance will have to include value judgments. In that respect, philosophies of governance will express ideological bases and political visions.

In western (capitalist and democratic) societies, there are in principle three distinct principles of governance that may be coupled with three distinct political ideologies. These are the socialist (here: social democratic), neo-liberalist (or, more correctly, libertarian), and conservative principles. The design and implementation of specific market solutions may require just as much careful planning as government intervention, and it is thus justifiable to talk about a principle of governance even when the market provides the solution. In a democratic country, governance is in principle the result of choices – even though both the degrees of awareness and liberty varies. One may make a distinction between principles based on government intervention, on the market economy and on the main pillars of the civil society.

The *socialists'* principle is focused on the struggle with "the capital". An ungoverned capitalism leads to crises, inequality and poverty and the market has to be tamed by political intervention. The social democrats acquired a tool for achieving this from the Keynesian theory of macroeconomic management in which counter-cyclical manipulation of government expenses affects domestic demand (Keynes 1936). This is a way of governing that *regulates* the market through laws, formal settlements and economic incentives to *compensate* for the inequalities and biases and, finally, to *add to* the areas of the economy where the market is unable to provide public goods. This principle of governance may be termed *state interventionism* (cpr. Habermas 1975, 1981, Offe 1984b).

The *neo-liberalist* principle has its basis in the theory of a free, self-regulating market (Friedman 1980). Capitalism has never been put to a test, either because several illegitimate allocations have already been made, or because politics distort the market mechanism. Actors on the marketplace may make mistakes, but so do politicians and their faults have much greater consequences. That the defects of the market are always less than the *defects of politics* is the postulate of the public choice school (Buchanan 1985). Philosophically, this is substantiated by stating that the individuals' exchanges on the market are not violating any of their basic rights, and that this is the case with all other principles for the allocation of resources (Nozick 1974, Hayek 1960). The neo-liberalists gained increased self-confidence with monetarism, according to which inflation is kept down by strict monetary policies. The theorem that supply creates its own demand – supply side economics – was practised in the United States and Great Britain under Reagan and Thatcher.

The *conservative* principle has a less clear methodological founding. It corresponds with the neo-liberalists' in the sense that market solutions are better than government solutions, but there is often a preference for the middle ground (Oakshott 1962). Even so, the difficulty of defining the conservative philosophy of governance stems from the fact that a society does not only consist of a market and a government, but also of a *civil society*, comprising family, social networks and voluntary organizations of all sorts (Bell 1976, Bellah et al. 1985). The conservative opposition towards any kind of radical or total change gives rise to a concept of governance where the tampering with natural, spontaneous processes is seen as harmful. Politics is to play a minor role. Today, conservatives are lamenting government policies' detrimental effects on societal norms. Policies are weakening social bonds, informal networks and the ligatures – the cement of society – by favoring an egoistic, hedonistic and narcissistic approach to life. The conservative philosophy may be linked to the concept of *remoralization*; politics has to revitalize the old virtues and norms, especially the old work ethic, in order to cope with the disintegration and the large, complex problems of loneliness, crime, suicide and divorce. Some Norwegian social scientists support such a description, and also some known supporters of the left.

We may see the development of DNA in relation to the three principles of governance. What is characteristic of the traditional way of governing, and whither has it moved in the 1970's and 1980's?

Modernization and Humanization

DNA came originally to power under the slogan 'All people at work'. Its three-year plan of 1933, inspired by the Soviet five-year plans, was directed against the conservatives' policy of public saving that (allegedly) led to economic depression. The three-year plan was a program for setting the unemployed to work through increased public consumption. The project of DNA is closely connected to growth and modernization through industrialization and readjustments, but also to democratization and the humanization of the work place. This is not simple in a society where there is private ownership of the means of production. The experience of the crisis of the 1930's, of the later war and cold war seems to have shaped a situation for a successful combination of the initially conflicting areas in the 1950's and 1960's. The instruments for the realization of "the vision of a new and better Norway" (E. Gerhardsen, former prime minister), were macroeconomic planning and interest group participation.

The theoretical basis for this model was Keynesianism. The idea is that increased public spending and the stimulation of demand in general will lead to economic growth. Counter-cyclical measures and deficit budgets could be justified theoretically against the conservative policy of saving, because temporary government deficits would be fully compensated for in the long term. Keynesian theory incorporates the multiplier effects of public spending, it is a theory of *demand*, focusing on the problem of unemployment.

It is an unsettled question whether this way of governing rep-

resented a step away from socialism towards a peaceful coexistence with capitalism, or if it represented the best road to socialism (Østerud 1971:23, Bergh 1991:6). In any case, it implies the
idea that more planning and order would create a more safe and
rational society. The free play of the market forces was to be
tamed. It was an attempt to stabilize the antagonism between
labor and capital in a game where the cake grew while it was
distributed. The "new government" regulates both distribution
and production. The potentials of the business sector were to be
maintained, simultaneously guaranteeing the security of the individual.

On the one hand, DNA's principle of governance reflects
growth and innovation through the regulation of capitalism. On
the other hand, we find a universal concept of solidarity, where
the former welfare state's means test is supplanted by general
rights. This principle is based on an egalitarian concept of justice
and a high degree of political and economic realism. This link
between humanization and modernization is often termed a
compromise of the welfare state. It is a compromise between
labor and capital: The laborers are granted rights of organization
and negotiation, and capital owners are granted rights of ownership and control. The government has both a regulating and a
compensating function. The result is *the mixed economy*, a strong
public sector and an almost paternalistic welfare policy. The
situation was pro-state and optimistic. Capitalism had been controlled. The success of this program and the absence of an effective opposition led to an expansion of the area where the market
economy was assumed not able to function.

The Disintegration of the Market and the "Negotiational" Economy

The early post-war period was characterized by the transition
from microeconomic regulations to macroeconomic planning.
The primary tool for constructing an economic policy became the
National Budget, which, by systematic analysis of the development of demand and production, provides a solid basis for choice
of policy instruments. This kind of planning puts economists in
the front line and increases legitimacy of political governance.
The idea of nationalization was soon abandoned, and the instruments for economic policy were liberalized in tune with developments within the western trading area: GATT, OECD, EFTA,
EC. Liberalization of trade and a positive attitude towards multi-

national capital are keywords. Increased public regulation was parallel with the introduction of general-purpose instruments and indirect economic policies by manipulation of the money and credit markets.

The model for governance was based on the close, down-to-earth cooperation between the parties on the labor market. The "class-compromise" was institutionalized through encompassing negotiations covering large numbers of workers and firms. The parties of the labor market were included in the political decision-making by participating in various committees and public commissions. Such a model was able to function as long as the supremacy of the government was not disputed (Rokkan 1966, Eriksen 1990).

In the 1970's the *logic of the organizational society* led to the break-down of this "social contract". The early 1960's saw the introduction of a selective industrial policy and government support schemes for troubled firms, and this became the hallmark of the 1970's. Government policy was increasingly motivated by social and political needs, in addition to economic calculations. In 1976 one fourth of industrial funding came from the government so that there was government support "behind every fourth industrial worker" (Østerud, 1979:93). The establishment of capital support schemes, labor subsidies, tax-exemption schemes, the public trust for regional development, The Industrial Bank, etc., was motivated by short-term cycles and social concerns, but quickly became a hindrance to long-term structural change. The government became a guarantee for a firm's survival, for the survival of local communities, profits, jobs and careers, but also a protective shield for professions and a barrier for rearrangements. The mixed economy had become a *negotiational* economy. The role of the state had been increased in relation to the principle of the mixed economy where the government compensates for the accidents, risks and costs incurred by the market economy. There had been a transition to reallocation through institutionalized negotiations. The social democratic model had begun to crack. It resulted in *perversions*, by producing free-riders, *structural problems* by stopping necessary readjustments and *problems of governance* by creating too many decision-makers, confusion of responsibilities and obscure relationships between means and goals (Hernes 1978, Olsen 1978, Berrefjord , Nilsen og Pedersen 1989).

Reform Zeal and State Fixation

The period that ended with the 1970's was marked by an impatient desire for reforms in most areas of society and by humanization of the work-place. The retirement age was lowered in 1974, work-hours were reduced in 1976, a new bill regulating most aspects of company-employee relationships was introduced in 1977 and a new bill for compensation for sick-leave was passed in 1978. This resulted in major formal settlements between the parties of the labor market, both in the private and public spheres. The company-employee bill is one of the most comprehensive in the world. The economy was made more democratic in the sense that public control of the forces of capital was greater than in any other West European country. The period from 1975 to 1981 marked the peak of the "social democratic state" (Lafferty 1986).

The 1970's marked the peak, but also the end, of this principle of governance. It was the peak, because this was the period of major labor reforms and of the largest counter-cyclical measures seen in Norway so far. It was the period of "combined wage-negotiations", where the government took part in the annual salary negotiations, resulting in major government expenses that were financed by spending income that was to come from the oil sector. Per Kleppe, former Minister of Finance, says today that the same effect could have been achieved by far less spending. DNA was probably attempting to regain some of the voters it had lost since 1972, when the party lost in the referendum on EC-membership. A sharp increase in the price of oil with subsequent optimistic prognoses for incomes helped fuel the expansive policy.

Higher inflation, rising interest rates and numerous possibilities for tax avoidance gave rise to speculation on the currency and led capital abroad. The internationalization had made Norway's open economy vulnerable and increased subsidies stimulated imports, rather than domestic production. It was the time of selective industrial policies, growth in real incomes and regional development, but also of an escape from the marketplace and a fixation on governmental solutions. The rate of investment declined, while subsidies and public guarantees of business investments increased. Whereas the other European countries changed their policies during the early 1970's, the turnaround in Norway came later, when it turned out that the increase in inflation was not followed by increased employment. *Stagflation* had eventually reached Norway.

A Pause of Reforms and a Period of Self-Scrutiny

A growing liberalist movement and a declining rate of growth led, together with the stagflation, to an economic counter-revolution. In terms of economic theory, Keynesianism had been on the defensive side since the 1960's. In Norway, this model for government was widely used up to 1977. The revised National Budget of that year signalled the turnaround; it was now important to "...maintain a reasonable development of the competitiveness of the Norwegian industries." The interest rate rose and "credit-socialism" was demolished (Mjøset, 1986: 250). The "dynamic tax policy" of the 1980's was introduced by the labor government at the end of the 1970's, and the regulation of the interest rates was abolished on December 1st, 1977. Thus, the conservatives' deregulations of the 1980's were actually initiated by DNA.

In several countries, the theory that the rate of inflation is closely linked to the money supply, had gained popularity. Starting with the end of the 1970's, the monetarist rhetoric was heard increasingly often – also in Norway. With its simple analogy to the family budget – do not spend more than your income allows – it justified a tight fiscal policy. Only such a policy would provide lower production costs, increased competitiveness and, in the long run, increased employment. The wave from the right had reached Norway.

From 1982, the rejection of counter-cyclical policies was made explicit, and the public sector was to diminish its share of the economy. The non-socialist parties liberalized the financial markets, abolished the radio and TV monopoly, and deregulated the housing market. The growth of the export-related industries was paramount. The acceptance of the latter point by the DNA, marks its turn to the right, as does its pause of reforms in this period. Of course, political ambitions were also lowered by the dramatic drop in oil prices in 1986.

Lacking an alternative policy and faced with a diminishing support, the DNA embarked on a period of self-scrutiny, introduced with a programme for "freedom" (*Aksjon Frihet*) in 1985, where criticism of bureaucracy and ideological renewal are key words. The conservative coalition government introduced a program for modernization of the central government in 1986, and DNA came up with a reform program entitled "The New Government". The conventional interpretation of this turnaround is that DNA tried to brush up its image and moved towards the right in order to attract support. "Central tenets of the right-wing agitation against the public sector and government regulations are accepted" (Overrein, 1988:207). The party had to change its "supply" in order to increase its support, without putting off its traditional voters (Lafferty, 1987:52) and party secretary T. Jagland said that "the DNA must never abandon being a 40 % party".

The Lost Decade

The 1980's is the lost decade, said the leader of the party's youth organization in 1990: DNA saved the economy, but lost the battle of opinions.[2] The 1980's is the decade where social democracy left its original foundations and adopted the terminology of the neoliberalists. Some claim this was the decade of vanishing solidarity and a grand decade for market liberalism and right-wing ideologies. It was the decade when individual freedom conquered the ideology of equality.

Abolishment of government-owned industries, the introduction of unit-pricing in hospitals, increased market-orientation of government provisions, decentralization and liberalization of government services, are all examples of the movement toward the market. Several of the early proposals of the liberalist populistic party – *Fremskrittspartiet* (The Progress Party) – have now been accepted by DNA, even though the DNA as late as 1987 characterized some of them as "blueprints for the destruction of the welfare state.. that may tear apart unity and solidarity. . . and renew destructive divisions between groups and classes".[3]

The terminology for the restructuring of the public sector is neo-liberalist. The stress is put on service, consumer sovereignty, increased effectiveness and decentralization. Quoting Lafferty, a "neo-liberalist modernism is now characterizing the Norwegian social democracy" (1990:90). Clichés for the 1980's are rampant. The 1970's, on the contrary, are seen as "pure and red", as marking the peak of social democratic government where Norway, thanks to counter-cyclical policies, remained an island in a sea of unemployment .[4]

The Distance to the Neo-Liberalists

Many commentators have seen DNA's transition as a defensive one, and as an adoption of central neo-liberalist tenets, where balanced budgets, competitiveness and inflation are put in focus.

The cleaning up after the conservatives' alleged "bankruptcy" of the early 1980's has followed the same recipe. The new DNA-government of 1986 did not return to the traditional way of governing. On the contrary, the new government started the largest economic turnaround since the war, in order to beat inflation, drastically cutting both private and public expenditure. B. Furre (1991:428) claims that the new government " . . finished what the conservative government had said they would do, but did not manage to do". There are, however, several counter-arguments to such an analysis:

1a) After the deregulation of the financial markets, it was impossible to return to the old economic policies, because of the international credit market. The tools of government had been weakened .

1b) Partly, the turnaround reflects the general consensus of Norwegian politics. While the 1970's were marked by an eagerness to reform, without any strongly voiced opposition from the right, the 1980's saw a similar consensus on competitiveness being the most important problem and on cuts in government spending being the solution. A new consensus was established in the areas of housing (1982) and interest rates (1987-8) and opinions on unemployment and agriculture were also greatly changed from 1988 to 1991 (Cappelen et al. 1991:105).

1c) Well-documented flaws in both the efficiency and quality of public services, as well as the recognition of unnecessary regulations, centralization and standardization, led to the efforts for readjustment and renewal of the public sector. The problems of coordination, the power of the professions, the queues, the overconsumption, etc., of the public sector, were well known. Seen together with technological innovations and structural changes of the international economy, it became increasingly difficult to stick to old models of governing.

2) There is also a difficulty in separating neo-liberalist ideas on abolishing monopolies and letting tax-payers get more value for their money on the one hand from social-democratic ideals of consumer participation and economic democracy on the other. In addition, decentralization cannot be seen only as a strategy for governing, but may also be a goal of its own. Readjustments are usually a *twin process of democratization and rationalization* (Eriksen, 1992).

3) The process of adjustment towards the EC gained speed by the end of the 1980's and the negotiations between EC and the EFTA-countries were started. This meant that deregulation had

to continue. It is, of course, possible to see this as just another evidence of DNA's neo-liberalism, but it is more reasonable to see deregulation as a way to achieve another goal – closer ties to the EC. As early as 1953 the party's program said that "with all its history, Norway is connected to the western cultural sphere which democratic socialism originated in. The Norwegian Labor Party wants Norway to support measures leading to closer co-operation within Western Europe."

The Pragmatism of DNA

4) The distance from the neo-liberalists is best seen from the fact that DNA never adopted their glorification of the market. DNA has not adopted the hostility towards trade unions, the critique of the welfare state or the general dislike of social rights. Liberalists see the market not only as the most efficient way of governing, but also as an area of freedom where the individual may realize his or her potentials. DNA agrees only on the first point and its pragmatism is expressed this way in the party's program for the 1989 general election:

> "Duties that have once been public duties may not always have to be public. The same goes for private duties. The choice between public and private has to be made on the basis of the interests of the consumers and of society."

Thus, the movement towards liberalist ideas and solutions means that public solutions are no longer a priority. The "liberalism" of DNA seems to lie in the lack of a principled attitude towards what is to be governed by the state or the market. After 1945, DNA has not been dogmatic on this point, and it has never opposed private enterprise as such (cpr. Grønlie 1989:91).

5) A final point putting DNA apart from the neo-liberalists is their *paternalism*, so typical of the Norwegian social democratic principle of government. This is a matter of general intervention in the civil society; the institutions of society gradually become legally controlled and invaded by professional expertise. Examples are the ban on corporal punishment within the family, psychiatric aid to victims of catastrophes, the ban on smoking in public buildings, etc. All this is contrary to the basic idea of liberalism that the individual cannot be "saved" by anyone except himself and the idea of the protection of the civil society from government intervention. As the economic liberalism of

DNA progressed, the "caring state" was extended rather than reduced.

How then, can we characterize DNA's principle of government? Its economic policy is more liberalist than is the case for other fields of politics. Are we facing a social democracy with lost visions spiffed up with a few market solutions? There are more fundamental reasons for DNA's change than the general political swing to the right in Norwegian politics.

The End of Utopia?

The self-scrutiny that started in the mid-1980's was not only a pragmatic adjustment of ornaments to attract new voters, but was also a search for a new basis. There was a sincerely felt need for a new identity in a changing world. The entire social democratic project had been shaken, and this process had started in the late 1960's and was only partially a result of the wave from the right. The core idea of social democratic thinking of economic growth in a capitalist society, and of compensation for unwanted side-effects of the growth process, ran into problems. Humanization and modernization no longer go hand in hand because the limits to growth and the unintended consequences of growth become apparent. The conflict between labor and capital, having been checked by the compromise of the welfare state, is increasingly turning up in non-economic areas and becomes politically manifest through new social movements. Increasingly, innocent groups have to pay the bill. In addition. the general level of reflection has increased and social valuations and identifications have changed. Improvements in welfare and increased equality lead to differentiations and ways of life that shatter the old model of governance.

The costs of industrial growth turn up in the party programs as early as the end of the 1960's: "...in 1969 a flow of new concepts entered the programs: conservation of nature, pollution, sulphurous fumes, traffic accidents, "environment", etc. ....the flow of new words is one of the reasons to make the period around 1970 mark the beginning of a new period" (Bull 1979:167). The fragmentation of the trade unions and the explosion of higher education and services contributed to the undermining of the class-based foundations of DNA. Together with the growth of the public sector and increased geographical and social mobility, it changed the anatomy of the party. It became clear that man was

Norwegian Prime Minister, Gro Harlem Brundtland.

not only a laborer and a voter, but also a client, a consumer, a citizen and a private person.

At the same time it became increasingly apparent that the consequences of the economic growth were unclear both social-ly, culturally and in terms of ecology. The traditional philosophy of government is undermined throughout the 1970's by opposition to EC-membership, spontaneous strikes, mass movements, civil disobedience, and by new political parties, minority governments and, not least, by demonstration of the darker sides of the welfare state. The social democratic project was already seriously undermined at the end of the 1970's, making it easy for the parties on the right to gain influence.

My point is that the very principle of government was in a crisis, and that the increased reservedness on behalf of the state that we see in the 1980's is not only a strategic move to attract voters. The unintended consequences of the welfare state was common knowledge and the political instruments and the reforms contributed to undermining the social basis of the party. One was puzzled by the "non-solidarity" of the public sector. Social democracy had built a welfare state where an increasing number of people saw alienation, isolation, egoistic misuse of rights, and dwindling willingness to assume responsibility. The "zeitgeist" was described by social democracy's literary man Kjartan Fløgstad, as the time when "...everybody had realized that moral was equal to the absence of socialism". The society had developed in such a way that a lot of people may "... live a life without having to face moral tests ...":

> Greed. Savagery. ......Who may say these words today?
> Behind every child an ombudsman.
> Behind every refugee a counselor.
> Behind every bus a bus with catastrophe psychiatrists.
> Behind every old person a team of social workers.
> Behind every woman a rape center.
> (Fløgstad 1991: 220, 105, 221.)

The Conservative Element and the Limits of Remoralization

Thus, there are grounds for asking whether the conservative principle of governance sheds as much light on the development of DNA as does the neo-liberalist. Egoism and lack of responsibility are criticized and solidarity is wanting. Increasingly, one is scrutinizing the ways in which public policies undermine the possibility of collective action. Through this process, DNA discovered the civil *society* outside the state and the market. Voluntary organizations became popular in the 1980's and gave rise to statements like: "It is now of utmost importance to guard and increase the status of the popular communities in between the state and the market".[4] A white paper on voluntary organizations put forth by the conservatives in 1988 was praised by the DNA and the ideas turned up in a parliamentary report (Stortings-melding nr. 4 1988-89) where it is said that "many tasks may be solved through communal cooperation and by voluntary organi-zations". The prime minister herself praised this kind of work highly. The speech given by the vice-chairman of the party Einar Førde – at the party conference in 1987 – was a clear indication of the extent to which the conservative cultural diagnosis had been accepted:

"During the last years we have been shown what may happen if one makes self-interest and egoism the fundamental principles. A modern economy where managers, workers and consumers are lying, stealing and cheating wherever possible in order to satisfy one's own interests, will end in economic chaos. ...An increasing number of people are concerned about the importance of moral standards in a good society. A society without ideology, religion, patriotism and true local communities is liable to become a so-ciety without a lot of freedom."

The vital issue is now to create a new ideological foundation for the party by revitalizing the classical virtues. At the begin-ning of the 1990's, the conservative critique has gained a mo-mentum within the DNA. Today's debates on "kind-ism" (snil-lisme) is the most significant expression of this (Gerhardsen 1991). The questioning of the effects of social policies are like blueprints of the conservative critique.

Even so, it is hard to see how it will be possible to succeed with such a strategy. First of all, the old labor society has disap-peared. Secondly, moralism will never be a viable strategy. The society has been through processes of *learning and democrati-zation* that cannot be reversed. DNA itself has contributed to the destruction of both social and political hierarchies and has nur-tured a new system of norms. This has displaced both the bour-geois-protestant work ethic and the simple social democratic ide-ology of equality. Moral norms are only effective when we believe in them and feel they are true. They are not binding when they are only "useful", i.e. when the consequences of following the norms are good for society. Consequences like that are only side-effects: One does not believe in God because it leads to a more healthy society or shorter queues for operations. A remoral-istic policy, be it a return to the protestant work ethic or to simple social democratic virtues, is in effect, a totalitarian project: "A

moralizing policy is absolutely not less gruesome than a machia-
vellian policy" (Heller 1983:4), because it entails the enforcement of meaning upon an individual. In any case, as a political
project it is futile: It would be just as futile as trying to enlighten
a dog by letting it eat books (Hegel 1969:13).

Complexity and Reason

The state is no longer seen as a neutral instrument for the realization of the good society, but more like an apparatus that has to
be used with more cleverness and reflection than before. DNA's
philosophy of governance of the late 1980's reflects this dilemma
for government planning: "The market strikes back when set
aside, but follows unprioritized roads when let loose" (Østerud
1979:97). There is no efficient countermeasure except moderate
Keynesianism. A unilateral return of competence to social networks, to voluntary organizations and community leagues is so
much at odds with the self-image of social democracy and its
antipathy towards charity that this does not seem to be any alternative. Thus, DNA's philosophy of government must be interpreted as a continuation of the party's traditional pragmatism and
technocratic paternalism. The swing to the right in recent years
reflects just as much neo-liberalist as conservative ideas. What
remains is a philosophy of government that sways between traditional social democratic regulations, neo-liberalist market solutions and a conservative restraint on behalf of the government. Is
there any reason to be found behind this?

The society of today is so complex that different institutions
and ways of governing are needed for different purposes and for
different causes. Whereas the *market* has to be used to stop unnecessary bureaucratization and to provide efficient production,
and the *state* has to govern the arena for market transactions and
stop informal tyrannies, the civil society outside state and market
has to be engaged and informal social networks maintained.
Simple solutions in a complex world are to no use. The return to
one principle, to one philosophy of governance implies regres-
sion because it represents a return to something of the past,
something transgressed. Only by grasping the *logic of differentiation* may one stop the new vagueness from leading to irrationality.

The problem with this principle of governance is that in itself it
has no appeal, it lacks a message that arouses the voters and a
guiding principle between the three models of governance. The

dilemma of DNA reflects the problems of the modern society in securing the autonomy of various institutions, so that freedom, community feeling, and solidarity are not destroyed by technological and economic imperatives. Only from this understanding may one pursue a reasonable project for maintaining the idea of humanization and modernization in a world where ecological pressures, poverty in the south and the disintegration of Eastern Europe are increasingly present. The social democratic idea of solidarity may offer a way to tackle these global problems in a relatively civilized way.

Some maintain that the social democratic project has depleted its potential and that it is ready for the garbage heap. This is probably somewhat premature, considering any modern market economy has to be regulated to a certain extent. It may be balanced out by feudal norms, religious beliefs, or civil culture. In a secular and fragmented world these kinds of counterforces tend to lose ground. The advantage of the social democratic counterforces is that they are based on real interests (the conflict between labor and capital) and are being supported by trade union power. The success of social democracy lies in an effective balancing out of market power by organizations, allocation of rights and government regulations. When it comes to making a market economy function, the emerging regimes in the east and south have much to learn from the social democratic model.

Notes

1. Another version of this article was published in Nytt Norsk Tidsskrift no. 1 1992 entitled The Governmental Philosophy of the Norwegian Labour Party in the 1970's and 1980's.
2. Turid Birkeland, Dagbladet, July 12, 1990.
3. Quoted from Olsen (1988:12) .
4. "The Labour Party into a new century", quoted from Lafferty (1987:54).

References

Bell, Daniel. *The Cultural Contradictions of Capitalism.* New York, 1976.
Bellah, Robert. (ed.). *Habits of the Heart.* Berkeley, 1985.
Berrefjord, Ole, Klaus Nielsen og Ove K. Pedersen. "Forhandlingsøkonomi i Norden – en indledning". In K. Nielsen og O. Pedersen (eds.), *Forhandlingsøkonomi i Norden.* Oslo, 1989.
Bergh, Trond. "Arbeiderpartiets styringsfilosofl etter krigen", i R. Slagstad og T. Nordby (red.): *Fagstyre og sosialdemokratisk politikk,* Universitetet i Oslo/ LOS-senteret 1991.
Buchanan, James M. *Liberty, Market and State.* Wheatsheaf, 1985.
Bull, Edvard. *Norge i den rike verden. Norges historie,* bd. 14. Oslo, 1987.

Cappelen, Ådne, Per Richard Johansen og Knut Moum. "Nasjonalbudsjettet som styringsinstrument og ideologisk tumleplass". B. E. Rasch og R. Slagstad (eds.): *Parlamentarisk styring og økonomisk politikk: symboler, signaler, realiteter.* LOS-notat 1991:1.

Eriksen, Erik O. "Towards the post-corporate state?" *Scandinavian Political Studies,* no. 4:345-364 (1990).

Eriksen, Erik O. "Fra målstyring til selvstyring". *Tidsskrift for samfunnsforskning* no. 3 (1992).

Fløgstad, Kjartan. *Kniven på strupen.* Oslo, 1991.

Friedman, Milton. *Free to Choose.* New York, 1990.

Furre, Berge. *Vårt hundreår. Norsk historie 1905-1990.* Oslo, 1991.

Gerhardsen, Einar. *Samarbeid og strid. Erindringer 1945-55.* Oslo, 1971.

Gerhardsen, Rune. *Snillisme på norsk.* Oslo, 1991.

Grønlie, Tore. *Statsdrift.* Oslo, 1989.

Habermas, Jürgen. *Legitimationsproblemer i senkapitalismen.* 1973. Translation. København, 1975.

Habermas, Jürgen. *Theorie des kommunikativen handelns. Band 2. Zur Kritik der funktionalistischen Vernunft.* Frankfurt, 1981.

Hayek, Frederick A. *The Constitution of Liberty.* Chicago, 1960.

Hegel, Georg W.F. *Vorlesungen über die Philosophie der Religion 1. Werke in zwanzig Bänden 16.* 1832–45. Reprint: Frankfurt, 1969.

Heller, Agnes. "Politikk og moral", *Samtiden* vol. 92(1):2-13 (1987).

Hemes, Gudmund (red.) (1978): *Forhandlingsøkonomi og blandingsadministrasjon.* Oslo, 1978.

Keynes, John M. *The General Theory of Employment, Interest and Money.* London, 1936.

Lafferty, William. "Den sosialdemokratiske stat". *Nytt Norsk Tidsskrift* vol.3 (no. 1):23-37. (1986).

Lafferty, William. "DNAs nye retning". *Nytt Norsk Tidsskrift* vol. 4 (no.4):46-55. (1987).

Lafferty, William M. "The Political Transformation of a Social Democratic State. Neoliberalism as Modernism in Norway". in R. Slagstad and T. Nordby (ed.): *Fagstyre og sosialdemokratisk politikk,* Universitetet i Oslo/LOSsenteret 1990.

Mjøset, Lars (ed.). *Norden dagen derpå.* Oslo, 1985.

Mjøset, Lars. "Norges økonomiske integrasjon i den første verden", i L. Alldèn et al. (red.) *Det norske samfunnet.* Oslo, 1986.

Nozick, Robert. *Anarchy, State and Utopia.* Oxford, 1974.

Nyhamar, Jostein. *Arbeiderbevegelsens historie i Norge bind 6. Nye utfordringer.* Oslo, 1990.

Oakshott, Michael. *Rationalism in Politics.* New York, 1962.

Offe, Claus. *The Contradictions of the Welfare State.* London, 1984.

Olsen, Johan P. (ed.). *Politisk organisering.* Oslo, 1978.

Olsen, Johan P. *Statsstyre og institusjonsutforming.* Oslo, 1988.

Overein, Arne. "Sosialdemokrati mellom stat og samfunn". *Vardøger* no.18:68-115. (1988)

Rokkan, Stein. "Norway: Numerical Democracy and Corporate Pluralism", in Dahl, R. A. (ed.): *Political Oppositions in Western Democracies,* New Haven: Yale University Press, 70-115, 1966.

(St. meld. nr. 4 (1987-88): *Perspektiver og reformer i den økonomiske politikken.* Finans- og tolldepartementet.

St.meld. nr. 4 (1988-89). *Langtidsprogrammet 1990-1993.* Finans- og tolldepartementet.

Østerud, Øyvind. *Samfunnsplanlegging og politisk system.* Oslo, 1972.

Østerud, Øyvind. *Det planlagte samfunn.* Oslo, 1979.

8

Norwegian Families

Øystein Gullvåg Holter

The Family as the Moral of Society

When Henrik Ibsen described the hypocrisy of the bourgeoisie of the 1880s, he followed a Norwegian tradition, portraying family conflicts not just as private matters but as a public concern. He described the patriarchal family and the plight of women like Nora as symptoms of the conditions of society as a whole.

Family matters have in some respects always been more 'public' in Norway than in many other European countries, including even the other Nordic countries. In Ibsen's later days there was a debate among Nordic male intellectuals on women's rights, and men's role toward women – with the focus on men's use of prostitutes. Not only were the Norwegian men in this debate, like Bjørnstjerne Bjørnson, more equality-minded than the Swedish and Danish participants, like August Strindberg and Georg Brandes, they were also much more critical towards the idea that men's use of prostitutes was a private matter only.

Norwegian culture puts emphasis on outdoor activities and sports, often in a family setting. On Sundays the whole family should go for a walk in the woods – or go skiing in the winter. Children should play outside and not stay around in the home all the time. – One could perhaps relate the 'public' character of family life to this outdoor orientation. Yet Norwegian families may seem closed and rather impenetrable, for example from the viewpoint of many Third World cultures. Norwegian family life has much of its historical background in the 'protestant ethic', where the home is a 'private world' and not primarily part of a local community. Relations between families may appear as rather distant, cold or even altogether absent. The family often presents a successful facade to the outside world which is not in tune with what actually happens inside it.

However, these traits and the Norwegian version of the 'protestant ethic' itself are more complex when one looks more closely. Norwegian families are products of very different cultural and historical traditions; what appears as a homogeneous culture is in fact a mixture of tendencies which often contradict each other. The greater emphasis on family life as a public matter in Norway compared to many other Western countries is one example. It co-exists with the opposite tendency of closing off internal matters behind a polished facade. The Norwegian "Jante Laws" may be mentioned in this contest: don't pretend you amount to anything special, don't stick your head out, stay safe in the ranks of the conformists. Some would cite this law as an example of the costs of putting emphasis on equality. To be *different* easily comes to mean being *difficult* in the eyes of others.

Norwegians bumping into one another on the street literally say *"Unguilt me!" (Unnskyld meg)*. In the protestant ethic and perhaps especially in its Norwegian version, sanctions centre around the notion of *guilt*. One is punished not primarily by some strong external authority, or by losing face in the community, but rather through an inner feeling of guilt.

Guilt (and unguilt) are strongly connected to a sense of *justice*. As mentioned, being equal and being just are associated in Norwegian culture. Here we meet an aspect of the family tradition where Norway does in fact differ from that of many other Western countries: the comparative lack of authoritarianism in personal relations. Or, put somewhat differently: authority and discipline in *indirect* forms, for example through each person's guilt and private conscience, rather than in *direct* forms. Alice Miller's books on the treatment of children in traditional Germany and continental Europe illustrate this difference. The childhoods described by Miller are filled with harsh direct discipline and physical violence. The all-ruling family head, the *patria potestas*, is a living reality. Such tendencies existed in Norway, too. But what Miller calls "the black pedagogy" could perhaps better be described as grey in Norway; things never went quite that far.

These differences all relate to one basic historical fact: Norway was never a feudal country – or at least never a fully feudalized country. The "vertical" feudal order with authoritarian relations from top to bottom of society never really became part of the social fabric of daily life. Norway is better described as a country 'under' a feudalism which always remained foreign. In the five hundred years of Danish sovereignty over Norway, the Danes never succeeded in creating a strong local feudal organization. There were some local aristocrats in the richest, southeastern parts of the country, but comparatively speaking it did not amount to much. Tax collection, for example, usually depended on travelling Danish bureaucrats. Like Switzerland, the mountainous and thinly populated country of Norway did not favour a feudal social order. This had great implications, not just for Norwegian family culture in the transition from the Middle Ages, but for the whole of Norwegian society, in modern times also. Norway never had feudal villages with the serf population living beneath the castle walls. Instead, Norwegians lived spread out across the land, with each farm or *gård* (farm) as a self-owning and (to a great extent) self-governing unit. This had been the case also in Viking times, and in other Germanic areas as well, but in Norway the pattern survived. Local political authority retained the sense of "first among peers" typical of kinship societies – again very different from the feudal sense of authority deriving from pope or king.

It has even been argued that the Norwegian household structure contributed to the break-up of feudalism itself and the transition to capitalism in northwestern Europe. In England, especially, Norwegians and other Scandinavians settled in great numbers during the eighth and ninth century. These were mostly peaceful settlers, arriving before the Viking attacks, and their culture left a great impact on the local communities. Whole areas in Yorkshire and other parts of central England still have Nordic place-names and family names, and historical documents show a household structure which was strikingly different from the feudal manor system elsewhere in England. As in Norway itself, the *gårder* were spread and not grouped in villages, with women as well as men owning, selling and buying land. English historians have noted the importance of women and the very early 'commercialism' of these areas (D.M. Stenton 1956). Later on, the earliest 'capitalist' patterns can be found in many of these regions, rather than in the more heavily feudalized regions of the south.

The relatively 'public' character of the Norwegian family can probably be connected to the relative importance of the household, compared to other institutions of society. In one sense the household was everywhere the main institution, up until the industrial revolution, since it was the primary producing unit. Yet this economic primacy may coexist with very different social patterns; families may be heavily subordinated or enclosed within a wall of privacy, as in classical Greece, in Islamic countries, etc. The importance of the household also depends on the political and social context. In the Norwegian tradition, the power of the household and of women as main producers within the household was symbolized by the *gård* wife's key to the *stabbur* (the storage house). This power was usually connected to a comparative lack of strong male institutions surrounding the household. Here is another pattern with modern-day connections: German men visit the Bierstube, the British go to the pub, etc. – Norwegians, however, go home.

To some extent, household power and self-sufficiency can still be seen today, especially in districts where the men have traditionally left the household in periods in order to get paid work, while the woman has been responsible both for the children and for the 'local economy' – the small *gård* or *småbruk*. Men's periodic absence and the importance of women's contributions to the household may give women a 'say' in family matters that is greater than one would expect, at least from an urban middle-class perspective where the two-career family seems the only road to gender equality (Borchgrewinck and Melhuus 1985; Heen, Holter and Solheim 1987).

It should perhaps be emphasised that all these differences are relative; Norwegians usually have gender equality as an ideal, but their practice may not be so different from what one finds in other Western countries. Yet recent cross-cultural studies confirm the difference in attitudes to equal rights' questions (in family life as well as worklife) between the Nordic countries and other countries. Among the advanced industrialized countries, these studies indicate an interesting triadic pattern – with the Nordic countries as the most egalitarian group, followed by a broad middle group which includes most of the English-speaking countries, and a third least-egalitarian group where Germany, Italy, and Japan are prominent – the former axis powers (Hofstede 1980; Williams and Best 1982; Holter 1989:35ff).

It is a strange paradox that the modern equality-minded Norwegian state has in many respects been a poorer provider for the family than the state in many other countries. Although the ideology of the Nordic governments has been similar, the Swedish state, for example, has done much more for the family than the Norwegian. Swedish couples of the 1980s would easily get daycare centres for their small children; Norwegians usually had to wait, or do without. The paradox is not so strange, perhaps, given the Norwegian idea of the family as a public sphere by itself – so while the Swedes and others concentrated on providing for their young families, Norwegians discussed how husband and wife should share the burdens equally.

Family Demographics

As in other Western countries, family research and divorce statistics especially made "the crisis of the family" a subject of public discussion in the 70s and 80s. Married Norwegian couples have been less divorce-prone than couples in many other Western countries, but the differences are diminishing, and the divorce rate continues to climb, if not as steeply as in the 70s.

There has been some speculation whether the 70s and 80s trends will be reversed, with a "New familism" and a return to conditions more similar to the 50s – low divorce rate, higher birth rate, more adults living in family households, etc. Although there has been an increase in the birth rate over the last five years (again, on par with many other countries), the increase probably does not signal a return of this type. One main difference, of course, is the proportion of employed married women, which is much higher today than it was in the 50s. But there are also other important dissimilarities.

About one in four of all adult women aged 20-40 live in "paperless marriages" as unmarried cohabitants – fifteen years ago it was only one in twenty. Two out of three women live with a partner, married or unmarried, today, as against three out of four fifteen years ago. The married proportion of the population has declined dramatically, and there has also been a decline in the total proportion living with a partner.

The increasing proportion of single households may seem to imply more social isolation and loneliness. A rising suicide rate, especially among young men, might be taken as evidence of this. On the other hand, statistical "loneliness measures" do not point to any significant change, except perhaps a greater proportion of men lacking close friendships. One out of four men lack an intimate friend, as against one out of seven or eight women. Statistical measures like these are, however, somewhat crude, and they are usually more influenced by the set-up and context of the interview or questionnaire than the researchers care to admit. Other indicators – like drug and alcohol abuse – tend to show an increase over the last fifteen years, as they do in other countries, with a clustering of such problems among the less well off in the cities especially.

During the last years, economic problems have reemerged on the agenda of many Norwegian families in a way unknown since the thirties, with day-to-day money difficulties for many, and unemployment and personal bankruptcy for some. In a recent

Two fathers on a stroll

survey it was estimated that one of four households in the cities needed welfare support in order to keep their houses or apartments. Although the economic depression has been less deep than in countries like Denmark and England, it has left a serious impact on many families, with long-term unemployment among young people as an especially serious problem.

Three Family Cultures

Norwegian family patterns traditionally have shown significant regional differences. Nonmarried cohabitation, for example, always was more accepted in northern Norway than elsewhere, and the proportion is still somewhat higher here than in the south. Strongly religious regions, on the western and southern coasts especially, have traditionally had a much lower divorce rate and a higher birth rate, than the rest of the country. These differences have diminished over the last fifteen years, but there still exists several "family cultures" in Norway, based primarily on regional and social class differences.

In a broad postwar perspective, three major "family cultures" may be identified. What is interesting about these cultures is their variation not only on formal measures like the proportion married or the divorce rate, but the different ways in which informal interaction and communication is structured. Each contains its own "social logic", with tacit rules about proper behaviors.

For some family researchers (and for some social researchers), it is difficult to imagine a social relation which is not an *exchange* relation or where the communication has an aspect of *negotiation*. Terms which are derived from the market sphere of society are used rather indiscriminately for all social affairs. Yet family life, in particular, is something very different, and it is more different within some family cultures than others.

In what might loosely be termed *the urban middle class family culture*, the principles of market exchange are perhaps not that foreign to what actually goes on in families. Here, partners tend to emphasize a fair and just outcome for each, rather than the common result of family interaction. The individual rather than the group is the basic unit. Like all exchange relations, the relation between husband and wife can be dissolved, when it no longer is deemed fair and just.

Things are different in *the urban working class family culture*. Social class differences have not disappeared in the family field (H. Holter et al. 1976), and the economic difficulties over the last years may even have strengthened the contrasts. The bond between man and wife in the working class family is also dissolvable, but for typically different reasons – lack of solidarity, rather than unfair exchange. Of course this may in practice be one and the same thing, but the different frameworks for interpretation are nevertheless important. The common good and the value of being together are emphasized by the family members, rather than the outcome for each individual.

A third type may be called *the rural family culture*. Although this type is in fact even more diversified than the two first, some common traditional traits especially within families in Southern Norway may be distinguished. Once again, the family is not the place for negotiations. While the urban middle class couple would emphasize "fruitful discussions" and the working class couple would talk about the necessity of sometimes venting the air, the rural couple would like to be described as harmonious. Often, this relates to the importance of keeping up a facade and not being the object of gossip in the village (*i bygda*). Traditionally, divorce was frowned upon, and the informal sanctions against divorce probably are still higher than in the cities. Gift principles, rather than market or solidarity logic, often seem of basic importance to the interaction. In one study of such couples, for example, the women especially emphasized the significance of "silent gifts" – if the act of giving is made visible or mentioned outright, the gift loses its "gift value" (Heel, Holter and Solheim 1987). Being worthy of respect (and self-respect) is an important theme in Norwegian culture generally, but it seems especially relevant here (T. Ødegård in Haukaa 1991).

As mentioned, family statistics imply that some of these differences between family cultures have diminished. This is probably the case with the urban-rural dimension, but not necessarily with class. As before in history, it seems that greater homogeneity has been achieved primarily through the diffusion of urban middle-class family values. Quite a bit of modern family research unintentionally forms part of this process by ascribing urban middle-class values to other family cultures and finding them lacking when realities don't match up.

One especially persistent issue here is the idea that working class families are more backward, limited, authoritarian, etc. than middle class families. In-depth analyses of such questions have reached widely different conclusions. Yet I believe family researchers would agree things are *not that simple*. Working class families may, for example, seem more restricted in their verbal communication, but have a richer communicative process on other levels. They may put greater emphasis on discipline towards children, when asked through questionnaires, but participant studies may reach the opposite conclusion that they do in fact give more freedom to children, with less of the indirect control typical of middle class families. In sum, families still are *qualitatively* different, even if at first there seems to be a variation in quantity only.

Ideals and Reality

The present-day cultural image of "family living" in Norway is in many ways ambiguous and to some extent self-contradictory. There is a huge gap between the equality ideals expressed by most Norwegians, and the gender relations portrayed in commercial culture. Greater equality seems to have strengthened the need for a renewed cultural gender polarization in some areas. Advertisements for women's underwear, for example, no longer sell underwear only; instead the emphasis is on feminine beauty and sexuality. Women are pictured as they would want men to see them – at least in the advertiser's mind. This may be old news in other countries, but in Norway one especially visible compaign of this type recently created a public debate. Men, on the other hand, are portrayed as more 'androgynous' characters, care-persons as well as breadwinners. Here too the picture is ambiguous, for the emphasis on masculinity, the masculine body and muscles especially, is perhaps greater than ever.

Could there be such a thing as too much equality? Some Norwegians believe the women's struggle has had a negative impact on family relations. If men and women become too alike, the love relationship will suffer, since love depends on different, or as some would say, complementary qualities. The result would be a drab, monotonous private life. Family research does not quite confirm this argument. Researchers point to similarity between men and women as a major force creating love relations (Moxnes 1990). Also, divorces seem to occur more frequently among dissimilar couples than among relatively homogeneous couples. The man's control or dominance is still a frequent reason for divorce among women (Ø.G.Holter 1989:207-225). Feminists would say that the struggle for equality between the sexes has in fact only begun; Norwegians still live in a culture based on 'patriarchal premises', and the Norwegian economy especially cannot by any stretch of the imagination be called egalitarian. Also, when women in some fields attain positions of power, they usually have had to adopt the masculine world view and behaviors in order to do so.

This debate on the future of equality is of course unresolved. It seems relevant to ask what equality should be like, since it is often overlooked in the debate that equal rights and influence in private and public life does not necessarily mean that men and women should be more similar to each other. In fact they could as well be more different; this is not really the issue. The confusion of the question of rights with the question of similarity, and the fact that equal rights seem possible to attain only by women becoming more like men, does perhaps confirm the feminists' claim that the basic premises of society remain unchanged.

Children

Most Norwegians would like to see a greater priority given to children's needs, and studies do indicate some positive changes in adults' relations to children in everyday family life (*Tidsnytting* 1990-91; Holter and Aarseth 1992). On the other hand the press has frequent reports on sexual abuse and maltreatment of children.

Some of these negative traits are probably new and specific to our times. This is not, of course, a specifically Norwegian phenomenon, since recent abuse studies have shown surprisingly high levels in a number of countries, but it certainly does not fit with Norwegian family ideals or even with the 'official' picture of the Norwegian family. Although the overwhelming majority of men deny being in any way excited by sexual violence, family statistics and studies show other realities beneath the surface. Approximately ten percent of Norwegian adults were victims of sexual abuse during their childhood according to one representative study, which also indicates that these experiences have strong negative long-term effects on the victims (Sætre et al. 1986).

At this point family ideals and realities may be bewildering, not just to the casual observer but to researchers too. Seemingly, family life goes "totally off the hinges" within a substantial minority of households, resulting in various kinds of abuse, neglect, violence, betrayal, etc. And the background is probably less tangible today than it once was; economic difficulties and childhood traumas in adults' biographies are seldom sufficient explanations for abuse.

Some would point to the connection between violence, sexuality and exploitation in parts of commercial culture, in order to explain the abuse and violence statistics. The experts may quarrel over the influence of commercially portrayed violence, but to most people it seems clear that videos, for example, glorifying violence and speculative sexuality, must have negative effects.

Family violence and abuse is to a great extent a male problem in the sense that most offenders are men. According to some studies, these men are not – as was once believed – wildly different from the "normal" man. Therefore some feminist researchers believe male abuse or oppression may be a matter of opportunity more than personal background. On the other hand most of the backgrounds of these men remain unknown, and a number of relevant questions have not really been investigated. Further research may uncover marked differences between offenders and other men as regards experiences of authority, personal alienation, relationship towards the other sex, etc. Many men may have a 'potential' towards some form of oppression in relationships where they are in the strong position; yet most men are not involved in abuse or violence.

The gap between ideals and reality may seem to be one of the greatest problems of Norwegian families. Adults would like to do things 'for the sake of the children'. In reality other matters often carry greater weight. They would like an egalitarian relationship without male dominance. – Such ideals are perhaps problematical by themselves, since they tend to blur the realities involved, especially when combined with the traditional tendency of presenting a nice family facade towards the outside world. Yet studies show that the change of ideals – the greater emphasis on gender equality and on children's needs – have been a major force of change over the last twenty years, even if practical changes have been smaller and more slow-coming than many would admit.

Greater realism in public education and in political debates on these issues would probably help many young couples trying to establish a new family. Many young women discover to their dismay that gender equality has not been achieved once and for all, as they learned in school. They still end up in lower-paying and more strenuous jobs than the men of their generation; when they marry these men, the relationship still often has a "vertical" aspect – the two are not quite on the same level, after all. In modern families, this becomes visible especially when one looks at the priority given to his job versus her job. In one recent study, two thirds of women living with or married to men in high-paying "dynamic" jobs said the demands connected to their husband's job stopped them from getting a job for themselves or restricted their paid work (Ø.G.Holter 1990).

According to many researchers, the situation of official equality and unofficial inequality often leads to a kind of private 'ideology production': we are not really unequal, his job counting more is just a temporary matter (Haavind 1982). Although social psychologists point to internal processes creating inequalities in the relationship, for many couples these are better understood as unwanted consequences of external practical and economic conditions. Inequality still pays, at least in some parts of the population, since a "one-and-a-half job orientation" with the man's career as the primary goal of both may result in a better standard of living. This is most notable in the private sector. In the study of couples with the men in dynamic jobs mentioned above, the men sought to compensate for some of their job-related dominance by giving more say to the women in the internal family negotiations. What is different, in this and other new studies, is the emphasis given to the equality ideal among men as well as women (Ø.G.Holter 1989B).

Some of these contradictions also appear in the case of children. Parents should be friends, and not primarily authorities, towards their children. They should appreciate the contact with children not just for the sake of the children, but for their own personal development as well – a point emphasized especially in the middle class (Tiller et al. 1983). The idealization of children may be greater among men than among women; to some extent it is a result of a lack of real contact with children. Thus, men working long hours often express a greater longing for more family time than women working short hours – another example of the kind of "half-fact" which is so typical in this field. Sometimes the idealized child seems to function primarily as the *investment object* of the parents. The commercialized child culture which worries many kindergarten teachers and child care workers cannot be seen only as a push-down effect from the international consumer industry; it has some real basis in the commercialized relations of children's lives.

Conclusion

Over the last generation, men and women in Norwegian families have tried to redefine what "family" should be about, with ideals differing from those of earlier generations. Formerly different family cultures have to some extent been supplanted by a more homogeneous middle class culture, with greater emphasis on the individual and the individual's freedom and rights. Gender equality has not been achieved, but even if the change of ideals has been greater than the practical changes, there has been progress on both levels. While the 70's and early 80's were a period of change for women especially, during the last years more emphasis has been put on increasing men's family participation and their contact with children.

With "serial monogamy", a high divorce rate, and a high proportion of singles etc., Norwegian family patterns have become more similar to those in countries like Britain or the United States. As one recent study of dating advertisements shows, there has been a marked shift in romantic ideals over the last twenty years. In the early seventies, the emphasis was still on the 'natural' qualities of masculinity and femininity. Today, gender appears more as one of many dimensions in each person's individuality (Ø.G.Holter 1990B).

Paradoxically, the increased individualism may also have meant an increased "disregard of subjectivity", at least on some levels. Disregard or disrespect for personal integrity seems to be a common factor behind a number of new trends relating to the family. These include cultural symptoms like growing fields of pornography and prostitution, family symptoms like violence and sexual abuse, and psychological symptoms like anorexia and rising suicide rates. On investigation, most cases of violence and misuse against oneself or other people tell a sad story of personal neglect, of people never having been respected and loved as subjects – but rather as objects for the use or misuse of others. The case of the woman as "sex object", then, is in this interpretation only one rather visible consequence of a more common pattern. None of these patterns are specifically Norwegian; but they are perhaps less taken for granted here than in many other countries. Instead they become matters of public concern, as they were in Ibsen's days.

Some would see a more exploitative attitude in the individualistic family culture as the primary background factor of the new (or renewed) family problems. It is a culture for the successful and the winners, which does not enhance the sense of personal integrity for the rest. At the same time, more individualism has undoubtedly meant greater freedom, at least compared to the rather strict informal discipline and sanctions of traditional Norwegian family life. In Norwegian political debate, freedom and equality are often seen as alternatives, but family history shows that this is not the whole truth. Young urban couples are more individualistic today than they were in the radical 70's, at least in their outspoken ideals; yet their sense of justice and equality in personal relations is probably sharper than it was twenty years ago. It is not, therefore, just a case of an old culture of equality and solidarity being wiped out by liberalistic individualism, even if that is one popular portrait of the situation. There are also new forms of solidarity and equality, based on greater personal responsibility instead of conformity, and the outcome of these complex changes in the family sphere is an open question.

References

Borchgrewinck, Tordis and Marit Melhuus. Familie og arbeid: fokus på sjømannsfamilier. *AFI rapport* 27/85, Oslo, 1985.

Heen, Hanne, and Ø. G. Holter and Jorun Solheim. *Hjemmeliv og Nordsjøliv.* AFI, Oslo, 1987.

Gullestad, Marianne. *Kitchen-table Society.* Oslo, 1984.

Haukaa, Runa, (ed.). *Nye kvinner – nye menn?* Oslo, 1991.

Heen, Hanne, and Ø. G. Holter and Jorun Solheim. *Hjemmeliv og Nordsjøliv,* del 2. AFI, Oslo, 1987.

162   ØYSTEIN GULLVÅG HOLTER

Holter, Øystein Gullvåg. *Menn.* Oslo, 1989.
– Likestilling 1989. SIFO-rapport, Lysaker, 1989 (B).
– *Arbeid og familie – en studie av teknologkulturen.* Oslo, 1990.
Holter, Øystein Gullvåg and Helene Aarseth. *Menns livssammenheng.* AFI, Oslo, 1992 (in print).
Levekårsundersøkelsen 1988, Statistisk sentralbyrå, Oslo, 1989.
Moxnes, Kari. *Kjernesprengning i familien,* Oslo, 1990.
Sosialt Utsyn 1989. Statistisk Sentralbyrå, Oslo, 1989.
Stenton, D. M. *The English Woman in History.* London, 1956.
Sætre, Marianne, Harriet Holter and Ellen Jebsen. *Tvang til seksualitet – en undersøkelse av seksuelle overgrep mot barn.* Oslo, 1986.
Tiller, Per Olav, Lars Grue (eds.). *Å vokse opp i Norge.* Oslo, 1983.

9

Sami: The Indigenous Peoples of Norway*

Tove Skotvedt

Introduction

Nomads far north beyond the Arctic Circle, striding around with their tents and reindeers in the cold and dark polar night. The image of this exotic and colorful part of the Norwegian population is an easy tourist attraction to sell.

Is this a fair picture of Norway's indigenous people? The answer is both "yes" and "no". The Sami identity has been, and still is, strongly attached to their traditional way of life that permits close contact with nature, reindeer herding, fishing and hunting, reindeer fur clothing and speaking the Sami language. The traditional picture can be true of the Sami communities in northern Norway, but the Sami have moved to other parts of Norway as well. Oslo, 2,000 kilometers away from the Sami homeland, represents the largest "Sami Community" with approximately 5,000 Sami. However, one almost never sees them wearing their traditional costumes nor hears them speaking their language. Are they still Sami or are they Norwegians, or maybe both?

With a population of approximately 40,000, the Sami represent a minority with a unique status. This special position has been underlined by the Norwegian Minister for Sami affairs at the conference of the World Council for Indigenous Peoples that took place in Norway during the summer of 1990:

In 1988 the Norwegian parliament amended the Constitution of 1814 by inserting a new article that is incumbent on the authorities of the state to create conditions enabling the Sami people to preserve and develop their own language, culture and societal life. The Sami people and the Norwegian government should both work on the distinct understanding that the Sami

---

* Until recently, the Norwegian indigenous peoples were called Lapps by the Norwegian majority and throughout the world. The word Sami has now replaced Lapps as the officially recognized name and the name the Sami have always referred to themselves by.

culture holds possibilities for development in accordance with its own premises. The Sami shall neither be Norwegian in language or in culture, nor shall they be kept as a "living page in the book of history". The Sami must rather make their own choice as to which extent they shall take up new cultural elements. The role of authorities can only provide the conditions for making this development possible. Shaping the actual contents must be the role of the indigenous peoples themselves.[1]

Formal instruments for integration exist and are financed by Norwegian authorities. Is this sufficient for a successful integration? For whom is integration successful: the Norwegian authorities or the Sami?

In order to attempt to answer the questions mentioned above, one needs to look into the history of these people that populated Norway long before the Norwegian national state was established in 1000 A.D. It is a history that for the Sami includes centuries of isolation, oppression by the Norwegians and the Sami uproar and fight for recognition. It was not until 1989 that the big national and international indigenous event took place: Olav V, the late king of Norway, formally inaugurated the first proper Sami Assembly (*Sametinget*) in Norway.

Origins and the Present Demographic Situation of the Sami.

The word *Sápmi* exists in every Sami dialect and it signifies both the Sami land and the Sami people. *Sápmi* comprises the northern regional parts of Norway, Sweden, Finland as well as the Kola peninsula in Russia.

Early written sources dating back to the 9th century confirm that the Sami people have inhabited the same areas in the Nordic countries and in Russia for over 1000 years. Archeological findings, believed to be Sami, prove that settlements have existed in these areas as early as 800 A.D.

Archeological findings also show that the Sami Iron Age, roughly until the early 1500's, constituted a relatively coherent and uniform culture. Findings conclude that this population came from the northern part of Russia which spoke a Finno-Ugric language. They later developed into a Sami speaking population.

Since the last century, more or less reliable figures have appeared regarding the size of the Sami population in the different countries. However, none of the countries within *Sápmi* has a satisfactory official registration of citizens based on ethnicity. [2]

The total population of Norway is 4.2 million. The Sami population consists of approximately 40,000. Less than 10 percent of the Sami population are reindeer-herding Sami. The Sami are living as a scattered minority in local communities all over northern and central Norway. In two municipalities, in the county of Finnmark in northern Norway, the Sami people form the majority of the population, thus making this area a Sami heartland.

In Sweden the Sami number 17,000, 2,700 of whom are employed in reindeer herding. About half of all Swedish Sami live in the traditional Sami areas in Northern Sweden.

The Finnish Sami population is small, about 5,700. 3,800 live in the Sami heartland in the northern regions. Half of the Sami in Finland depend on reindeer herding.

The situation in the former Soviet Union is uncertain. However, based on two criteria, self-identification and language, the Sami number about 2,000. Approximately half of the Russian Sami have Sami as their first language. Living mainly in the Lovozero region on the Kola peninsula, they depend heavily on reindeer herding and fishing. However, urban centers seem to be increasingly more attractive to the Russian Sami.

As far as subsistence goes, farming, trapping, fowling, fishing, trading, small-scale industries, service industries and public services are also important economic activities for the Sami. The Sami can be found in most occupations today in all the countries mentioned.

Due to bitter historical experiences, many Samis do not want integration but assimilation into the majority population. In their opinion, stigma and racism are attached to the Sami identity. Others again prefer segregation, visioning the revival of the once existing *Sápmi*. In spite of the losses caused by assimilation, the total Sami population has continued to grow.

The number of Sami has to be seen in relation to the other population groups present on Sami territory. For example, in the last centuries, due to decline in Norwegian settlement, the Sami constituted a majority in the Finnmark region in Norway. However, in the beginning of this century, an upswing in Norwegian settlement resulted in twice as many Norwegians as Sami in the Finnmark region.

Cultural Oppression

In the Norwegian part of *Sápmi*, the Sami were under Norwegian rule from the year 1000 A.D. Despite the gradual loss of their political and economic independence, the Sami were more or less left in peace until the 19th century.

New in the 19th century was a Norwegian policy towards cultural assimilation of the Sami population. The paternalistic attitude of the church became the general attitude towards the Sami. Sami traditions and beliefs were not taken into consideration and the Sami were looked down upon as inferiors.

In the process of cultural assimilation, the Norwegian language was essential. Even in Sami parishes, Norwegian was introduced as the only language in which instruction was to take place. To the children in the area, Norwegian was a completely unknown language at the time they started school. The language at home as well as in the community was Sami. This form of Norwegianization resulted in a suppression of the Sami language and a weak academic career for the Samis. Even as late as in the 1950's, Sami pupils were punished for uttering a single Sami word at school.

What made the situation even more difficult was the fact that the majority of Sami pupils lived at boarding schools during the seven years of primary education. This was due to the enormous distances between schools and the home, as well as to the nomadic life style which many Sami families led. The unfortunate part of boarding school life was that the rule of using only the Norwegian language was implemented even during the pupils' leisure time.

In their eagerness to "help" the Sami children to Norwegianize, some children were even taken by Norwegian authorities and placed in Norwegian foster families in the southern parts of Norway. This was done without the consent of the Sami parents. These activities as well took place as late as in the 1950's. This is a black spot in Norwegian social history, and as such is not often referred to.

Affecting both children and adults during this period of cultural oppression, was the attempt to suppress the Sami's traditional way of singing, the *joik*. In actuality, the *joik* is not a song, but a tune with special sounds attached to it - a chant in monotone. What is unique to the *joik* is that each *joik* is made as a personal and special greeting from the person who makes it to the person who receives it. It is often made by a mother to her child. Thus the *joik* represents a precious cultural manifestation.

Other measures of Norwegianization were in the form of active assistance given to Norwegian settlers in traditional Sami areas.

In 1902, a law was introduced stating that only a person who knew and used the Norwegian language could be the owner of land. This act was formally in force until 1965. The Sami did own land in spite of the law, but it made the Sami more likely to conceal their cultural identity.

Norway is usually known as a country with long humanitarian and democratic traditions, fostering people like Fridtjof Nansen, known world wide as a great explorer and a helper of refugees. How could this paternalistic and even racist behavior from Norwegian authorities be explained? How did the Norwegian authorities justify the treatment of the Sami?

The answer lies partly in defence. Norway feared its neighbor Finland, at the time under Czarist Russia, and thus feared the "Russian threat" through Finnish immigration to Norway. Unable to distinguish the Finns and the Sami, the Norwegian authorities chose the safe, but thorough cultural assimilation policy towards the Sami.

Norway also lacked a minority policy. A multicultural society would not have been acceptable at that time as nationalism was evolving into an ideology of conformity.

Cultural Self Defence: The Process Towards Self-Determination And a Sami Assembly.

Since the Second World War, there has been a growing tendency towards liberation from colonial rule and oppression. We have also been witness to a continual process among indigenous peoples and other ethnic and religious groups to fight for cultural, religious and/or political rights. Indigenous peoples use the term "self-determination" to describe their ethno-political struggle.

The Sami have been no exception; they did not accept the Norwegian campaign for assimilation. The cultural self-defence of the Sami started officially through the Sami organizations which were first established in 1903. Activities included the publishing of magazines and newspapers in the Sami language. Activities towards self-determination soon reached a nordic level covering the whole *Sápmi,* with the exception of the Soviet Union. The Nordic Sami Council was thus founded in 1956.

Cultural self-defence was, at the beginning, a struggle where only the intellectually or politically conscious elite participated. The courageous ones, not seriously affected by the stigmatized ethnic identity of being a Sami, turned the identity as Sami into a symbol of pride. The vast majority of the Sami were of course not at all in that position. Hiding one's Sami identity remained of major importance to those who lived in mixed societies together with Norwegians. Only the Sami living in areas dominated by Sami felt free to express their identity through language, traditional dress and customs.

In the early 1960's, the few Sami that had the courage, continued to organize and to protest against the official policies of Norwegian authorities. Then allies began to appear, particularly among local officials and social scientists in Norway. Interventions were done partly for humanitarian reasons, and partly by referring to the Sami as an indigenous people.

A most unexpected and important ally was the United Nations (UN). The UN suddenly turned Norway's criticism of apartheid in South Africa, towards Norway itself, pointing at the conditions of the Sami people. This event in particular helped to form and found the National Association of Norwegian Sami in 1968. The ethnopolitical struggle took a new step forward.

In 1979, other allies appeared on the scene. An important environmental struggle built up in connection with a dam construction in the Sami area. This attracted the attention of environmentalists in Norway as well as abroad. Dramatic demonstrations took place in the polar night. It was a long lasting and bitter struggle involving police and military forces. In addition, many a Sami family was divided due to differences of opinion about the dam question.

The struggle was settled in court, stating the right of the Norwegian state to continue the dam construction. This event, however, had a positive and interesting result. An official committee, The Sami Rights Committee, was formed and started its work outlining Sami rights.

In 1987, the Norwegian parliament adopted a bill concerning the establishment of a Sami Assembly, whose sphere of work would comprise all matters affecting the Sami people in Norway. The first election took place in September 1989, as a direct election among the Sami in Norway.

A New Era: Towards Integration?

The establishing of a Sami assembly reflects a completely new attitude from the Norwegians and the Norwegian authorities. The key concepts are cooperation, mutual respect and recognition of the rights of indigenous peoples to continued use of their traditional land as a necessary basis for the furthering of their culture.

Norway's former King Olav V opening the Sami Parliament.

Norway, by signing an international convention regarding indigenous peoples, stresses that the Sami shall have the right to decide their own priorities for the process of development and to exercise control as much as possible over their own economic, social and cultural development.

Norway has changed during the last decades due to the accumulation of events leading to the Sami Assembly. Another process has taken place in Norway parallel to this: the change into a multicultural society due to immigrant and refugees coming to Norway. Norwegian immigrant policy gives the new and recently immigrated minorities certain rights as to the conservation and development of their own culture and language. How-

ever, the Sami, with their status as indigenous peoples, are ensured other formal instruments. The Sami are at the threshold of
a sensitive era.

Cultural Revival

Going through the history of the Sami, one ends up with a tiny
group of approximately 70,000 people scattered in four different
countries, 40,000 of whom live in Norway. Does the glimpse into
Sami history and the life of the Sami in contemporary Norway
indicate integration? Integration is an awkward question, awkward in the sense that so many contradictory interests are involved. The Norwegian authorities state that their Sami policy is
a policy of integration and a generous one at that. Most Sami
would agree. However there are still many Sami who conceal
their identity and will continue to do so. The following incident
preceding the election to the Sami Assembly in 1990 illustrates
this:

> To participate in the election, one had to register. This was, of
> course, not a forced ethnic registration, only voluntary infor-
> mation in order to be allowed to vote as well as to stand for
> election into the Sami Assembly.

The switchboards in the central and local administrations literally
broke down when the system of registration was announced. The
dramatic and alarmed pleas from the Sami were completely un-
foreseen. Until this point, these Sami, known as Norwegians in
their surroundings, were afraid to have their ethnic identity revealed: "My wife will leave me!"- or "My mother-in-law will
make a hell of a trouble".

The Sami possess the strongest formal instruments to succeed
in their goal of a successful integration. It all depends on whether
the Sami in general intend to make use of these instruments.
Some have been separated from their language and culture too
long. The participation at the elections to the Sami Assembly
shows that it is still the intellectual and politically active elite in
the Sami society that are the driving force. In spite of a long and
intensive information campaign addressed to the Sami, the percentage of Sami participating in the election was low.

This might lead to the conclusion that the Sami elite are integrated, in the sense that they are Norwegian citizens but still with
a strong and proud Sami identity. What remains to be seen, is
whether this elite will encourage the assimilated and hidden Sa-

mi, little by little, to regain their Sami identity without feeling that stigma is attached to it.

The flourishing revival of Sami culture might also encourage the hidden Sami to come forward and declare their Sami identity. It all depends on whether the revival will last. It is true that Sami cultural activity has been booming during the last 10 years, helped by the growing interest among the Sami and sponsored by Norwegian authorities. Sami theater, literature and artists are making their entry. It is interesting to note that this recent cultural manifestation has developed not only in quantity but also in quality. Sami culture has been successful even internationally: The first movie in the Sami language directed by a Sami and with Sami actors, "Ofelas", better known in English as "The Pathfinder", was even nominated for an Oscar prize a couple of years ago.

Two obstacles are, however, evident in this integration process. One is the relative scarce human resources which the Sami have at their disposal, being a small linguistic group. From this group, they have to produce what they need of writers for their literature, songs, theater, translations, etc. The other obstacle, and maybe the most serious one, is the overwhelming influence of the dominating languages, Norwegian and English, through different kinds of modern media. The fight against majority languages starts from early childhood, as children become invaded by television, movies, etc., in other languages than Sami. The publishing of the cartoon "Vulle Vuojas", the Sami version of "Donald Duck" is one example of the attempt to preserve the Sami language.

Fortunately, the cultural revival is well represented by the younger generation: The young vocalist Mari Boine Persen, is making the Sami language known on hit lists both inside and outside of Norway; the director Nils Gaup, and the main actor Mikkel Gaup, of the film "Pathfinders" are two young Sami men who have toured the world launching their film, dressed often in the traditional Sami *kofte*.

Sami language, culture and tradition is kept alive first and foremost in the Sami homeland. Nature encourages it as well as the social surroundings. Almost everyone speaks Sami in everyday life. One wears the traditional *kofte* when going to church on Sundays and for other special occasions. However, this is not always the case in other areas of Norway.

In Oslo, the capital of Norway, some 2,000 kilometers south of the Sami homeland (equalling the distance between Oslo and Rome, Italy), the Sami number approximately 5,000 people. This is a number that is swallowed up in the remaining 495,000 living in the city. It suddenly becomes odd to wear the traditional costume and go to the theater or for a drink with friends somewhere downtown. If a Sami sends his or her child to kindergarten, the child will probably be the only Sami among the other 20 children. The Sami family will often be the only Sami family in the local community, and as such will have to counter both the influences from the Norwegian neighborhood and the influences from all kinds of Norwegian and other foreign mass media. This may seem an impossible struggle, but the Sami in Oslo had one solution, they opened the first Sami kindergarten in the capital.

In the struggle to protect and encourage the use of Sami language, the so-called "Sami Language Act" became operative from January 1992. The act states that in 6 municipalities with a concentration of Sami, the Sami and the Norwegian language are both official languages. One may thus address an official institution either in Norwegian or in Sami, and one has the right to get an answer in the language of preference.

Language is, of course, vital. But in spite of a limited number of Sami living from reindeer herding exclusively, this traditional way of life is the other cornerstone of the Sami culture and identity. Reindeer herding thus has great symbolic power in the integration process.

The population is growing also in traditional Sami areas. Reindeer herding demands vast territories for grazing. A Sami family will need at least a flock of 500 animals in order to make a sufficient income. The flock of a rich reindeer herder might exceed 3,000 deer. With a growing number of deer and a fixed territory, the result is a lack of grazing ground. The average weight of the reindeer has been falling, forcing the reindeer owner to increase his flock in order to sell the necessary amount of reindeer meat. This in turn has resulted in further excessive grazing due to too many animals in one area. It seems a vicious circle. It should be added that this vicious circle is a recent phenomenon. In earlier times, there was an ecological balance in the region. This balance has been set off course by Norwegian laws and regulations that have failed to regulate the number of animals. This has not only resulted in a falling weight of the reindeer, but has created some serious conflicts among the Sami themselves and internal problems in the organization of reindeer herding. The ecological balance has been further disturbed by nuclear tests and industrial pollution in the northern areas of Russia. The reestablishing of the ecological balance will have to be a shared responsibility between the Norwegian and the Russian authorities.

Another challenge is the gradual transfer of power from the Norwegian authorities and institutions to the Sami Assembly. Up until now, the assembly has had only an advisory function. This transfer will not continue without difficulties. Increased economic and political power is a demand from the Sami Assembly members. One of the target questions in the future will be the rights to land and water in the central Sami areas.

As one can see, possibilities and obstacles are mixed when describing the situation of integration. If the integration process does not succeed, the consequences will be severe and wide-reaching. Should the Sami in Norway disappear as an ethnic group, there will be no more Sami. Their brothers and sisters in the rest of *Sápmi* are too scarce in number to survive as a distinctive ethnic and linguistic group.

It is a heavy responsibility both for the Norwegian authorities and for the Norwegian Sami to carry on with their cooperation. So far, the mutual understanding of give and take amongst the Samis and the Norwegians during recent years has created a good climate for integration. However, this social experiment, as well as all human coexistence has to be evaluated and readjusted continuously.

Notes

1. Kjell Borgen, Norwegian Minister for Sami Affairs, August 7, 1990 at the World Council for Indigenous Peoples Conference in Tromsø, Norway.

2. A list exists from elections to the Norwegian Sami Assembly where individuals voluntarily registered on ethnic grounds.

References

Eidheim, H. *Aspects of the Lappish Minority Situation,* Oslo 1971.
IWGIA Document Nr. 45: Robert Paine: *Dam a River, Damn a People?*, Copenhagen, 1982.
IWGIA Document Nr. 58: *Self Determination and Indigenous Peoples. Sami Rights and Northern Perspectives,* Copenhagen, 1987
Keskitalo, A. "The Status of the Sami Language", Einar Haugen, J. Derrick McClure and Derick Tomson, (ed.). *Minority Languages Today.* Edinburgh, 1980.
Norwegian Ministry of Justice: Summary of the first report from The Norwegian Sami Rights Committee (NOU 1984:18 Om samenes rettsstilling).

Nordic Sami Institute: "The Sami People", Kautokeino, 1990.
NOU 1984: 18: Om samenes rettsstilling.
NOU 1985: 14: Samisk kultur og utdanning.
NOU 1987: 34: Samisk kultur og utdanning.
Paine, R. "Coast Lapp Society", Tromsø museum, 1957.

10

Recent Immigration to Norway

Long Litt Woon

Introduction

Despite its peripheral location on the outer rim of Europe, Norway has been a destination for immigrants for as long as Norwegians themselves have left the country[1]. The character of immigration to Norway, however, is slowly changing. This change implies new challenges for Norwegian society. In this article I shall concentrate on describing the changes and the challenges posed by recent immigration to Norway.

Recent Statistical Trends[2]

The foreign population in Norway – general trends

Compared to other countries in Western Europe, the number of foreigners in Norway is small (fig.1). However, the proportion of foreigners seen as a percentage of the total population has increased steadily in the last decade, from 2,0 % in 1980 to 3,3 % in 1990 (fig. 2). The composition of foreigners (based on citizenship) residing in Norway has also changed during this period. In 1976, 16% of the foreign population in Norway were citizens from Asia, Africa and Latin America. In 1990, the figure was 41%, the largest change being in the increase in the number of persons from Asia. However, among the foreign population, Danes and Swedes still represent the largest groups in Norway (fig.3). In general, the foreign population is much younger than the nationals. Foreigners, especially those from the so-called Third World countries, are mostly young adult men (fig.4).

1. Foreign citizens in some European countries, 1989. Percentage of total population.

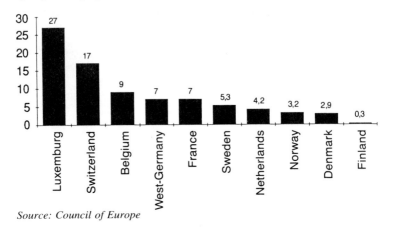

Source: Council of Europe

2. Foreign citizens in Norway from 1910-1990, absolute numbers and as a percentage of the total population.

Year	Foreign citizens in Norway	Foreign citizens as a percentage of the total population
1910	40 396	1,7
1920	63 537	2,3
1930	15 114	1,2
1946	15 912	0,5
1950	15 797	0,4
1960	24 823	0,6
1975	ı4 982	1,6
1980	82 076	2,0
1990	140 312	3,3

Source: Central Bureau of Statistics

Residential patterns

It has often been the case that foreigners in Norway have mainly settled in the larger cities which also are the economic, political and administrative centers. However, with the advent of

*3. Foreigners in Norway by citizenship. The ten largest groups.
1 July 1991.*

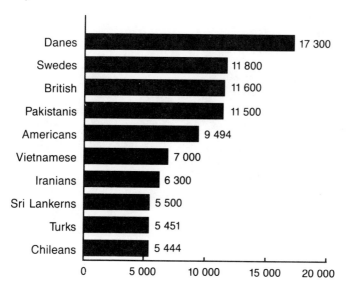

*4. Total population and foreigners in Norway, by sex and age,
and by percentage. 1 January 1990.*

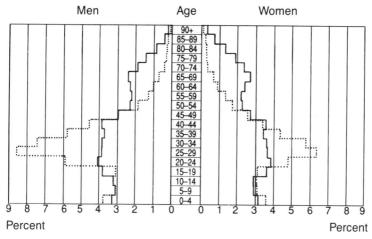

the 1980s – often called the decade of refugees – municipalities
all over Norway accepted small quotas of refugees for settlement. The official policy has aimed to ease integration by taking
into consideration ethnic background (in addition to prospects for

Class of immigrants.

employment and educational opportunities) when resettling refugees who need assistance in starting their lives in Norway.
Over recent years, this policy has led to the establishment of
relatively sizeable communities in several municipalities
throughout the country. The policy of establishing reception
centers for asylum seekers in various parts of the country, has
also led to foreign citizens living throughout the whole of Norway, including the more remote regions. Nord Trøndelag and
Sogn og Fjordane are the counties with the least foreigners.
However, the largest concentration of foreigners (43.6 % of the
foreign population) is still to be found in the counties of Oslo and
Akershus. In Oslo, foreign citizens make up 10 % of the population. The other counties with the highest numbers of foreigners
are Rogaland (13,553), Hordaland (10,770) and Buskerud
(8,326) (CBS, SU nr. 37, 1991).

Educational background

Persons who have immigrated to Norway have a wide variety
of educational backgrounds. Compared to the rest of the population, this group has relatively more persons with higher education. This is especially true in the case of women where 54% of
all women with post-graduate education (ie. nineteen or more

years of education) in Norway are foreign-born. However, it must be also noted that there are relatively fewer foreigners than nationals who have completed primary education. About 5% of women born in Asia and Africa have not been to school at all (CBS, SU nr. 42, 1991). Foreigners in Norway represent, in other words, a wide spectrum of educational backgrounds.

5. Level of education of foreign citizens born in Norway and in selected countries. Age 30-44 years. 1 October 1989.

Country of birth	Percentage with university educ.	Number of persons (age 30-44)
Norway	24.3	880 444
Switzerland	48.4	312
Philippines	47.5	1 407
Nigeria	46.5	155
Pakistan	11.1	3 843
Turkey	10.9	1 461
Morocco	7.5	770

Source: Central Bureau of Statistics

Employment

Foreigners are over-represented in some sectors of the economy. These are the oil and gas industry, the hotel and restaurant sector, and sanitation and cleaning services. Most of the foreigners (91%) in the oil and gas industry are from Europe, North America and Oceania, whilst 58 % of the foreigners in the hotel and restaurant sector and 74% of the foreigners in sanitation and cleaning services are from the Asia, Africa and Latin America. (Kjelsrud, 1992).

Employment statistics show that, compared to the total population, relatively fewer foreign-born men and women are employed. A significant factor in these statistics appears to be the number of years of residence in Norway. The higher the number of years of residence, the better the chances of employment (fig.6).

Unemployment

Rising unemployment has become a problem for Norwegian society, including its foreign population. Compared to the total

*6. Employment percentage of foreign-born immigrants accord-
ing to years of residence in Norway, 2nd quarter, 1987 and
1990. (The figures here refer to foreign-born immigrants with
mothers born in a foreign country).*

Employment
percentage

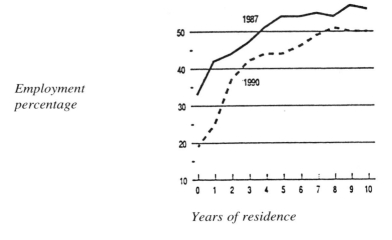

Years of residence

Source: Central Bureau of Statistics

population, relatively more foreigners are registered as unemployed. Among the foreign population, unemployment patterns
are different for persons coming from various regions (fig.7).
There is reason to believe that the figures are actually higher
because many foreigners do not register themselves as unemployed.

*7. Registered unemployed, total and foreign population.
September 1987, 1990, 1991. Absolute figures and percentage
of work force.*

	1987	1990	1991
Total population	29723 (1.4)	86784 (4.0)	97888 (4.6)
Foreign population	1653 (3.0)	5383 (8.6)	6625 (10.3)
Nordic countries	312 (1.5)	816 (3.9)	1056 (5.0)
Europe, N.Am, Oceania	457 (2.1)	1395 (6.2)	1607 (7.2)
Asia	647 (6.4)	2073 (15)	2639 (18.1)
S./Central America	89 (7.4)	407 (15.8)	475 (17.4)
Africa	148 (7.0)	640 (20)	811 (23.5)

Source: Central Bureau of Statistics and the Directorate of Labour

The immigration ban (1975)

Like many other industrialized European countries in the 1970s, Norway imposed an immigration ban in 1975 just after similar restrictions were enforced in Sweden and Danmark. The main effect of the ban is felt most strongly by potential migrant workers from countries like Pakistan, Turkey and Morocco who had been allowed to immigrate to Norway to work in the early 1970s. After the ban, immigration from the Third World still continued, though it changed in character: worker migration was replaced by family reunification and asylum seeker streams (fig.8). This remains the case also after the immigration ban of 1975 was incorporated into the provisions of the new Aliens Act (1991) regulating the entry of foreigners to Norway, the issuing of residence and work permits, etc.

Asylum seekers

The number of asylum seekers in Norway was small throughout the first half of the 1980s. However, this trend changed with the dramatic increases in 1986 and 1987. The percentage of asylum seekers who are granted permission to stay, either as refugees or on humanitarian grounds, has also changed in this short period,

8. Asylum seekers in Norway. 1983-1991.

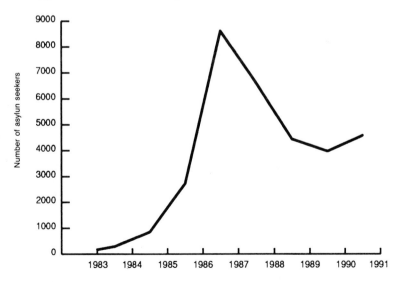

Source: Directorate of Immigration

from about 81% in 1983 to 44% in 1991 (fig.9). Several factors have been important for this: the time taken for processing applications has been shortened, thus reducing the number of applications that previously fell into the special category receiving "amnesty" (the so-called 15 month rule); information about asylum seeker producing countries is now better, thus making it easier to reject applicants who have no legitimate claims for protection. Asylum seekers who have been granted permission to stay in Norway have come mainly from Chile, Sri Lanka, Iran, Iraq, Ethiopia and Somalia.

9. Outcome of asylum applications. 1983-1991.

Year	Negative outcome	Positive outcome (Humanitarian + asylum) grounds		
1983	18.7	81.3%	(52.3%	+ 29%)
1984	24	76	(52	+ 24)
1985	23.9	76.1	(56	+ 20.1)
1986	20.8	79.2	(56	+ 23.2)
1987	24.2	75.8	(68	+ 7.8)
1988	33.2	66.8	(64.5	+ 2.3)
1989	42.2	57.8	(52.9	+ 4.9)
1990	60.8	39.2	(36	+ 3.2)
1991	56	44	(41	+ 3)

Source: Directorate of Immigration

Refugees

Norway also resettles a quota of refugees directly from abroad, mostly from the UN High Commisioner for Refugees (UNHCR) every year. This number of refugees is determined by the Norwegian Parliament [3]. In 1986, the number received was increased from 250 to 1000 per year. From 1988 onwards, this number is in effect even larger because family members who are received are not included in the quota. Lately, most of the UN registered refugees who have been accepted by Norway have been Vietnamese from UNHCR camps in Southeast Asia and ethnic Kurds from Iran and Iraq. Current efforts to develop policy in this area so as to make it more flexible to meet acute global refugee situations will probably affect the intake of UN registered refugees to Norway in the future.

10. Arrival of refugees resettled in Norway directly from abroad. 1983-1990

Year	Number of persons	
1983	879	
1984	668	
1985	774	incl.family members
1986	843	
1987	1043	
1988	765	
1989	1051	excl. family members
1990	973	
1991	1114	

From 1988 onwards, the figures do not include family reunification. In 1990 and 1991, 1191 and 849 persons were reunited with their families in Norway respectively.

Source: Directorate of Immigration.

Naturalization

Since 1977, over 40,000 foreign citizens have become Norwegian citizens. Recent trends (1988 onwards) show a marked increase in the number of people who have been naturalized (fig.11). Mainly, the largest groups are former citizens of Vietnam and Pakistan. As the probability for several immigrant groups to return to their original homelands continues to remain low, and the numbers who in time will fulfill the required length of stay for application for naturalization steadily increases [4], we can expect the number of new Norwegian citizens to rise in the future.

11. Naturalizations in Norway. 1977-1991.

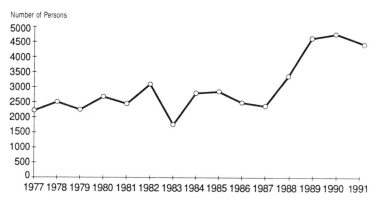

Repatriation

Voluntary repatriation is a relatively new phenomenon in the
Norwegian context. Between 1990 and 1991, about 400 Chilean
refugees in Norway were repatriated. This trend is in line with
the current policy of the UNHCR to bring refugees back to
countries like Namibia, South Africa and Chile where the political situation has improved.

12. Voluntary repatriation from Norway. 1990.

Home country	Number of persons
Iran	8
South Africa	1
Paraguay	2
Vietnam	3
Chile	186
Total	200

Source: Directorate of Immigration

Migration flows

The foreign and national populations are both represented in
the migration flows in and out of the country. The inflow of
foreign nationals increased steadily throughout the 1980s,
reaching a peak in 1987 and 1988, due mainly to the increase in
the number of asylum seekers and to immigrants from neighbouring countries being employed in expanding Norwegian industries. The outflow of foreign nationals, though smaller in
number than the inflow, has also increased steadily during this
period.

By way of comparison, the inflow and outflow of *Norwegian*
nationals, though also increasing, show the opposite trend: the
outflow of Norwegian nationals is larger than the inflow. Thus,
from a demographic point of view, the foreign population of
Norway has grown in importance as the natural growth of the
national population has declined and as the net outflow of Norwegian nationals has increased (fig.13).

"Native" Norwegian minority?

We can observe a continuous outflow of foreigners leaving
Norway and a new trend of increasing repatriation. However, it

13. Total number of immigrations and emigrations by citizenship 1978-1990.

Year	Foreign citizens		Norwegians		Total	
	Immi-gration	Emi-gration	Immi-gration	Emi-gration	Immi-gration	Emi-gration
1978	12 183	7 624	6 642	7 227	18 825	14 851
1979	11 213	7 619	6 618	7 466	17 831	15 085
1980	11 833	7 288	6 943	7 417	18 776	14 705
1981	13 061	7 252	6 637	7 270	19 698	14 522
1982	13 990	7 218	6 478	7 510	20 468	14 728
1983	13 090	7 955	6 973	7 823	20 063	15 778
1984	12 837	7 617	6 851	8 310	19 688	15 927
1985	14 906	7 522	6 952	8 108	21 856	15 630
1986	16 534	8 424	7 662	8 321	24 196	16 745
1987	23 793	8 591	7 356	8 789	31 149	17 380
1988	23 041	9 320	8 923	10 501	28 964	19 821
1989	18 384	10 563	7 463	16 737	25 847	27 300
1990	16 694	9 768	9 800	14 016	25 494	23 784

Source: Central Breau of Statistics

seems that the significance of these trends is overshadowed by the increasing numbers of persons from Third World countries who are settling permanently in Norway. There is, therefore, a common fear that "native" Norwegians will become a minority in Norway in the near future. A recent study shows that this fear will only become reality if today's immigration policy changes drastically in the direction of liberalizing entry regulations (Sevaldson, 1991). Judging from the current political climate, this seems unlikely to happen in the near future.

Living with Immigration

Immigration has become a topic of social interest in Norway. It is discussed everywhere (at home, at work places etc.) at all times (during lunchbreaks, over the dinner table etc.), often arousing much emotion. Therefore, though the absolute numbers of new "visible" ethnic minorities are relatively modest and, in most probability, will continue to remain so in the future, this does not mean that Norway has avoided the dilemmas and debates which many countries in the industrialized world have faced as a result of major global migrant worker flows in the 1960s-70s, and refugee and asylum seeker flows in the 1980s (Long, 1992).

In Norway, conflict situations – from simple misunderstandings because of the lack of a common language to violent juvenile gang fights – are seen as signs of the changing times and of the social problems connected to recent immigration. There is little public confidence regarding the many issues and questions which beg to be addressed. On the one hand, Norwegians are unsure if they are racist. On the other, they do not know if they are being too naive or too generous towards the new immigrants. Accusations of racism in particular seem to cause Norwegians much discomfort and embarrassment. These accusations are at odds with their self image of being tolerant, moral and righteous members of the international community.

Partly, this uncomfortable mood is the result of a general lack of knowledge of basic facts and figures. There is, in addition, an evergrowing stock of wandering stories about immigrants and the Norwegian immigration policy which get elaborated every time they are passed on. Furthermore, public debates over popular topics like border regulations, criminal activity among foreigners, mother tongue instruction, Islam, racism etc. have also functioned as contests in political correctness or populism. As such contests, public debates about immigration have also been occasions for political posturing and for showing which "side" one is on. Not unexpectedly, the media has played a contributive role in perpetuating this simple and polarized mode of approaching the complex issues connected to the phenomenon of immigration.

On the one hand, there is the side which is anti-immigrant and anti-immigration. This side wants to limit "the immigrant problem" by having even stricter entry regulations. They feel that many of the social problems connected with immigration can be solved if the immigrants adopt the Norwegian lifestyle as soon as possible. They are concerned about expenditures related to immigration and they define equality on the majority's terms: immigrants should only be entitled to the same services as Norwegians. Positive discrimination or affirmative action is seen as unfair to Norwegians. More radical streams on the anti-immigrant/immigration side demand that immigrants should not be entitled to exactly the same services and rights as Norwegians; they should be entitled to fewer. For example, they should stand at the end of the queue for jobs, housing etc. The arguments of the anti-immigrant/immigration side try to appeal to the common man's sense of justice and fairness. Surely, they argue, it is not fair that immigrants (who "have not made any contribution to society") are entitled to goods and services which they themselves have difficulty in obtaining?

The side which is pro-immigrant and pro-immigration, on the other hand, focuses particularly on the problems faced by immigrants. They argue that social problems implied by immigration are not caused by immigrants; in fact, immigrants bear the burden of the problems which are caused first and foremost by inequality. Equality is defined as equal opportunity: if immigrants do not have the same opportunities as Norwegians in competing for jobs, housing, education etc, then special measures need to be taken. The main focus is on the handicaps and obstacles faced by immigrants when adjusting to life in Norway. This is an attempt to appeal not only to the host society's sense of duty and morality, but also pity and shame. They argue that we have to be more tolerant and to make better efforts to make immigrants feel welcome. Furthermore, the immigrants represent important resources for society [5].

The *consequences of a polarized and unfruitful debate* are more serious than many (including those who have actively contributed and those who have remained silent and, thus, passively contributed) care to admit:

1. As effective occasions for political posturing, the symbolic value of political arguments tends to overshadow the arguments themselves. This has practical consequences because *the exploration of alternative, viable solutions does not become a priority.* An example of this is the recent debate about mother tongue instruction in Oslo, a minor item in the total municipal budget. The financial aspect is, in other words, not significant. However, the debate provided a good occasion to show how much who cares for the needs of the immigrants or, by the same token, how much who cares about popular Norwegian demands that immigrants should become as Norwegian as possible as soon as possible. The polarized mould of the debate effectively put a stop to any discussion about, for example, ways in which immigrant children could learn and master both their mother tongue and Norwegian.

2. Another effect of a polarized public debate about immigration is the wide exposure of populistic arguments in a frame of argument where *truth is seen as just another counter-argument.*

When two opposing sides engage in a sharpened, polarized debate, they exaggerate or leave out arguments and statistics which do not serve their cause. The result is that half-truths are claimed to be whole truths, and myths and false claims continue to remain in circulation.

3. When the pro-immigrant/immigration side defends the immigrant "cause" at all costs it leads to the image of being unrealistic and absurd. Contrary to the aim of converting individuals with prejudicial attitudes towards immigrants, politically correct zeal of this kind is perceived as being simple and naive. In addition, many people feel that their questions and doubts about immigration are neither addressed nor taken seriously. They feel that there are too many nagging issues which are dismissed by the well-meaning pro-immigrant side. In short, *the pro-immigrant/ immigration side lacks credibility* because their highly moral stance does not seem to be rooted in reality and real concerns.

4. The resonance that anti-immigrant/immigration arguments have had with the public has led to populistic perspectives dominating the political discourse. If leading politicians from the whole spectrum of political parties had been equally interested in immigration issues, we might have avoided the current situation where *the political agenda is set by the side which is against immigration and immigrants.* Most of the mainstream political parties have been re-active: they have responded to the issues brought up by the anti-immigration/immigrant side, rather than taking the lead themselves. They have avoided the minefield of immigration until forced to take a stand (Birkeland, 1992). As mentioned, there are several examples where mainstream political parties have actually adopted the issues initially brought up by the anti-immigration/immigrant side as their own[6]. It is, therefore, not completely untrue when the Progress Party (Fremskrittspartiet) accuses the Labour Party (Arbeiderpartiet) of stealing their political issues.

5. In a debate where the dividing line between "us" and "them" is absolute, there is *no space for exploring the common interests* which both the host society and the immigrants share in trying to work out living arrangements acceptable to all. Measures taken are often only seen to be in the interest of either the immigrants or the host society.

6. Within the restrictive context of a polarized debate, the *development of official policy is hampered by the problem of non-credibility.* It becomes a policy which few people identify with; it is criticized for being either too liberal or too restrictive. Government efforts are spent defending isolated aspects of the policy. The necessary relation between the regulative and integrative aspects of the policy does not become a focus of debate. Consequently, this hinders the development of an integrated, overall approach in official policy.

What role does such a debate climate leave the immigrants? Apart from the handful of active immigrants supporting the arguments and the "style" of the pro-immigrant/immigration side, there seem to be few other public roles. This raises the problem of representation and image: many Norwegians think that the few active immigrants speak on behalf of and represent all the immigrants in Norway.

If the frame of the debate continues to remain as restrictive and as predictable as it has been, we cannot expect that Norwegian society will find it any easier to live with the phenomenon of immigration. However, there seem to be signs of change and there are several issues which can be tackled in order to speed up a positive development.

Challenges and Future Issues

Compared to most of the countries in Western Europe, Norway is in an exceptional situation in terms of the possibility for effective action in this area. The scale of immigration to Norway is relatively modest. Migrant flows to Norway came slightly later than to ex-colonial powers like Britain, France and the Netherlands. Furthermore, Norway has relatively good control of the national borders. Thus, the feeling of crisis and panic so common in other Western European countries experiencing problems of rising illegal immigration is absent in Norway.

Given this situation, there are several issues which need immediate attention. The following is a list of suggestions (in order of priority):

1. The most important challenge for the pro-immigrant/immigration side is that it needs to *reset the political agenda.* This cannot continue to be left to the anti-immigrant/immigration side. The

pro-immigrant/immigration side will need to address the common man's uncertainties, doubts and fears seriously without stealing viewpoints and arguments from the Progress Party (Fremskrittspartiet). This will mean that it cannot avoid the dilemmas of setting limits (to border entries, to unacceptable practices and behavior etc.). This will require constructive thinking and clarification of values and principles. A likely spin-off for serious efforts here is increased credibility for the pro-immigrant/immigration side.

2. Activities by organized racist organizations in Norway seem to be more open and to be on the increase today. Their international links are a source of confidence and inspiration to like-minded groups. Their activities have influenced the atmosphere in society. There is a feeling that general attitudes towards immigrants have hardened. A recent study (Nystuen, 1991) has shown that legal action against racial discrimination in Norway is almost non-existent. The few legal proceedings in this area seem to suggest that the interpretation of the law is narrower than the UN Convention for the Elimination of All Forms of Discrimination (CERD) which Norway has ratified. Though the means of literally turning their backs to racism has seemed to be able to mobilize large crowds at anti-immigrant rallies in both Brumunudal and Oslo[7], there is a need for an *active enforcement of the law against racial discrimination*. The Norwegian legal system needs to contribute towards ensuring that people are legally protected from being unequally treated or even attacked just because they are members of particular ethnic groups.

3. Most of the discrimination which immigrant groups are subjected to, however, is neither intentional nor overt. Normal routines, procedures and rules covering all aspects of daily life can function as structural barriers to immigrants. The result of such unplanned *institutional discrimination* can only become apparent in statistical gaps between immigrant groups and the host society. In order to avoid the development of a marginalized "dishwasher caste" of Third World immigrants in Norway, active measures need to be taken. It is not enough to focus on individual, complaint-oriented measures. The practices of organizations need to be examined. Statistical gaps need to be uncovered, acted upon and monitored. Resources must be spent in developing and evaluating different working models. The efforts at the levels of central and local government need to be consistent and coordi-

nated. Education (including language instruction) and employment are important sectors to concentrate efforts on in order to encourage self-help among the immigrants.

Today a Norwegian living in Oslo is likely to ride to work in a tram-car driven by an Indian man, buy fruit for lunch from a Vietnamese woman, have his office cleaned by an Albanian family and shop for daily provisions from his local Pakistani grocer. In many ways, it can be said that immigrants are integrated in Nowegian society. However, unless the political agenda is reset to tackle the problems of legal protection from racial discrimination and the structural problems of ethnic discrimination, today's socio-economic differences between the host society and the recent immigrants, especially those from the Third World, will be reified by the coming generations.

Notes

1 Hanseatic traders in the 1200s were early immigrants in Norway. Other significant immigration streams include Danish administrators and civil servants, Swedish railroad builders and construction workers, Finnish slash-and-burn cultivators, specialists like German mining engineers and artisans from Central Europe etc. Between 1865-1930, 900,000 Norwegians emigrated, mainly to U.S.A. In the European context, Norwegian migration was second (relative to population size) only to emigration from Ireland.

2 I am indebted to Lars Østby's recent report: International Migration to Norway, 1990. Report for the Continuous Reporting System of OECD. (SOPEMI).

3 The numbers of UN registered refugees who arrive in Norway do not correspond with the figure set by the Norwegian Parliament for the various years because of the time taken to administer and implement the quota. This implies that many people who arrive in one year might have been given a place in the previous year's quota.

4 Currently, efforts are being made to decrease the length of required residence for naturalization applications from seven to five years. This will make Norwegian requirements for length of residence similar to requirements in, for example, Sweden and Finland.

5 However, no matter how well argued such views are, many people are still left wondering about the populist issues which have been brought up by the anti-immigrant/immigration side. How much truth is there in claims about the free cars, flats, furniture, clothes etc. which immigrants get at the taxpayers' expense? See eg. "Hva får asylsøkere, flyktninger og innvandrere" (Kommunaldept og Utlendingsdirektoratet, juli, 1991).

6 For example, Rune Gerhardsen from the Labour Party (Arbeiderpartiet) made several statements warning against naive generosity ("snillisme") towards immigrants. This has been one of the main arguments of the anti-immigrant Progress Party (Fremskrittspartiet).

7 Brumunddal: 31st August 1991, Oslo : 9th November 1991.

References

Birkeland, T. Oppgjør med den moralske eliten *Kommunalrapport,* 25.1.1992

Brox, O. *Jeg er ikke rasist, men...* Oslo, 1991.

Kommunaldept. og Utlendingsdirektoratet. "Hva får asylsøkere, flyktninger og innvandrere". Oslo, 1991.

Kjelsrud, M. Arbeidsmarkedet: Innvandrere rammes hardest av lavkonjunkturen. *Samfunnsspeil* nr.1/1992.

Long, Litt Woon. Innledning *Fellesskap til besvær?* Om nyere innvandring til Norge. Oslo, 1992.

Statistikk over utenlandske statsborgere 1. juli 1991 SU nr. 36/37, 1991 Central Bureau of Statistics.

Utdanningsnivå for utenlandsfødte. 1989 SU nr. 42, Central Bureau of Statistics, 1991.

Sevaldson, P. *Tallet på innvandrere og deres etterkommere fram mot år 2050* Central Bureau of Statistics, 1991.

Nystuen, G. *Rasediskriminerende Ytringer oq organisasjoner* Inst. for offentlig rettsskriftserie nr.4/1991 University of Oslo, 1991.

Østby, L. *International Migration to Norway, 1990. Report for the Continuous Reporting System of OECD(SOPEMI)* Central Bureau of Statistics, 1991.

11

The Norwegian Legal System

Arne Fliflet

The Fundamental Principles of the Norwegian Constitutional System.

The Norwegian legal system is based on a written Constitution originating in 1814. The Constitution has been changed several times since then. The laws laid down in the Constitution have also been changed or modified through the practice or conventions of the highest bodies of government. These laws are considered to be of both a legal and a customary nature.

The Constitution contains the basic rules concerning the organization and procedures of the highest state authorities: The King and the Council of State (*statsrådet*), The Norwegian National Assembly, (*Storting*), the Supreme Court (*Høyesterett*) and the Court of Impeachment (*Riksretten*). Further, the Constitution contains important rules concerning the political and human rights of the individual.

The Constitution sets limits to the power of the state authorities in relation to the citizen. If a statute, administrative regulation or administrative decision in a court of law is considered to be contrary to the Constitution, the statute, administrative regulation or administrative decision will be considered to have no legal effect. The constitutional provisions also play an important part in the interpretation of statutes since statutes are often interpreted so as to be in accordance with the Constitution.

Our present constitutional system is based on the so-called Principle of Legality. In the Norwegian legal tradition this principle means that all decisions taken by public administrative authorities must have their basis in law. "Law" is defined in this connection as constitutional provisions, statutory law or by-laws.

The Norwegian Constitution is further based on the principle of the supremacy of the people and the protection of fundamental human rights.

It is of fundamental value that citizens know their legal situa-

King Harald V and Queen Sonja of Norway.

tion. This contributes to a feeling of security and stability for the individual. As long as the society is based on sound egalitarian social conditions, the value of legal knowledge will be of great importance to the citizen. The Principle of Legality contributes to the safeguarding of this.

As mentioned above, the written Norwegian constitution dates back to 1814, when Norway gained its independence from Denmark. In the Treaty of Kiel settlement the Danish king had to sue for peace by ceding Norway to the Swedish king. The Norwegians did not accept this and a constitutional assembly was summoned in April 1814. This assembly adopted a new Constitution for Norway and elected a Norwegian king.

After a short war with Sweden in the summer of 1814, the

newly elected Norwegian king was forced to abdicate. However, the Swedes accepted the new Constitution and the new national legislative assembly, the *Storting*, as representative of the people. In the autumn of 1814, the *Storting* accepted the Swedish king as the common king of Sweden and Norway.

The Norwegian administrative and judicial system is different from the Swedish and Finnish systems, but is closely related to the Danish system. Although Norway was linked to Sweden in a union from 1814 to 1905, this union left few traces in its legal and judicial system. The 400 year union with Denmark, which ended in 1814, had a more lasting effect on the legal and judicial system than the subsequent union with Sweden.

The Norwegian Constitution of 1814 was a democratic constitution with the king as the head of state and as the leader of the executive power. The king had no longer absolute power. He was now a constitutional monarch sharing the political power with the National Assembly. The legislative and fiscal power, the power of the purse and the power to audit and control the executive power was from then on vested in the Storting.

The "King in Council of State" (*Kongen i statsråd*), is the Government of Norway. All formal decisions to be taken by the Government must be made by the King in Council. The decisions will in fact be made in cabinet meetings under the leadership of the prime minister, and formally decided either by the King in Council or by a minister in accordance with delegated authority. The king himself will in accordance with old-established custom never exercise personal power.

The Constitution is further based on the principle that the courts shall be separated from, and independent of, both the Executive and the Legislative branches of government. The Constitution contains the basic rules of the organization of the Supreme Court and the Court of Impeachment, and further presupposes that the court system should be a hierachical system with the Supreme Court as the final instance.

The Supremacy of the Storting

The Norwegian national assembly, the *Storting*, has the superior position in today's Norwegian constitutional system. First of all, the *Storting* is the only constitutional law maker. It is only the *Storting* that possesses the power to amend the Constitution. The Government normally takes no part in the constitutional process, and in amending the constitution, the *Storting* is only bound to comply with the rules of procedure laid down in the Constitution itself. As regards the contents of the amendments, the *Storting* is only bound to seek to comply with the spirit and the fundamental principles of the Constitution. Article 112 of the Constitution prescribes that amendments to the Constitution must never "contradict the principles embodied in the Constitution, but merely relate to modifications of particular provisions which do not alter the spirit of the Constitution". The courts have the power to decide whether or not statutes passed by the *Storting* are contrary to the Constitution.

The *Storting*'s supremacy and the *Storting*'s power to allocate funds further ensures that all major political issues and matters will be decided in the *Storting*. This means that the *Storting* not only has the power to legislate and the power to tax, it also has the power of the purse and the central auditing and controlling power. The *Storting* can also take up and discuss any administrative matter in whatever manner the assembly prefers.

The Supremacy of the *Storting* is the hallmark of the Norwegian Constitution. On the other hand, this important principle must be seen in relation to the so-called "prerogatives" of the Executive. The King in Council is the head of the Norwegian state church. Internal church matters concerning liturgy and faith must, in accordance with Article 16 of the Norwegian Constitution, be dealt with and decided only by the King in Council. The principle of the royal prerogative in internal church matters was laid down in a Supreme Court judgment in 1987. It is also a prerogative of the King in Council to pardon criminals.

The Interpretation of Statutes. The Significance of Court Practice and of International Human Rights Obligations.

The Norwegian legal system is today very much based on statutory law. Legislation is, in both private and public law, the most important source of law for judicial and administrative decision making. However, important legal principles and rules have also been introduced and laid down by court practice (i.e. judge-made law). For example, an important decision of the Supreme Court of Norway in 1977 declared that a patient had a legal right to see his or her own medical file.

In the interpretation of statutes, the courts usually give weight to statements and opinions from the legislative history. In particular, pre-parliamentary material, e.g. reports of committees reviewing and recommending changes, parliamentary committee reports and minutes of parliamentary debates will be given consideration in the application of the statutes.

As mentioned above, conventions on international human rights have also played an important part in the practice of the Supreme Court. Norway is a party to the European Conventions for the Protection of Human Rights and Fundamental Freedoms and also to International Covenants on Economic, Social, Cultural, Civil and Political Rights. The Supreme Court has in several judgments looked to the rules and principles embodied in the human rights conventions. The international human rights conventions are not incorporated in Norwegian law, but it is recognized that the conventions – and particularly the European Convention on Human Rights – are both a "legitimate and important aid to the interpretation of domestic law".

Even if legislation plays an important part in the Norwegian legal system, the Supreme Court practice is also of importance both for the interpretation of statutes and in the development of the law in general. In administrative law, the practice of the administrative agencies is considered to be relevant for the interpretation of administrative regulations.

Legal literature also plays a part in the interpretation of statutes, but it is difficult to give an accurate description of the relevance and weight of this.

Legislation and the Legislative Process.

According to the Constitution and the *Storting's* "Standing Orders", a Bill will pass several stages before it becomes an Act of the *Storting*, called "Lov". In fact the road from start to finish is in practice more complex than prescribed in the law. Important legal matters will, as a rule, be elucidated and reported on by a committee consisting of experts and representatives of different interest groups. In some cases, and particularly in less important legal matters, the ministries themselves will prepare the Bills.

In many cases the Department of the Ministry of Justice will go through the Bill before presenting it to the *Storting*. All Bills are discussed in cabinet meetings and the King in Council will formally make the decision to present the Bill to the *Storting*.

The *Storting* is a unicameral assembly. All the 167 representatives are elected to the *Storting*, but in legislative matters the

Storting divides itself into two chambers. Formal legislation will be dealt with and discussed in these two separate chambers of the *Storting* – the *Odelsting* (the lower chamber) and the *Lagting* (the upper chamber). All Bills are introduced in the *Odelsting*, which consists of 119 members.

After having passed the *Odelsting*, the Bill goes to the *Lagting*, which consists of 48 members. After having passed both chambers the Bill will be presented to the King in Council for the royal assent. In practice the king will always give his assent. After 1905 it has happened only once (1976) that the king has rejected/vetoed a Bill. It is however correct to say that this veto was made in accordance with the will of the *Storting*. The Bill concerned an industrial action and was aimed at ending a strike. After the Bill had passed the *Odelsting* and the *Lagting*, but before it was presented to the king for the royal assent, the dispute was resolved.

The *Storting* also has the fiscal and granting authority. The budget and tax bills are introduced to the *Storting* in plenary sessions. The annual tax bills are not subject to royal assent. These bills concern only the rates of taxation. The legislation concerning the assessment of taxes will be subject to ordinary legislation (in *Odelsting* and *Lagting*).

The central Government, ministries and directorates, local authorities and public corporations, all have delegated power to issue either administrative regulations, ordinances or by-laws to enable them to perform their administrative functions.

All acts of the *Storting*, all administrative regulations passed by the King in Council, ordinances and by-laws, are set forth in the Norwegian Law Report (*Norsk Lovtidende*).

The Organization and Administration of the Executive Branch of Government.

Norway is a unitary state. However, the country is divided into counties and municipalities. These local units are organized by local administrative agencies under the control of popularly elected bodies. The legal basis for the organization and rules of procedure of the local administrative corporations and bodies are to be found in statutory provisions. The principle of the so-called "local self-government" is based on statutory provisions and is not a part of the Norwegian Constitution.

The executive power of the state administration is vested in the "King", which in fact is the Government. (Article 3 of the Constitution). Because of the dependency of the *Storting* it is, however, necessary to stress the influence of the *Storting* both through legislation and decisions concerning budgetary matters. The Government is a collegium of the ministers who are both members of the Council of State and normally also heads of ministries. The Prime Minister is not head of any ministry.

The responsibility of the Government is not only to run the central administration and to carry out the tasks laid upon the Government in constitutional and statutory provision, it is also the duty of the Government to indicate legislation, tax bills and other budgetary proposals. The Government proposals to the *Storting* are called "Propositions to the *Storting*" (*Stortings-proposisjonen*). Proposals in legislative matters are called "Propositions to the *Odelsting*" (*Odelstingsproposisjoner*) and are put forward to the *Odelsting*.

An important responsibility for the ministries is to prepare all cases for the King in Council. A matter before the Council of State will always have to be handled by the ministry in advance. The ministry will prepare a so-called "Submission to the Council of State". This applies both in cases to be decided by the Government and in cases to be put forward to the *Storting*. The decisions made by the King in Council are called "Royal Resolutions" (*kongelig resolusjon*).

The ministries also have an independent authority to decide matters vested in the ministries according to statutes and Royal Resolutions. The competence to delegate authority to the ministries is only limited by Article 28 of the Constitution saying that "matters of importance shall be presented to the Council of State". All propositions to be put forward to the *Storting* must be presented in the Council of State irrespective of the importance of the matter.

As a general rule the administrative procedure is written. The traditional mode of work is that the ministry official prepares a proposition for the head of the division of the ministry, who may decide the matter himself if the case is not of importance. Important matters will be presented to the Director General or even the Secretary General or the Minister himself. Formally, all ministry decisions are made on behalf of the Minister who also will take the blame or praise.

There are also several directorates, state corporations outside the ministries. The independence of the directorates varies from directorate to directorate. Some directorates are departments of a ministry. Other directorates, such as the Price Directorate, have a more independent status.

In the central public administration there are also boards and committees in charge of the state corporations. Some boards or committees have as their only task to settle disputes, such as the Social Security Court. The Price Council, the Central Taxation Board and the Norwegian Patent Office are examples of more independent administrative bodies.

It is worth mentioning that many boards and committees have interest group representation. The administration needs practical experience and special skills, and it is also often considered to be an advantage to have cooperation across the different occupational groups.

On the regional level the county is the most important administrative unit. The County Governor (*fylkesmann*) is the superior state representative. The County Governor has important administrative functions and also has power to decide in various areas, such as in building matters, family matters, divorce cases, alimony cases and child care matters. The County Governor is also responsible for the Government's supervision of the municipalities.

On the regional level there are also other state agencies with special administrative tasks, such as the Chief County Tax Inspector, and the Chief County Agricultural Officer. There are also regional boards and committees with administrative tasks. In addition there are locally elected bodies with the responsibility for administering secondary education, health, road planning etc.

The County Council is the highest popularly elected authority in the County. The Chairman of the County Council (*fylkesordfører*) is the legal representative of the County and the leader of the administration of the County Executive (*fylkesrådmann*).

On the municipal level there are several popularly elected bodies. First of all there are the Municipal Councils and the Boards of Aldermen. The main tasks of the municipalities are to be responsible for primary schools, medical care, construction and maintenance of roads, water supplies, electricity, public communications etc.

The Administrative Form of Procedure.

After the Second World War many administrative reforms have been carried out aimed at improving the legal position of citizens in relation to the public administration. First, there was a desire to improve the legal position of the individual in relation to the administration by laying down rules for the administrative process. In the Act of February 1967 relating to procedure in cases concerning the public administration (The Public Administration Act) important rules of administrative procedure were laid down. Before 1967 the rules of administrative procedure to a great extent were not written. Some statutory rules were given, but the main aim of these rules was to protect public interests.

In all public administration the most common form of procedure is written. All decisions as a general rule shall also be in writing. Individual decisions may be appealed to the administrative body which is the immediate superior of the administrative body that rendered the administrative decision. The time limit for lodging an appeal is three weeks.

The Public Administration Act of 1967 contains detailed provisions concerning the requirements as to impartiality, the duty of the administration to provide guidance within its sphere of competence, the completion of cases without undue delay, the parties' right to call on the assistance of a lawyer, the duties of the administration not to disclose information relating to an individual's personal affairs etc., the duties of the administration to inform and notify the parties, the duties of the administration to ensure that the cases to be decided are clarified as thoroughly as possible, the right of the individual to acquaint himself with the documents of the case, rights of appeal and costs of litigation.

Second, there was also a desire to improve the general public's (rights of) access to information concerning the administrative process. In 1970, the Freedom of Information Act was adopted.

Third, there was a desire to improve the citizen's possibilities for ensuring that the rules which were intended to strengthen their position in relation to the administration were enforced. In 1962, a parliamentary ombudsman for public administration was established with the task of ensuring that citizens did not suffer injustice from the public administration.

The Highest Courts of Justice – The Court of Impeachment and the Supreme Court

The highest courts of the state are the Supreme Court (*Høyesterett*) and the Court of Impeachment (*Riksretten*). The Court of Impeachment, which according to the Constitution consists of members of the upper chamber of the *Storting* – the *Lagting* – and members of the Supreme Court, was established by the 1814 Constitution. The Supreme Court was established by a Royal

Resolution in 1815. It was later constitued by an act of the *Storting*.

The Court of Impeachment is a Criminal Court acting in cases against ministers of the crown, members of the *Storting* and members of the Supreme Court. The Prosecution authority is vested in the lower chamber of the *Storting* – the *Odelsting*. The Court of Impeachment has been convened eight times, all cases against ministers. No prosecution has been made against members of the *Storting* or judges of the Supreme Court.

In a famous case in 1883/84, the Court of Impeachment ruled that the charged ministers should lose their ministerial posts because they had advised the king not to give assent to an amendment of the Constitution allowing ministers to take part in the proceedings of the *Storting*. In practice this case laid the foundation for our present parliamentary system where the ministers are responsible to the *Storting* and must resign upon a vote of noconfidence.

The last impeachment trial took place in 1926/27. Several ministers were charged for having given financial support (loans and deposits) to one major Norwegian private bank in 1923 and 1924, without informing the *Storting* about it and without having the *Storting's* consent. The ministers were all acquitted (mainly because the prosecution was made too late).

The Court System in Ordinary Civil and Criminal Cases

Like the administration, the court system is hierarchically structured with the Supreme Court at the top. There are two other main levels in the Norwegian court system. The courts of first level are the so-called Urban and Rural District Courts *(herredsretter og byretter)*. The courts of second level are the High Courts *(lagmannsretter)*. The Supreme Court consists of a President and 17 permanently appointed justices. In each case five justices are sitting. In the judgments of the Supreme Court each judge will give his own reasoning in connection with his vote. It is the practice of the judges to be very "open" in the argumentation and it is therefore easy to trace the reasoning.

In some cases it may be decided that the Supreme Court should meet in plenary session. If important constitutional principles are in question it may be decided that the Supreme Court should render its judgement in plenary session. This happens one or two times a year. The Supreme Court hears both civil and criminal cases. The number of criminal cases presented before the Supreme Court is substantially higher than the number of civil cases. Legislators and the Supreme Court have both considered it important that the Supreme Court plays a substantial role in the application of the criminal law and the assessment of sentences.

The Appeals Committee of the Supreme Court is composed of three justices. The Committee is a court and it has the power to grant appeal permissions to the Supreme Court. The Committee may also in certain circumstances pass judgments both in civil and criminal matters.

There are five High Courts (*lagmannsrett*) with their seats in Oslo, Skien, Bergen, Trondheim and Tromsø. The President of the court is called *lagmann*. The High Court has civil and criminal functions. In civil matters the High Court is an appellate court. In criminal cases, the High Court is a trial court of first instance in more serious cases.

There are about 100 Urban and Rural District Courts in Norway. These courts also have both civil and criminal functions. In civil matters an action normally must start with the Conciliation Board before it is taken to court. The aim of the Conciliation Board is to mediate and if possible reach a settlement with the parties. If the parties do not agree, the case will continue in court.

In civil cases the parties may ask for lay judges to adjudicate the dispute together with the judge. Such demands may be made both in the Urban and Rural District Court and in the High Court, but never in the Supreme Court.

Lay judges always take part in criminal cases, except in cases decided in the Court of Examination and Summary Jurisdiction on the basis of a confession of the accused. In the Urban and Rural District Court, there are two lay judges in addition to the judge. In the High Court it is a "dual" system. In the cases starting in the High Court, a jury of ten members will decide the question of guilt. The sentence will be decided by the three judges and four of the jury members.

An appeal case or a retrial in the High Court is decided by three judges and four lay judges.

The rules of Court Procedure in civil and criminal cases are based on different Acts and the court procedure also differs to some extent. The procedure in civil cases is laid down in an Act of 1915. For criminal cases an Act of 1981 repealed the Act of 1887 concerning Rules of Court Procedure in Criminal Cases. Formerly both civil and criminal procedure to a great extent was based on customary law.

The present acts on court procedure both in civil and criminal cases are based on the principles that proceedings shall be oral and that evidence shall be presented before the trial court.

Although the rules of procedure to some extent differ in civil and criminal cases, the courts are now the same. The Act of 1981 concerning criminal cases has in many ways made the difference between criminal and civil cases less significant.

In 1887, a public prosecution authority with a Director General (*Riksadvokat*) as head and district prosecutors (*Statsadvokater*) under his command was established. The Director General and the district prosecutors are all jurists, and are appointed by the King in Council. Police officers with a legal degree and district sheriffs (*lensmenn*) are also part of the prosecution authority.

Decisions to instigate criminal proceedings are made either by the King in Council, the Director General, the State Advocates or the senior police officers, depending on what kind of criminal offence has been committed.

The Legal Profession

The functions and characteristics of a country's legal profession will to a great extent be determined by social conditions, history and tradition. One important characteristic of the Norwegian legal profession is the common educational basis. It is now possible to take law degrees at the universities in Oslo, Bergen and Tromsø, but the material difference in education is not significant. The study of law normally takes about six years. The law degree, candidatus juris (cand. jur.), is obtained on the basis of 4 or 5 main written examinations.

Having obtained the law degree, the candidate has a variety of possibilities. A law degree is required for prosecuting officials in the police department, junior administrative officials, associates in law firms and in legal departments of private and public companies.

There is a long tradition that the young Norwegian lawyer practises as a "deputy judge" in an urban and rural district court. As a deputy judge the young lawyer is allowed to act in the capacity of a judge. The deputy is acting on behalf of the ordinary judge and will normally obtain useful practice for his future legal work.

To be an advocate, one needs a licence. Such a licence is given by the Ministry of Justice. To obtain the licence it is, among other things, obligatory to have specific kinds of legal practice for at least two years.

12

Education in Norway

Oddvar Vormeland

Historical Overview

Education has a long tradition in Norway. The oldest organized education we know of dates back to the 12th Century and was related to the religious teachings of the church.

In 1989, Norway celebrated the 250th anniversary of the first national decree regarding education. The background of this decree was the introduction of confirmation within the church in 1736 and the resulting need for catechism before confirmation.

Norway's constitution from 1814 inspired, obliged and challenged officials to work for the then, new democracy. The goals and ideas put forth were to be realized through training and teaching. Concepts such as freedom, equality, likeness and personal development therefore were an integral part of the development of the educational system. The younger generation was expected to take a central part in the building, protecting and development of Norway for the coming generations.

Religious and humanistic values, social services, societal information and appraisal had to be developed in the school and its teachings. The curriculum became more varied and extensive as the school freed itself more and more from its ecclesiastical duties. The values and main goals of the church were, however, quite clearly carried over to the 20th century school system.

The postwar decades (after 1945) witnessed an explosive development in the Norwegian educational system. It became increasingly clear that there was a need for experimentation and research within schools and education. In 1954, a council was formed for furthering research. The dismantling of this council thirty years later (1984) marked the end of an experimental and research expansive period in Norwegian education.

School Politics: Trends for the 1990s

From the advent of the present decade, there are a number of trends in school politics which are clearly emerging and are expected to influence further development within the different types of schools and educational levels.

Decentralization has been for a number of decades a heated issue in school politics. This came as a counterweight to the centralization wave of the 1960s and 1970s. At that time, many of the smaller local schools were closed down to accomplish greater school unity across the nation, and thereby to allow for a more varied curriculum at each school. Pupils, especially, in the elementary schools, were then bussed to municipal schools. To be able to realize other goals, however, for example equal education opportunities, it has been seen as optimal to provide opportunities for schooling as close to the pupils' homes as possible.

Municipalities (*kommuner*) decide themselves the number of elementary schools they should have and must have, where these schools should be located and how they should be organized. Even the contents of the obligatory years of schooling (from first grade through ninth grade), are under a certain amount of influence from local government and schools.

Now, however, the question has been asked whether the decentralization of Norwegian education has gone too far. Is it at all possible to maintain a somewhat unified and equal school system when over 450 different municipalities decide the content of primary education?

With a background in the above question, the entire governing system for Norwegian schools and education has been under evaluation. Parliament has given the government and the Ministry of Education, Research and Church Affairs (KUFD) authority to reorganize so as to ensure more rational policy making, and thereby for the possibility of more unified and superior reforms. In this way, it is possible to maintain and to develop continuously better and more effective educational opportunities. The tendency is to turn once again from decentralization to the direction of a more central control, with the pros and cons that come with this. We can see similar tendencies in a number of other countries where decentralization has been applauded as a principle for some time.

Democratization is another principle which has been emphasized. At all steps in the educational process, the users have had a large influence on its control, content and development. In the primary and secondary schools, it is chiefly the parents and local politicians who have influence. In upper education, colleges, universities, technical institutions, representatives from business and society are coming more strongly and clearly into the influential sphere.

The Norwegian belief in education as a democratic right is most clearly visible in the wide range of pedagogical opportunities to anyone regardless of socio-economic background, religion, gender, ethnic background or locality. Learning and opportunities for personal development are to be accessible to everyone. This democratic openness shows itself in the fact that all classes in public schools and educational institutions are tuition free, from primary school through university. More than 96% of all pupils are found in the public primary schools and lower secondary schools.

Classes are organized as mixed, both in terms of gender, socio-economic background and ability. Any tendency to depart from this principle is quickly curbed by the central administration.

Delegation is often seen as a form of decentralization. There is a wide consensus that too many details have been attended to, and less important decisions too often made, at the central level, or at least at an unnecessarily high administrative level. Therefore, there has been an increasingly clear tendency to delegate authority for decision making to the lower levels of the system. "Decisions should be made as much as possible at the point where the questions and problems arise".

This development towards a larger delegation of responsibilities and decision making, makes it necessary, however, to establish clear rules for appealing decisions. School laws contain such regulations.

In the spring of 1992, Parliament dealt with proposals for reforms in municipal and county administrations. These reforms are in the direction of larger delegation and decentralization within the area of school and education. It is obvious that the pendulum of centralization vs. delegation/decentralization is still swinging freely.

Values and Discipline

Regulations governing primary school teaching stress that the school has a double goal: 1) knowledge, learning and information, and 2) moral upbringing.

The Evangelical-Lutheran religion is Norway's state religion; consequently the norms and directives for upbringing, behavior, rights and responsibilities are based upon it. As in many other countries, the question of values has once again come into focus in the Norwegian schools and educational system. Schools are asked to emphasize the teaching of values and the ways in which these can be put into practice.

At the same time, the school has been ordered to "promote intellectual freedom and tolerance" so that all children and parents, irrespective of values and religious belief, will feel accepted while cooperating with the schools. The teaching of Christianity and other religions is to give knowledge and not to be a form of indoctrination

The question of discipline is also being discussed more and more intensely. The background for this can be seen, for instance, in terms of a pronounced breaking away from what is considered acceptable societal behavior. The school is seen by different authorities as a place where one should try to find ways to promote morals and social behavior both now and in the future.

Society's discipline problems are reflected directly in the schools. Earlier, this was seen primarily in the higher grades, but now already in the first year of school, conflicts and unacceptable behavior are seen more frequently and in a more serious fashion.

The School: A Part of Society

As is the case today, the school and educational system in Norway has been a corner stone in society's devlopment from both an historical and a traditional perspective. The schools are a social issue of which all political parties and groups see the importance, despite disagreement concerning details and directions of development.

There are differences of opinion as to how strongly liberalistic ideals and principles should enter into the educational sphere. The temperature for such debates can be expected to rise throughout the nineties. Traditionally, the state has had the responsibility for practically all education in Norway. The church is called the mother of our schools, but society at large has been responsible for the rest of the child's development.

As mentioned earlier, nearly all pupils attend public primary and secondary schools. This gives, of course, the public school system a clear and direct responsibility to develop the system both quantitatively and qualitatively. The public school is and wishes to be the people's school. Therefore, it needs to compare favourably with other options of education.

All the same, there is room for private schools and other educational enterprises. Even in the primary school, there is no obligatory attendance. There is, however, between the ages of seven and sixteen years obligatory learning. If a child in this age group does not use his/her right to attend school, the parents or guardians are obliged to find similar education outside of the public school system.

A private school law (1985) gives private persons and organizations the right to establish schools and instruction and to stipulate tuition fees. These can be subsidized by the state; however, there are conditions for, and limits to, the financial support even within a liberalistic philosophy.

Current debates on schooling continually show examples of how individuals and groups feel that the boundary between liberalism and state intervention should be moved in one direction or the other.

Societal development influences both political and curriculum priorities within the school. A good example of this is the instruction on environmental issues. Just a few years ago, one scarcely spoke of the teaching of environmental issues. Now it is close to becoming an obligatory course at all levels. Developing methods and a curriculum for this has become an increasing state priority.

Equal rights between the sexes is an issue which the schools are required to actively engage in. This is done in, for instance, career counselling. Textbooks are examined closely to create a balance between the sexes in different situations.

Emphasis has recently been placed on the importance of understanding both the working and business worlds. The two main trade unions (LO and NHO) advocate that the schools should have a major part of the responsibility in this area. Other interest groups also wish to influence the school curriculum either directly or indirectly. Who is to decide what part of the curriculum should be replaced by the new issues?

This question can cause political and professional disagreement. In addition, unions would like to have more say as to the use of time at school, working hours and salaries. In these and other situations, politicians and professionals often are on opposing sides.

In the past few years there has been an increasing demand to strengthen Norwegian, mathematics, and foreign languages in the school. The sciences also have had numerous promoters. These initiatives, especially when sufficiently strong or supported by Parliament, often result in changed priorities in the pupils' curriculum.

Structure of the Educational System

The Norwegian school system can broadly be divided into the following levels:
- Kindergarten/Preschool: under 7 years of age
- Primary and lower secondary school: 7–16 years of age
- Upper secondary school: 17–19 years of age
- Higher education/Universities and colleges
- Adult education (at all levels)

Kindergarten/Preschool is not formally a part of the public school system. It is, however, being currently discussed whether or not children should begin schooling at the age of 6 instead of 7. Most preschool centers are owned and run by private organizations, but receive public support.

Primary and lower secondary schools cover the compulsory school age, 7–16 years. If a child in this age group does not attend public school, it is required that he/she receive the equivalent training in a private school or, say, from teaching at home. Local municipalities are responsible for ensuring that every child of school age has a place in the public school system. Most 16 year olds apply to upper secondary schools. The goal is to be able to offer this education to everyone. Every year, however, there are many young people who do not get into upper secondary schools for lack of space. The counties have the responsibility to establish and run these schools.

Higher education/universities and colleges are the responsibility of the state. Private institutions offering instruction at this level most often receive state subsidies.

Adult education with state subsidies is given by local and regional public school systems, different types of voluntary organizations, correspondence schools, and media companies.

Primary and Lower Secondary Education

Primary and lower secondary education is compulsory for all Norwegian inhabitants, irrespective of citizenship, from the ages of 7 to 16.

Individual local municipalities are responsible for securing necessary school facilities and running the schools according to existing national laws and regulations.

The nine year compulsory school is divided into two stages:
- Primary stage: grades 1–6 (ages 7 to 13)
- Lower secondary stage: Grades 7–9 (ages 13 to 16).

Some municipalities, alone or together with a neighbouring municipality, may also establish an additional voluntary tenth grade. There is no repeating of grades. As part of a reform suggested by the government for lowering the school entrance age to six, possibilities for extending the compulsory school to the tenth grade was discussed.

As a consequence of decentralization, there is a general aim to secure school facilities as near the family home as possible. Norway has a large number of small schools, especially in remote and sparsely populated areas. Approximately one third (or 1,200) of the total schools nationwide have more than one age group in each class. Some schools have as few as six pupils, where all pupils are together in the same classroom regardless of which grade they are in.

The class is regarded as an important unit, both socially and educationally. It is kept together as much as possible in a homogeneous unit, at least from the first to the sixth grade, in many cases even to the ninth grade. A class teacher is responsible for each class, even when subject teachers are brought in (which is rarely the case at the primary level).

The compulsory school is completely comprehensive. This is clearly stated in paragraph 7.1 of school law: "All pupils have the right to receive instruction in accordance with their abilities and aptitudes". This principle applies equally to the education of gifted and highly motivated pupils as to the physically or mentally disabled. Consequently, the main approach in teaching as well as in learning must be individual differentiation.

Curriculum Guidelines

The Model Plan (M-87) includes an outline of the basic principles and objectives of compulsory education, as stated by Parliament. Furthermore, it gives the framework of the content of the various subjects, allocation of teaching periods and suggestions as to adequate lines of activities.

At all levels of the compulsory school, pupil participation has become increasingly more important. This means varied and active social learning in meaningful settings. The pupils are regarded not only as listeners and individual schoolworkers, but as active participants in what happens and what is accomplished in the school as well. As an example, right from the start of school, pupils meet together with their parents to discuss their own situation and development with their respective teachers. This not only means more openness and frankness between pupils, teachers and parents, but will hopefully foster responsibility and fairness as well.

At the school, all parents are members of a "parents' council" that elects a working committee. There is also a coordinating unit where parents have two members in addition to two representatives from teachers, one from the other staff, the principal, and two representatives from the pupils' council. The last member of the coordination unit is elected by the municipal school board. This council is another example of practical and social democracy.

The curriculum guidelines (M-87) also include a section on Sami education. The guidelines aim at giving an adequate and non-discriminatory education. In addition, Sami history and Sami culture are topics which all Norwegian pupils should be familiar with.

Correspondingly, it is stated that other language minorities and immigrant groups must be given the same opportunities as Norwegian pupils. Emphasis is put on the necessity to provide teaching in both the child's mother tongue and the Norwegian language. There are, however, some disputes regarding the legally defined obligation of the national school system to offer mother tongue teaching, at least as it is currently offered.

The main foreign language at the primary and lower secondary level is English, at present introduced at the fourth grade, or at the age of 10. A second foreign language is no longer compulsory but is offered at the lower secondary level. A country with a relatively small population, in need of international contact and exchange, should be especially on the alert for promoting foreign language teaching. Voices from trade and industry, among others, are repeatedly emphasizing this.

Upper Secondary Education

Upper secondary education covers all education between compulsory school and higher education, or grades 10–12. These

"Russefeiring": The traditional way of celebrating the end of upper-secondary education.

levels include general and vocational education as well as apprenticeship training.

The pupils are normally between the ages of 16 and 19. Older students are becoming more common, however, as adults return to school to supplement or improve their educational status.

The traditional European theoretically-based school has been replaced by a school open for anyone who has graduated from the lower secondary school. All types of education for the ages of 16 to 19 are now part of the same comprehensive system covered by the same law (from 1974, implemented in 1976).

According to the law, the upper secondary school should prepare the students for further education as well as for later professional and community life. Promoting personality development, extending knowledge and the understanding of basic Christian values, the national cultural heritage, democratic ideas, are all elements of the upper secondary school, in addition to working methods, a scientific way of thinking, etc.

The responsibility for planning and running upper secondary schools rests with the various county and municipal authorities. In principle, the upper secondary school is open for all and should be available as near the pupils' place of residence as possible. In cases of competition for school places or special courses, grades from the lower stages of schooling are considered.

In 1984, disabled pupils in need of adapted instruction were given legalized priority for admission. To what extent such students may be given special education is then up to the school to decide, dependent on available facilities and resources.

Presently, there are ten areas of study in upper secondary education, comprising general as well as vocational subjects:
– General subjects
– Technical and industrial subjects
– Aesthetic subjects
– Fishing trade subjects
– Maritime subjects
– Physical education
– Commercial and clerical subjects
– Home economics
– Social services and health subjects
– Agricultural subjects

The areas of study which meet the requirements for admission to universities and other higher educational institutions are: General subjects, commercial and clerical subjects, and physical education. Music within aesthetic subjects, and some combinations of general subjects and vocational areas of study meet the requirements for admission as well. All areas of study have the same basic structure: foundation courses taking one or two years to complete, then advanced courses for one or two years implying specialization.

Apprenticeship Training

Within a wide range of crafts, trades and industries, apprenticeship training is a traditional way of vocational education. The training is based on close cooperation between schools and places of employment. The students can receive all their secondary vocational education at a place of work, or they can receive their entire education at a school. A combination of these two possibilities is the third, and often regarded as the best, alternative: a two year foundation school-based course, followed by a third year at a trade.

Development of the apprenticeship training system has been a key issue in government policy to ensure coordinated theoretical and practical education and training. The aim is to provide skilled workers in the various crafts and industries, and to reduce unemployment among youth.

Higher Education

Traditionally, higher education has meant academic education at prestigious universities at home and abroad. The University of Oslo is Norway's first university (founded in 1811) and it is still the largest (20,000 students) and most comprehensive in terms of the range of subjects. The three other universities, established in the post-war period after 1945, are located in Bergen, Trondheim, and Tromsø. A certain degree of specialization is found among the universities. The University of Trondheim is the major centre for technology in the country, while the University of Tromsø has developed higher education and research in fields like fishery, science and arctic studies.

– In addition to the four universities, there are six specialized colleges at the university level:
– The Agricultural College of Norway (Norges Landbrukshøyskole)
– The Norwegian College of Veterinary Medicine (Norges Veterinærhøyskole)
– Norwegian School of Economics and Business Administration (Norges Handelshøyskole)
– Norwegian College of Physical Education and Sports (Norges Idrettshøyskole)

- Norwegian State Academy of Music (Norges Musikk-høyskole)
- Oslo School of Architecture (Oslo Arkitekthøyskole)

The universities and the scientific colleges mentioned above have a dual purpose of teaching and research. They are all run by the state, with no charge for tuition.

The universities offer degrees at three different levels: Lower degree (4 years), Higher degree (5–7 years) and Doctoral degree. In addition, there are 5–7 years of professional studies, for instance, in medicine, law, agriculture, and technology.

Increasing autonomy in the allocation of resources, within the general budgetary framework laid down centrally, has been given to the institutions. The main purpose of these reforms is to make the institutions and their activities generally more efficient and autonomous.

Regional Colleges

Regional colleges generally provide one, two and three year programmes in a wide variety of fields, such as business administration, engineering, science, language, nursing and social work. Some colleges also set up graduate programmes and do research and development work in relation to, and for, local enterprises.

The growth and development of regional colleges is closely related to the policy for decentralizing higher education in the country. In the view of the state, even higher education should be available in the districts. The purpose of this approach is also to convey professional competence to local and regional trade, industry and cultural life.

Comprising upgraded former colleges in the regions, there are approximately 110 regional institutions of higher education. In addition, there are 22 private colleges supported by the government. It is worth mentioning that several regional colleges are fairly small. Only 10 have more than 1,000 students. This is regarded as a weakness, and not only from an economic point of view; it also restricts possibilities for alternative studies at one and the same institution.

The current policy in regard to regional colleges is primarily to strengthen and consolidate what has been achieved. To a certain extent, this will imply improved contact between different colleges and between colleges and university institutions. Merging and even closing has, in some instances, been discussed. This means that new colleges will not be established.

Teacher Training

Teacher training is given both at regional teacher training colleges and at universities. In both cases, the major responsibility for the academic activities lies with the institution, and within the scope of the Teacher Training Act (1973). This act prescribes administrative and academic standards for programmes that qualify teachers in the pre-primary school, as well as in the primary and secondary school. Entrance requirements for training programmes are the same: three years of upper secondary education or its equivalent. Additional credits may be given for other studies and practical work.

There are three levels of educational qualifications for all categories of teachers ("lærer", "adjunkt" and "lektor"). The titles are awarded on the basis of 3,4, and 5–7 years of study, respectively. The latter two titles mentioned may be compared with the B.A. and M.A. degrees.

"The Norwegian Net" (Norgesnettet)

The Norwegian net is a concept coined recently, but already known to active participants and those interested in the future of the higher education system. The idea behind the concept is planned efforts to rationalize, to improve the efficiency and to raise the quality of the entire system of higher education. In some instances this will mean a reduction of units, or even closure. A further functional specialization will be blended with national integration. An effective system of cooperation (net-working) between higher education institutions should be one of the main vehicles towards the comprehensive goal. Another consequence anticipated by this reform is more qualified leading-edge competence within different fields. This, again, could raise the level of Norway's research, and thereby its scientific reputation internationally.

International Relations

In different respects the Government is putting stronger emphasis on internationalizing higher education. This aim is prompted by recent international trends and developments, in eastern as well as in western Europe. The more influential national trade and labour unions are presenting arguments for more comprehensive and bilaterally binding relations internationally. For this end they find a strengthening of foreign language education, at all levels, as a cornerstone.

Exchange of higher education students is another endeavor for widening the international scope. Norway has a long tradition for having students at universities abroad. In different ways, a small country especially, may profit from international experiences and impulses brought back by capable native students. This is a fact irrespective of possibilities for higher education in the home country. By now 8–9,000 Norwegians are studying abroad, while fewer than half this number of foreign students come to our higher education institutions. Norwegian authorities are aiming at a better balance between these groups preferably by improving conditions for foreign students in this country.

Adult Education

Adult education has a fairly long tradition in Norway. In its more modern version it is based on the current Act on Adult Education from 1976.

Like a large, well developed tree, it has many diversified boughs. The responsibility for strengthening and developing the system rests with different sources:
– voluntary organizations
– school authorities
– manpower authorities and work organizations
– universities and other educational institutions.

The general aim of adult education is, according to the law, "... to help the individual to attain a more meaningful life ..." and "... contribute to providing adults with equal access to knowledge, insight and skills which promote the individual's endeavors to find their own values and help in their personal development, and thus strengthen the basis for independent achievement and cooperation with others in work and community life". On this background the pupose is also to smooth out gender differences and dissimilarities between social, age and regional groups.

Special education for adults, labour market education, education for adult immigrants, refugees and asylum seekers are included, as well as education for trade union representatives and for particular groups with specific difficulties.

Basic adult education covering elementary, lower and secondary curricula is mostly given free of charge by public schools at relevant levels. Distribution of costs between state, county and municipality is the same as for similar education for children and young people.

Folk High Schools

Folk high schools are said to be the only really original Scandinavian educational institution. Inspired by Danish folk high schools, the first school in Norway was established in 1864 (in Hamar). The idea was primarily to raise the general educational level of countryside youth as they often had very few possibilities for attending other schools. The folk high schools have, for more than 125 years, been important links in our decentralized general education.

Traditionally, folk high schools have been residential. They consist today, as when they were first established, of two parts: school and boarding. Most of the near 100 schools are owned and run by different private organizations. They operate outside the system of upper secondary education, have no set curriculum and no formal examinations. The operation of folk high schools was regulated in 1984 by a specific law. The law guarantees these schools considerable educational freedom, but establishes guidelines governing their exterior framework for education (i.e. length of courses, number of students, etc.) and finances. The schools are tuition free, as they receive public support. Student expenses are primarily limited to room and board.

Folk high schools are open to all. The minimum age for admission is 17. The average age of students has increased during the past years, however.

There are now foreign students attending almost every folk high school. However, under the current immigration policy, only a limited number of student places are available for foreign students.

Since students live on campus, they share most of their school time and leisure time. There is no sharp division between formal class hours and leisure activities. No formal vocational or professional training is given; neither do the schools grant formal academic credits.

Generally, all students attend the same lessons and/or activities such as lectures on language, literature, current issues, Norwegian art and crafts, philosophy and/or Christianity. An information pamphlet on folk high schools concludes as follows: These schools "offer a unique opportunity to enhance each individual's human resources. The schools constitute small, educational societies where each individual makes a difference. Studying in a warm and open environment, working closely with fellow students and staff stimulates personal growth and development."

References

Dokka, Hans Jørgen *En skole gjennom 250 år*. Oslo, 1988.
Ness, Einar *Det var en gang – norsk skole gjennom tidene*. Oslo, 1989.
Adult Education in Norway. A Brief Introduction. The Norwegian Association of Adult Education Organizations (15pp.). Oslo 1985.
Den videregående skole (pamphlet) Rådet for videregående skole. Oslo, 1990.
Description of Teacher Education/Training in Norway. Manuscript by Hans Otto Mørk. 33pp.
Education in Norway. Ministry of Education and Research. Oslo, 1990, 36pp. (Order no. F–2600)
Folkehøgskolen i Norge. With an English Summary (pp.102). Oslo 1991. (Order no. F–2183)
Primary Education in Norway (pp.13). Council of Europe, 1988.

13

Nature and Conservation of Natural Resources

Kjetil Hindar, NINA*

Living nature has always meant a lot to people in Norway. Several thousand year-old rock carvings tell us that the early Norwegians hunted for moose and reindeer and fished for salmon and halibut. In the first written account about a Norwegian, Ottar tells King Alfred of England, 1100 years ago, how he and his people made a living from hunting and fishing in the extreme north of the European continent. Rich marine resources formed the basis of an extensive trade along the Norwegian coast for centuries, and even today, export of fishery products provides many coastal communities with all or most of their income.

In the 19th century, Norway's nature was discovered for its beauty, and attracted people from both near and far "in search of trout, reindeer, and the picturesque", to cite one classic source. The attractions are still there, although not always in their pristine state. Norway can still boast magnificent scenery, clean water, spectacular waterfalls, big salmon, and swift reindeer. But dams and pipes have replaced many waterfalls, acid rain has caused the death of fish in thousands of lakes, the big salmon may well be escapees from fish farms, and the wild reindeer suffered great damage from the Chernobyl accident in 1988.

The Norwegian territories comprise the mainland and the islands of Svalbard and Jan Mayen in the Arctic Ocean. The total area is approximately 387,000 km², whereof the mainland covers 324,000 km².

Nearly 40 percent of mainland Norway is situated more than 600 meters above sea level, 20 percent above 900 m. There are more than 1,500 glaciers covering less than 1 percent of the area. The Jostedalen glacier is the largest glacier on the European continent. Norway has, as many other areas which were glaciated, many lakes and rivers. More than 211,000 lakes are distribut-

[*Norwegian Institute for Nature Research. The authors are: Kjell E. Erikstad, Eli Fremstad, Kjetil Hindar (corresponding author), Harald Korsmo, Odd Terje Sandlund, Terje Skogland and Jørn Thomassen]

ed all over the country. Only 3–4 percent of the area of (mainland) Norway is cultivated, another 1 percent is built up land. Of the remaining area, forests cover 37 percent, and freshwater, fens, mires and other wetlands cover 11–12 percent. Approximately 47 percent is "unproductive land", that is mountainous areas, coastal heaths and other unforested areas.

The Svalbard archipelago is situated between 76° and 81°N and belongs to the high arctic. Due to relatively warm southerly air masses connected to low pressures passing the islands, they have a surprisingly diverse animal and plant life. This makes Svalbard unique in the Arctic. In the past, Svalbard was the target for whalers, hunters and trappers not only from Norway, but also from the Netherlands, Russia and Great Britain. Their uncritical resource exploitation almost led to the extinction of whales, walrus and polar bears on Svalbard. Later, greater emphasis was put on the exploration of minerals and coal on the island. Several countries had shown an interest in exploiting the natural resources on Svalbard and in 1920 the Svalbard Treaty was signed. The Treaty states that the Svalbard archipelago shall be ruled under the system of Norwegian government and Norwegian laws.

The Arctic is characterized by summer day and winter night, that is, the midnight sun in summer and almost total darkness in winter. The length varies according to latitude; in Svalbard the midnight sun period lasts for approximately 4 months and the dark period for 3 months. The animals and plants of Svalbard are adapted to this yearly cycle with an explosion in productivity in summer.

Approximately 165 species of plants are found on Svalbard, most of them in the fjord areas on the western and northern coast. Vegetation covers less than 10 percent of the land area. This is due to low precipitation combined with a short growing season, as well as to soil with a low nutritional content.

The Barents Sea has an enormous primary production of planktonic algae. This marine primary production is the basis for all animal life in Svalbard and also for much of the plant life. Millions of seabirds visit Svalbard every year to breed and raise chicks. Their faeces provide nutrition for well-adapted species of plants. The only overwintering bird living on the islands is the ptarmigan. Birds of prey and owls are absent from Svalbard, probably due to the absence of rodents.

The most common sea-living mammals are the ringed seal and the bearded seal. The walrus, being almost extinct due to 300–

400 years of hunting, has in recent years become more and more common in its traditional resting places. The white whale is a rather common smaller whale associated with shallow waters. Due to man's hunting for profit, the bigger whales, especially the greenland whale, are almost extinct from the Barents Sea.

Only three terrestrial mammals find a living on Svalbard: the arctic fox, the polar bear, and the reindeer, all of them having special adaptations to tackle the hard climatic conditions.

Half of the land area on Svalbard has good protection through regulations. There are two nature reserves, three national parks, plant reserves and bird sanctuaries. But Svalbard with its peculiar nature and its history of resource exploitation is vulnerable to all sorts of environmental encroachments. The major environmental problems are industrial exploitation of natural resources (mainly coal mining and oil prospecting), tourism and exploitation of living resources. In addition we see an increasing threat to the environment from long range air and seaborne pollutants.

Coal mining in Svalbard has a one hundred year-old history. Today mining activity occurs in the main settlements on the island, Longyearbyen (Norway) and Barentsburg and Pyramiden (Russia). The search for new coal mining fields also includes plans for road building and new ports for shipments. Oil prospecting and the possible exploitation and extraction of oil sources represent a more serious threat to the environment than the coal mining industry. Oil spills in the arctic environment can damage the ecosystem for decades and destroy animal and plant life that already live under extreme environmental stress.

Outdoor recreation and tourism are constantly in search of more challenge. Svalbard, as the most easily accessible high arctic area in the world, is the goal for various sorts of recreational activity. Natural and cultural monuments are in danger of being destroyed by tourists lacking the necessary respect and knowledge. The need for Norwegian authorities to regulate tourism and outdoor recreation well within the critical levels of Svalbard's environment is obvious, and a management plan for tourism and outdoor recreation on Svalbard has now been devised.

The coastal areas of the Norwegian mainland are characterized by deep fjords and steep cliffs. The adjacent marine environment of the Norwegian Sea is among the most productive in the world and forms the basis of extensive commercial fishing. In addition to important fish stocks like cod, herring, saithe and capelin, the area also includes dense populations of whales, seals and seabirds.

During the last 20 years the coastal ecosystem has gone through dramatic changes. In the late 1960s the huge herring stock, estimated at more than 10 million tons of spawning fish in the 1950s, collapsed because of overfishing. Since then the stock has remained at a low level for more than two decades. The herring spawn off western Norway in early spring, and the larvae then drift northwards with the coastal current. On their way northwards, the young fish reach northwestern Norway in the first half of July when they dominate the diet of the puffin. Due to the collapse in the herring stock, insignificant numbers of young herring have been available to breeding puffins at the Røst archipelago in Lofoten. During 1969–1990 the puffin have bred successfully in only four seasons and since 1979 there has been an annual decrease in the population of about 10–15 percent.

Since 1980, the capelin stock steadily declined from about 5.5 mill tons until it collapsed in 1987 to 20,000 tons. The exact cause of this collapse was not so clear cut as for the herring, but was probably a combination of heavy predation pressure by cod (in the absence of herring), sea-temperature changes and over-fishing. The collapse in the capelin stock had dramatic consequences on the whole ecosystem. The coastal cod fishery failed and cod taken by trawlers offshore were in extremely poor body condition. Fish-eating seabirds, especially the common guillemot, decreased by about 80% in the area and the coast was on several occasions invaded by tens of thousands of hungry harp seals. This further aggravated the situation for the coastal communities for whom fisheries are the prime source of income. Northern Norway was in a severe economic crisis.

In sharp contrast to the herring, the Barents sea capelin stock is already close to its pre-collapse level, and the capelin fishery reopened in 1991, after only three years' closure. This rapid recovery is due to the capelin maturing at a younger age than herring, good recruitment to the stock in 1988 and 1989, and unusually rapid fish growth during the last few years.

When natural populations fluctuate so severely under man's fishing pressure, why not breed them artificially and raise them under controlled conditions? For Atlantic salmon, rearing in a captive environment through the life cycle is a reality, and Norway now produces about 150,000 tons per year, or more than 100 times the weight of wild salmon caught in Norwegian waters. But the success in rearing salmon carries a burden for wild fish.

So many fish escape from containment that they now outnumber wild fish in many spawning populations of Atlantic salmon in Norway. The escaped salmon threaten natural populations by transmitting diseases, and by competing for space and spawning partners in the river. Following interbreeding with wild fish, the threat includes reduced genetic adaptation of the natural populations to their local environment. Whereas some of these effects may be difficult to demonstrate, we have already witnessed severe losses from the transmission of parasites and diseases to wild fish. It is evident that large-scale culture of Atlantic salmon, or of any other fish species, must be better regulated with respect to containment and disease control, so that aquaculture can be developed without compromising the ecological and genetic integrity of the wild source populations.

Alpine areas are close to the heart of every Norwegian. The local term for these high unforested areas and the mountain forest areas is *fjellet*. *Fjellet* plays a prominent part in our cultural traditions, in outdoor recreation and in the entire Norwegian way of being. In former times *fjellet* was extensively used for grazing and hunting, and it was essential for the survival of a large section of the rural population.

The most characteristic animal of the mountains is the Norwegian lemming, a small rodent which has its main distribution area here. In one year, the mountains may be crowded by them, and with their conspicuous yellowish coloration and hot-blooded cheeps, they cannot go unnoticed. In the next and following years, they may be impossible to locate and only the corpses and faeces tell us about a recent peak in the 3–4 year population cycle.

Ecologists have for ages speculated about the causes for the pronounced population fluctuations. Fifty years of research has not resolved this issue, and it is perhaps time to realize that no single factor is responsible for the fluctuations.

By mid-summer thousands of Norwegians go hiking in the mountains, and find pleasure in seeing spectacular birds of prey like the rough-legged buzzard, which is common, and the more sparsely distributed golden eagle and gyrfalcon. Every autumn, Norwegians go hunting in the mountains for willow grouse, ptarmigan, and the mountain hare. Centuries ago the Norwegian mountains attracted falconers from Central Europe. They lived in the mountains for several months each summer and captured live gyrfalcon and other birds of prey. Today all birds of prey are protected by Norwegian legislation.

One of the hottest environmental issues in Norway to-day concerns the management of the Dovrefjell mountains in Central Norway. Nowhere in Norway is the density of conserved wildlands as high as in this area, and nowhere is the research tradition in alpine ecology as long. The flora and vegetation of Dovrefjell were appreciated by Norwegian and foreign botanists as early as the beginning of the 19th century. In 1911, fifty alpine plants were protected by law. In 1923 the fens, *Fokstumyrene,* were protected. The rounded mountains of Dovrefjell have a light yellowish colour. This is due to lichens which cover the floor of open birch forests and dominate the heaths in the low alpine zone. The lichen heaths may seem monotonous, and usually such heath areas are poor in species. However, at Dovrefjell, lichen heaths sometimes form mosaics with calcareous, moist sites, and these mosaics make the mountains an exciting place for those who are interested in alpine flora. Moreover, Dovrefjell is the only area left in Europe where wild reindeer, arctic fox and wolverine coexist, that is, the only area where the large herbivores and top predators of the mountain ranges can be seen in their original habitat. Dovrefjell's value as a reference for our natural heritage is obvious, both in strictly scientific terms and in relation to appreciating plant and animal life in their pristine state.

In early 1992 the Norwegian government decided to use mines at Dovre for temporary storage of hazardous waste (e.g. chlorinated solvents, pesticides, and PCB). This use came on top of other encroachments in the area such as a military target field, watercourse regulation, and road-building. This prompted the question: How much can Dovre and its wild animal and plant life tolerate before the conservation value is gone? It should be noted that even in the absence of the above-mentioned encroachments, indirect threats occur especially in the form of fall-outs from long range airborne pollution. The wildlife at Dovre was hit hard by radioactive fall-outs from the 1988 Tchernobyl accident. This was primarily due to the fact that reindeer through their diet of lichens are extremely vulnerable to airborne pollution. Lichens accumulate not only radioactivity but also heavy metals, which are reflected in high contents of both radiocesium, lead and cadmium in the reindeer.

The problems at Dovrefjell show that conservation has both local and global dimensions. Whatever the outcome of the present debate over the use of this mountain range, the final word has not been said.

The forests in Norway consist of about 50,000 km^2 coniferous forest and 22,000 km^2 deciduous forest. The largest part of this resource is found in the southeastern part of the country where conifers cover more than 60 percent. Nearly 80 percent of the total forest area belongs to private owners, of which there are many. The mean size of a forest property is between 0.5 and 0.6 km^2.

Norway spruce and Scotch pine are the main species of conifers while birch, silver birch, and aspen are among the most important trees in the deciduous forest. The nemoral forests in the extreme south consist of oak, beech (rare), ash, elm, hazel, lime, alder, and some other broadleaved deciduous trees. Some of these species are also common in a transitional zone between the nemoral zone and the boreal zone, and in a similar transitional section stretching along the coast up to the Trondheims-fjord district. The outermost part of this section was deforested many hundred, even thousands of years ago. The practice of winter grazing and burning created a treeless landscape dominated by heather, a dwarf shrub which is also a prominent part of the heath landscapes of Britain. To-day the heaths are threatened by invasion of juniper, birch and pine due to changes in land use.

Modern forestry was introduced in the middle of the 1950s by use of clear felling techniques, site preparation and afforestation. Road building has often been necessary to meet the aim of the economical utilization of the resources. As a consequence of this development, a number of problems have been created, especially related to plant and animal life which depend on old forest for a living. Another problem for Norwegian forests is the ecological effect of long range pollution.

On the west coast, rising new coniferous land outside the natural range of spruce vegetation has altered the ecological conditions for tree growth where deciduous trees formerly grew, or where only heather was the main vegetation type. Dense spruce forest stocked by even-aged trees results in poor vegetation development from worsened light conditions and competition from planted trees. Modern forestry does not allow for long rotation periods. Pine trees are cut before they reach 1/3 or 1/2 of their maximal age, respectively. The morphology is also different in younger trees compared to older. Recently, the forestry authorities have become interested in practising multiple use which includes a more careful forestry and habitat protection as a supplement to conservation.

Mechanical impact caused by vast clear cutting and use of heavy machines causes soil erosion. The damage depends on soil type and texture. Extreme conditions appear in connection with high precipitation or strong snowmelts. To meet this problem a more careful method in forestry practice is necessary, which has to be developed for the various soil conditions.

Modern forestry also causes problems for flora and fauna. In Norway, one of the coniferous forest types most worthy of conservation is located on the Atlantic coast of Central Norway, containing oceanic spruce forest with a rare epiphytic lichen community not found elsewhere on the Eurasian continent. Fragmentation of old-growth coniferous forest may also cause problems to birds and mammals. For example, the capercaillie grouse is affected by forest fragmentation on both small and large geographical scales. On the small scale, the proportion of old growth forest determines the density of males during the breeding season when capercaillies are territorial. On the larger scale, the seasonal movement and dispersal of the young may be limited by clear cutting. Forty years of modern forestry have led to a reduction of the capercaillie grouse population which may end up with only remnant populations if this silvicultural practice goes unchanged.

Acid rain has become a severe problem during the last two decades. A combination of sulphur dioxide and nitrogen oxides together with hydrogen chloride and other compounds are mixed in the atmosphere with oxygen and water vapor. These form dilute solutions of strong mineral acids reaching vegetation and soil during mist and precipitation. Many symptoms of forest decline are evident in the more industrialized parts of Europe, but one can see the effect of long range pollution in Norway as well. During one generation ten times more acid has been measured in the southernmost part of Norway. This part of the country has very little buffering capacity owing to shallow soil and very acid bedrocks. Damage to the fine root filaments of the trees, miscolouring of needles, and a decrease in crown density are signals of the effect of long range pollution.

Lakes and rivers, tarns and streams, are characteristic parts of the landscape anywhere one goes in this country; Norway is indeed the land of thousands of lakes. The traditional image of water in Norway is that it is clean. Although this is no longer true in the densely populated areas and in areas influenced by acid rain, one can still drink from the brook one crosses when hiking in the mountains. Even in the forest areas outside the larger towns, like Oslo and Trondheim, most surface waters are potable.

Generally speaking, Norwegian lakes and rivers are nutrient poor, with low productivity. Nutrient rich waters and pollution causing algal blooms are restricted to the most densely populated areas. During the last twenty years, the construction of sewage treatment plants and restrictions on fertilizer use in agriculture have reduced the number of heavily polluted lakes and rivers around Oslo and in some other urban and agricultural areas.

In mountain areas with glaciers you may find lakes and rivers with greyish green water. The colour is caused by fine clay particles produced by the friction of the glacier against the bedrock. The more common mountain lake or stream has a crystal clear water, very well suited for swimming, except for the water temperature, which in the mountains only occasionally exceeds 15°C. In the forest areas, the typical lake water is brownish, due to the humic substances supplied by decaying forest litter and bog mosses. In spite of the brown tinge to the water, the normal forest lakes are perfectly clean for swimming, and even for drinking.

With this abundance of clean lakes and rivers, it is not surprising that many popular pastimes in Norway are connected to water. Angling and canoeing are among the popular family activities, and during the short summer weeks, people by the thousands may go swimming in their neighborhood lake. In most parts of the country, lakes are covered by ice during several months every year. Even ice-covered lakes, however, are popular for recreational fishing, when people drill holes in the ice and angle for trout or charr through the ice.

The fauna of Norwegian freshwaters is poor in species; there are only approximately 40 species of freshwater fish. The geological history of the country explains this. Some 20,000 years ago, the whole of Northern Europe was covered by ice. The ice eventually melted away, and from 10,000 to 8,000 years ago, the Scandinavian peninsula became accessible to immigrating life. Among the first fish species to enter rivers and lakes were Arctic charr, brown trout and Atlantic salmon. All three species spawn and live as juveniles in fresh water, but are able to survive for parts of their lives in salt water; thus they are called anadromous fish.

Being rid of the weight of the ice, the land kept rising (it still does), and in some parts of Norway, the sea level at the end of the glaciation period was more than 200 meters above the present sea level. The land elevation created waterfalls, closing the migration route from the sea to upper parts of the rivers. Arctic charr and brown trout were able to establish resident populations above waterfalls. Today, brown trout is the most common freshwater fish in Norway, and Arctic charr is also found in thousands of lakes. Anadromous trout, or sea-trout, is found in rivers from the Swedish border in the south to the Russian border in the north, whereas anadromous charr is found only in the northernmost counties: Nordland, Troms and Finnmark. Atlantic salmon, on the other hand, normally do not form freshwater resident stocks. Consequently, salmon are found only in the lower parts of the rivers accessible from the sea. The original distribution of freshwater fish has been greatly modified by humans, who have continually been introducing fish to create a food supply or angling opportunities in their nearby lake. Angling is in most Norwegian waters open to anyone, provided a licence has been obtained.

Acidification of Norwegian lakes and rivers has caused severe damage to freshwater ecosystems. Fish populations have been lost or strongly reduced in an area covering about 20 percent of Norway's mainland area, including thousands of trout lakes and twenty-five salmon rivers. The southernmost counties are those suffering most from acidification, but the areas at the Russian border are also polluted. Recent data suggest that the damage to fish populations caused by acidification continues apace. Artificial liming is now used to reestablish a water quality in which fish can live, and several watercourses once devoid of fish now support healthy populations.

Most Norwegian rivers used to have populations of otters. Unfortunately, the otter is rarely to be seen in rivers to-day, but it is fairly common along the coast in Trøndelag and Nordland. Another animal which is common along most Norwegian watercourses is the North American mink. Originally taken to many European countries for fur production in farms, some animals escaped, forming viable populations in the wild.

Although the climate in Norway prevents any dangerous waterborne diseases becoming common, some of the temporary inhabitants of freshwater may create a nuisance. Mosquitoes, which spend their larval stages in water, are common in most parts of the country during summer months. Swarms of blood sucking mosquitoes may destroy any lovely summer's evening, and chase everyone indoors. The problem is particularly serious in Finnmark, where mosquitoes are said to be twin-engined and to attack like dive bombers. In other parts of the country, blackflies and gnats may be a nuisance. However, the insects are not transferring any diseases, so as long as one is equipped with insect repellents, there is ample opportunity to enjoy a summer's night on a lake shore or along a river.

Conservation plans have been worked out for broadleaved deciduous forest, bogs and mires, and wetlands (as bird habitats) in Norway, and are being established for coniferous forests as well. During the last twenty years eighteen national parks and a large number of nature reserves and other categories of protection areas have been established. Still only 4 percent of the territory mainland is protected from encroachments such as road building, eutrophication of waters, extension of urban areas, logging, drainage, forest plantations, industrial development, and impacts from recreational activity and tourist development. A plan has recently been issued to double the area of conserved wildlands in Norway. But environmental threats such as long-range airborne pollutants cannot be dealt with by Norwegian nature management alone, and can only be counteracted through international cooperation.

Norway has few environmental problems compared with most other industrialized countries, and there are still large areas hardly influenced by humans. Nevertheless, it is of paramount importance that conservation of nature and natural resources be given high and never-ending priority, in the remotest areas as well as in our backyards. The acidification problem amply demonstrates that complacency has a high price. An international conference held in Norway in the autumn of 1990 strongly urged that objectives for conservation be established on national and international levels. Future generations will judge us by how well we pursued those objectives.

14

Norway and the World Since 1945
Helge Pharo

Introduction

As a World War II allied nation, Norway participated in the 1945 San Francisco conference which set up the universal United Nations Organization (UN). In 1949 Norway joined the North Atlantic Treaty Organization (NATO) as a founding member. Membership in a military alliance constituted a new departure for Norway. At the time many Norwegians, including many within the political elite, considered NATO membership a dramatic breach with past policies as well as with the terms of the membership in the UN. However, the 1949 decision should not be made unduly dramatic. As a sparsely populated and militarily weak state wielding sovereignty over a territory considerably larger than that of, e.g. Great Britain, Norway had endeavoured not to get involved in the conflicts of the great powers since her independence in 1905. On the other hand, Norwegian political cabinets (right, left and center), had assumed that Great Britain in her own interest would prevent other powers from gaining a foothold on Norwegian territory. Norway's security interests were seen to place her alongside the Western powers. The German invasion of Norway on April 9, 1940, proved that while Britain certainly wanted to keep competing powers out, it could not be achieved in an improvised manner. In the view of the wartime Labor government in exile in London, as well as those of the postwar years, the pre-World War II implicit western guarantee of Norwegian security should, when necessary, be replaced by a formal one. During the war, the London government promoted the setting up of a North Atlantic security system. The need for such an alliance was seen to diminish by 1944-45. However, if international tensions were to rise again to a level where war might be threatening, Norway would need a formal guarantee of its security from the North Atlantic powers. Military cooperation would have to be prepared in peacetime. Thus, while membership in a universal security organization based on the cooperation of the "Big Four" (France, Great Britain, United States, Soviet Union), was Norway's first choice, western alignment constituted the reserve position.

In the immediate aftermath of the war and into the early 1960s, the security issue was the predominant concern for Norwegian foreign policy makers. In addition, the direction of foreign trade and shipping interests, placed Norway squarely within the emerging western camp.

The issue of integration forms the second major theme in any study of post World War II Norwegian foreign policy. As far as political implementation goes, Western European as well as Nordic integration are exclusively postwar issues. It was introduced into the political debate already in 1947 as a consequence of United States' pressure for European integration in conjunction with the Marshall Plan.[1] It became a major political problem in the early 1960s and exploded in the 1972 referendum on membership in the European Community. The issue was then dormant until the late 1980s, when the plans for a European Economic Area and the end of the Cold War forced a new round of discussions which are to end in another referendum.

The integration issue cuts across three of the spheres of Norwegian foreign policy: the North Atlantic sphere; the Nordic sphere; and the European sphere. While Norwegian ideology and economic interests were oriented towards the Atlantic world as well as the Nordic area for reasons of security, Norwegian governments, politicians, the various economic interest groups and the population at large viewed continental Western Europe with considerable scepticism if not outright hostility. Economic and political integration turned into the most divisive issue in Norwegian politics. It remains so today.

Relations with the non-western world constitute a third, but relatively minor, theme in postwar Norwegian foreign policy. Its most prominent aspects are foreign aid and the question of decolonization. This third theme differs fundamentally from the first two. No immediate Norwegian interests are at stake, and important conflicts with the major allies or other great powers have been rare.

Security: The Paramount Issue

Norway's foreign policy from 1945 into early 1948 was dubbed "bridgebuilding" by contemporaries. The term has been retained to characterize the period even though it is somewhat misleading.

It conveys the impression that the Norwegian government tried to build and maintain bridges between the potentially antagonistic big powers from the anti-Hitler coalition. The first postwar Labor government, until about 1948, may have harbored such ambitions, but no significant efforts were made to put them into effect.

The government's primary concern was not to involve Norway in any conflicts between Britain and the US on the one hand, and the Soviet Union on the other. In terms of actual policies, Norway in 1946 declined a seat on the UN security council and frequently abstained on UN and peace conference votes when east-west cleavages were pronounced. Occasionally Norway shifted support between the emerging camps for tactical rather than substantive reasons when divisive issues were voted upon.

The government's underlying concept of postwar international relations must, however, be considered valid. Norway was situated in an exposed geopolitical position between east and west, and after the war had a common border with the Soviet Union.[2] At the same time, Norway was traditionally western oriented: Since 1905, Norway had depended upon Britain, and by the end of World War II also on the United States, to guarantee its independence and territorial integrity. An amicable relationship between east and west, or at least the absence of strong tensions, would serve Norway's interests best. Great power cooperation within the UN would make a formal alliance relationship with the US and Britain superfluous. While "bridgebuilding" thus gives a false impression of an activist Norwegian policy, the term reflects the perceived Norwegian stake in, and hope for, great power cooperation.

Yet a reserve position was kept: Strong functional links were maintained with Britain. There was never any doubt among the foreign and security policy elite that if tensions between the powers were to rise, Norway would turn to the west for support. The Soviets, on their side, appear to have harbored few doubts about Norway's future alignment: Norway was considered part of a western sphere of influence.

Among western leaders "bridgebuilding", however, raised serious doubt as to where Norway actually belonged. As late as September of 1947, Britain's Chancellor of the Exchequer queried the president of the Bank of Norway, "Does Norway belong to Western Europe?"[3]

International tensions were significantly on the rise. Responding to what they considered a weakening western position in

Greece and Western Europe, the Americans launched the Truman Doctrine and the Marshall Plan in 1947. The Marshall Plan in particular brought the Norwegian dilemma to the forefront. As the Soviets refused Marshall aid, participation would represent a move towards the west. Still the Marshall Plan did not constitute a military alliance, and avowedly neutral Sweden joined. The Swedes and Norwegians, after weighing the pros and cons of the realignment, agreed that declining Marshall aid would imply a far more significant step towards the other side.[4]

The British Foreign Minister's speech in the House of Commons in January of 1948 set the process towards a defence alliance in motion internationally, as well as in Norway. Calling for closer Western European cooperation, the British foreign minister's initiative led directly to the Brussels Treaty in March 1948,[5] and contributed to the creation of NATO one year later. In Norway, elements within the Labor leadership exploited the speech for pushing Norway towards the west. In the short run, the initiative proved abortive. However, in the wake of the communist coup in Czechoslovakia in February 1948, Soviet pressures in Finland the same month, and rumours of similar pressures on Norway, led the Norwegian government to approach both the British and the Americans to ask what, if any, protection they could offer.

The events of early 1948 thus forced the Norwegian government to move to its reserve position and establish some sort of formal ties with the west both for deterrence purposes and to effect measures of military preparation. Several options would be explored, but the solution to the problem had not at that time been presented. Only by the summer of 1948, as the U.S. Senate passed the Vandenburg resolution[6], was the eventual North Atlantic solution a realistic option. The possibility of joining the Brussels Pact was never seriously considered. Joining a predominantly continental alliance did not in itself appeal to the Labor leadership. Norwegian scepticism of the continental states was considerable. Furthermore, a continental alliance, even with Britain as a member, would have neither the capability nor the inclination to defend Norway. Alternatively the idea of an Anglo-Scandinavian defence arrangement was briefly looked at. It is highly unlikely that such an alliance could have made it beyond the talking stage: the British, as mentioned, lacked the military capability to engage in the defence of Scandinavia; the Swedes later demonstrated that they did not want a formal commitment that might conflict with their neutrality policy.

As it turned out, the Scandinavian option was the first to be seriously investigated. As Norway and Denmark approached the west in the wake of the events of early 1948, Sweden was faced with the option of isolated neutrality in the Scandinavian region or abandoning neutrality by moving along with its neighbors. Sweden then proposed a Scandinavian defence union. Clearly the move was preemptive as much as geared towards a viable solution of the Scandinavian dilemma. Sweden could neither alone, nor in alliance with Denmark and Norway, create a credible military alternative to a western security guarantee. The Swedes were willing to shoulder a disproportionate share of the defence burden for an extended period for their initiative to succeed. However, they were not willing to budge on the neutrality issue. A Nordic union must remain neutral. Neither formal ties nor informal understandings with the west were acceptable to the Swedish Labor government or to the overwhelming majority of the Swedish parliament.

While a majority of the Gerhardsen cabinet[7] considered some sort of a western alignment a *sine qua non*, they were willing to explore the possibilities for a Scandinavian union with Sweden and Denmark. The Scandinavian Defence Committee that was set up to study the question concluded that while a defence association could have a certain deterrent effect, it could not forestall an isolated attack. If the Scandinavians were attacked, outside assistance would be needed already in the initial phase. Even so the final round of negotiations between the prime, foreign and defence ministers of the three countries broke down in January of 1949 over the issue of a minimal opening to the west. From the moment the Swedish foreign minister launched the initiative in 1948 the Norwegians were continually pushed back from their initial desire for an unequivocal western guarantee. When talks finally broke down, the Norwegians had accepted an explicitly non-aligned defence union. However, the Norwegian defence minister questioned whether or not Sweden would then be prepared to discuss with the US government some form of guarantee from the western powers in case of war. Even this minimal opening was unacceptable to Sweden.

This relatively detailed analysis of the process leading to Norwegian NATO membership serves to highlight several important points. To Norway the Atlantic connection was of overriding importance in terms of security as well as foreign economic relations. For Sweden the Atlantic connection was much more a secondary consideration. Norway was strategically important at the crossroads of Soviet and western interests. Sweden, as was also demonstrated by World War II, was less vital to the competing groups of powers. Secondly, the Swedish and Norwegian governments differed widely in their views of the likelihood of western assistance, on the conditions for aid that the west would set, and on the need for peacetime preparation for wartime assistance. The opposing views reflected the different experiences of the two states during World War II. Sweden remained successfully neutral. Norway was occupied through the better part of the war.

The wartime experience had left the two Scandinavian opposites with widely divergent views on the necessities for military preparation as well as of the possibilities for small states to be heard in alliance councils.

Clearly some sort of a Scandinavian option was the preferred one for the Labor party and probably widely beyond. Yet, it was only a Scandinavian union with an opening to the west that could serve as a nationally unifying security alternative. Furthermore, the opening to the west ensured Norway of a secure supply of arms at favorable prices. The Americans made it clear that such a deal would not be available to neutrals.

Outside the Labor party, the Communists objected to all of the solutions that were being discussed. By parroting Soviet proposals and objections, they made themselves totally ineffectual. Among the bourgeois parties, opposition was modest while support for joining ran strong. That left the motley Labor opposition, ranging from former pacifists, old style neutralists/isolationists and small state believers to extreme left wingers in a weak position. There was no credible common platform for them to grasp. The German attack in 1940 had killed old style neutrality. The rigid Swedish policies left the Labor opposition with no viable option. Party unity was at risk. Only a small number of diehard opponents voted against membership in the North Atlantic Organization at the decisive party conference in February and subsequently in the Storting in March 1949.

Alliance membership has not been in doubt since then. Popular support has increased over time and the Storting has been overwhelmingly in favor, the exceptions being the representatives of the Communists, the Socialist People's Party, its successor the Socialist Left Party, and the far left of the Labor Party. With the exception of the 1970s and the 1990s, these groups were fairly marginal in the Storting, if not within the Labor party or the electorate. Foreign policy radicalism was quite strong within

Labor from the late 1960s and well into the 1980s. Since then the active NATO opposition has again crumbled. Partly, the decline has been due to international factors: the final discrediting and crumbling of the Soviet empire on the one hand, the uncertainties of the European security framework and of US policies on the other. Norway's Euro-scepticism has in this situation underlined the uncertainties involved, and possibly served to reduce NATO opposition. However, Labor government concessions to the opposition through the 1970s and the early 1980s probably also played a role.

Foreign policies, of course, are designed to cater to a domestic constituency as well as to secure an international position. To be successful they must meet minimum requirements with several audiences. "Bridgebuilding" did that for some time until the policy created serious doubt among the presumed protectors of Norwegian integrity. Domestically, the policy caused considerable dissension between its supporters and those who thought Norway's security was potentially at risk. Alignment with the west then provoked dissent on the left. Contributing to the sense of confusion and bitterness over NATO membership was the fact that the importance of the reserve position had been, at best, grasped only vaguely. Furthermore, while bridgebuilding and the subsequent western alignment were logically interconnected in the minds of the foreign policy elite, the Labor party, along with other parties still felt that the formal western alignment embodied in NATO membership, for better or worse, represented a fundamental break with the past. The fact that Norway functionally had been under British protection since independence in 1905 counted for less than the change in formal status.

Norway's new alliance policies also had to be designed with several objectives in mind. Achieving the western guarantee was paramount, but creating a new foreign policy consensus was important as well. The Labor government could not for long pursue a foreign policy that alienated significant sections of the party. Bridgebuilding was conceived as maximizing security by maintaining links to the west at the same time as policies were designed in order not to provoke the Soviet Union. After joining NATO the Labor government designed a similar policy for similar purposes, with the important proviso that Norway now was securely placed within the North Atlantic Alliance and the cabinet had no desire to have that fact doubted.

Norway's balancing act between NATO membership and a neighborly policy towards the Soviet Union may be characterized by two sets of dichotomies: deterrence and reassurance, integration and screening. Membership in NATO would have a deterrent effect while the limitations on participation by the Norwegian government would serve to reassure the Soviets of Norway's non-hostile intentions. Integration characterizes NATO membership and allied commitments to Norway, and screening characterizes Norway's reluctance to take on the most far-ranging NATO commitments.[8]

In terms of actual policies the postwar governments adhered to the bases declaration of 1949 which stated that foreign troops would only be stationed on Norwegian territory in times of war or when war threatened. There would be no permanent NATO bases in Norway. Military manoeuvers in Norway would not be held on territory close to the Soviet Union, in fact Norway's largest and northernmost county (*fylke*), which has a common border with the Soviet Union, only hosts small border patrol forces. German officers were not accepted at the NATO head-quarters near Oslo until the late 1950s, and during that period a return visit by the German minister of defence to Oslo was postponed several times. Both symbolically and in substance the Norwegian government took great care not to challenge or offend the great eastern neighbour.

The political and military leadership in Norway was not al-ways able or keen to control allied activities involving their territory. The Americans in the 1950s used the military airport at Gardermoen to launch a series of intelligence gathering balloons, declaring they were to be used for weather research. American U-2 intelligence planes used the airport at Bodø as a destination point after flying north and west over Soviet territory, unknown certainly to Norwegian political authorities. The U-2 plane that was shot down over Soviet territory en route to Bodø in the summer of 1960 caused the Soviets to make strong protests. While Norwegian authorities protested against these unan-nounced transgressions of Norway's declared defence policies, they may still have caused some damage to relations with the Soviet Union. They also caused civilian and military authorities to enforce more strict controls with allied movements.

The bases[9] policy was primarily directed towards the Soviet Union. However, it also served to modify the criticism of the domestic opposition and to reconcile the sceptics to membership. There was a constant tug of war between - at times also within - the government, the NATO sceptics and the left opposition over the implications of NATO membership for Norwegian defence policies. In the wake of the 1952 NATO council meeting in Lisbon - setting new force goals for the alliance - a lengthy struggle over the duration of compulsory military service ensued. The most dramatic fight took place over the issue of nuclear weapons in Norway. A considerable portion of the Labor political leadership, the better part of Norway's military leadership as well as a majority within the bourgeois parties thought Norway should accept nuclear weapons. A surprise proposal at the Labor party convention in 1957, however, sealed the fate of the plans. Nuclear weapons were banned from Norway by a convention decision. Yet the conflict continued to simmer into the 1960s as the left was perennially worried that the decision would be reversed. The nuclear issue, and NATO opposition generally, constituted the primary basis when the Socialist People's Party, based predominantly on Labor left wingers, was formed in 1961. The founders of the party feared that the Labor party was in the process of reversing the 1957 decision when the 1961 convention conceded the *Storting* the right to decide on Norway's nuclear weapons policy. In practice the Labor government as well as later governments from 1960 were engaged in a retreat from the option of also using tactical nuclear weapons in the defence of Norway during a war. The pressures within the party, particularly with the resurgence of the foreign policy opposition during the 1970s, led the Labor government in the early 1980s to endorse the proposal for a Nordic nuclear free zone.

We would be wrong, however, to conclude that Norwegian attempts to modify NATO policies were merely tactical moves to placate the opposition to the left. Fears and scepticism of nuclear weapons and scepticism of the easy recourse to armaments and military measures to solve political questions were certainly widely shared within the Labor party and the Norwegian population more generally.

Characteristic of Norwegian policies particularly during the the 1950s were the attempts to make NATO less great power dominated and more open to influence and insight from elected representatives. The attempts never led to substantial changes in NATO structures, but nevertheless are representative of a genuine Norwegian desire for democratization and representative control of a military and bureaucratic organisation. The concern for a democratic, North Atlantic and nonaggressive NATO profile also led Norway to protest against policies that were not of primary Norwegian concern. Even in the founding phase Norway was known to object to Italian membership. As the two countries were invited in at the same time, Norway could not pursue such objections. However, the Labor government protested against the inclusion of Greece and Turkey in 1951, and was reluctant to accept the Federal Republic of Germany as a member, even though the defence of Norway would be immensely strengthened by West German rearmament.

Most of the Norwegian objections were, however, voiced quietly and behind the scenes. The Soviets and the Norwegian foreign policy opposition only constituted part of the audience. The primary objective of Norwegian protests has generally been to achieve modifications or course corrections of NATO policies, not to give voice to protests in order to score propaganda points in other quarters. With increasing interest in foreign policy, this has probably become less true towards the end of our period. During the late 1970s and early 1980s the Labor government again protested against NATO nuclear policies in general, and again did not limit itself to issues of only direct concern to Norway.

The tenor of Norwegian objections and demands for special treatment, however, underlines the fact that they represent a quest for policy modifications. For the Labor governments especially it was important to pacify domestic opposition and reassure the Soviets of Norwegian defensive intentions. However, screening and reassurance must be considered secondary to integration and deterrence. Once Norway had joined NATO and civilian and military leaders realized the vulnerability of Norway and the modest prospects for real western support, they invested the major effort in nailing the main North Atlantic powers to the defence of Norway.

The central front took precedence when NATO strategies were worked out. For Norway then, the overriding objective was to make sure that the west was actually tied down to defending Norway, beyond the formal commitment as embodied in the treaty. Therefore great efforts went into securing a US or British Commander-in-chief at the NATO headquarters near Oslo. Earmarking of forces for Norwegian defence was seen as crucial. As Soviet naval capability has grown in the Kola peninsula, allied naval doctrine has assumed greater importance for Norway.

As historian Rolf Tamnes has pointed out, the combination of integration and screening with shifts in the general Cold War climate has held the potential for creating paradoxical results for Norway. Detente in one sense represents the fulfillment of Norwegian foreign policy goals. Detente on the other hand has caused the United States to allow the Soviets greater freedom of movement without making any protesting noises. For Norway as a neighboring country to the Soviet Union that meant less vigilance in the maintenance of Norwegian security interests. Thus while detente in a general way is considered to be in the interest of Norway, the practical consequences in the North may be less desirable. Periods of increasing tension on the other hand can yield equally paradoxical results. While the general thrust of Norwegian policy has been geared towards modifying high tension cold war policies, such policies on the part of the US in the narrow sense increase Norway's security as it has given the Soviet Union less room for manoeuver.

As the Cold War has come to an end so has the bipolar relationship that has dominated European security issues. The consequences for Norway of the end of the Cold War are far from clear. A new defence commission, the third since World War II, will have completed its recommendations during the first half of 1992. The commission dealt with what kind of potential military threat Norway will possibly face in the future, what force levels are necessary, and to whom, and to what kind of organization should Norway turn for a security guarantee. NATO still exists, but with the increasing likelihood of a significantly reduced US presence in Europe, NATO may not remain an adequate safeguard as the Europeans appear to want to pool their forces in the Western European Union. Norwegian indications of interest in that organization may be read as signals that Norway desires that the continental European powers take a greater interest in the defence of Norway.

No matter that the Cold War has come to an end, Norway still borders the militarily most powerful state on the western part of the Eurasian landmass, even if at present it presents itself in some disarray. The successor state has lost strategically important territories formerly belonging to the Soviet Union. The Kola base[10] then takes on even greater importance, and it still represents a formidable concentration of military power. Thus for Norway the end of the Cold War may present in another version the paradox that Rolf Tamnes has analyzed with regards to the Cold War. Generally reduced tensions do not necessarily lead to greater security for Norway.

Integration: The Awkward Issue

In proposing the Marshall Plan, the Truman administration

sought to gain several objectives. In the short run it was deemed
vital to stabilize Western Europe and contain the Soviet Union.
The means chosen were economic. With the establishment of
NATO a military guarantee was added. Secondly, by means of
the Marshall Plan, the Americans hoped to nudge or pressure the
Europeans more gradually towards closer economic cooperation,
even to the point of establishing a customs union or a common
market. In time political unification might take place. The Truman administration sought what it considered in the long run to
be the cheapest and most efficient way to make the Europeans
take care of their own defence requirements. As a goal in itself,
the Americans also wanted the Europeans to set up some sort of
framework for supranational integration.

Only within the nations of continental Western Europe could
there be found any interest in or enthusiasm for supranational
integration. When the Americans, supported by the continentals,
tried to push integration through the medium of the Marshall
Plan organization, the Organization of European Economic Cooperation (OEEC), they were faced with determined Anglo-
Scandinavian opposition. This group consistently sabotaged integration efforts, forcing the continentals to create their own
alternatives, the European Coal and Steel Community, Euratom
and the EEC, which were eventually merged through the creation
of the European Community in 1965. [11]

The anti-integrationists were in fact faced with a process which
they could neither control nor derail, neither escape nor, apparently for a long time, understand. For nearly fifteen years after
the end of World War II, Norwegian Labor governments fully
supported by the bourgeois parties, sought either to bypass the
issue, to ignore the consequences or to emasculate the emerging
supranational organizations. Norway did not join the customs
union study group formed under the aegis of the Marshall Plan.
The Labor government never even considered joining the Coal
and Steel Community. Together with the other OEEC members
Norway did join the negotiations for the Wider Free Trade Area
(WFTA) from 1956 to 1958, but EEC membership was not considered at that time. The creation of the European Free Trade
Association (EFTA), was for Norway and the other non-mem-
bers of the EEC, a second best alternative to the WFTA organization that had failed to materialize.

The anti-integration policies of the Labor government were
based on a number of somewhat divergent policy preferences as
well as fears of continental economic policies. Above all, the

Labor government was concerned that the overarching goals of economic policies and the policies themselves differed as between Great Britain and Scandinavia on the one hand and the continental states on the other. Foreign Minister Halvard Lange [12] in an important speech in 1949 contrasted the goal of full employment with continental trust in "the free play of the forces of the market". Alluding to the lack of public interest in the integration issue, he contended that informed Norwegians were sceptical about plans of integration which they felt would put their "...economy at the mercy of continental cartels." [13]

We find one of the most dramatic expressions of fears and scepticism from a senior Norwegian official in a letter to the foreign minister in 1950. He particularly disliked the economic policies of France, Italy, Belgium and The German Federal Republic. He much prefered the "Anglo-Scandinavian" stress on full employment, income equalization and social justice to the continental insistence on laissez-faire and trade liberalization for its own sake. [14]

Three salient points stand out as we study the early Norwegian attitudes towards the continental integration process. In the first place, Norwegian policymakers were heavily influenced by their interwar experience of mass unemployment. Postwar continental policies were considered wholly inadequate to deal with the issues of economic growth and an equitable distribution of wealth.

Secondly, during this initial phase only the foreign policy elite paid any attention to the integration process. There was at best only intermittent public debate, and even the policy-makers were concerned with the issues on an irregular basis. Thus Norwegian policies to a degree, and public opinion especially, tended to be shaped by superficially formed attitudes rather than by sustained informed analysis. It is true that the situation in Europe was to some degree confused and that Norwegian policies were, in fact, more egalitarian. However, the historically formed blinkers worn by Norwegians prevented them from seeing the complexities of the situation and the continental will and need to succeed.

Thirdly, the attitudes held by the policy elite in the late 1940s and early 1950s foreshadow those expressed by the anti-integration popular movements of the 1960s, 1970s and 1990s. In that sense the victory of the anti-forces in the referendum of 1972 represents an element of continuity in Norwegian politics. The views expressed and the arguments made were nearly identical to those the foreign ministry expressed in the first postwar decade.

The Labor government could not simply oppose or ignore US

demands for and European initiatives towards European integration. During the Marshall Plan period Norway would then run the risk of forfeiting American aid, and with regard to the integration process there was always the risk of becoming isolated from the rest of Western Europe. The Labor government chose several partly supplementary, partly alternative, strategies. In response to the US demand for a European customs union, Norway called for a Nordic one already in the fall of 1947. In response to the continental process, Norway within the Organization for European Economic Cooperation joined with Great Britain, Denmark and Sweden in the Anglo-Scandinavian cooperation committee, dubbed UNISCAN. More importantly Norway tentatively worked to create a wider North Atlantic framework, encompassing both the OEEC and NATO.

Negotiations for a Scandinavian solution were initiated by Norway three times over, in 1947, 1950 and 1954. The first initiative was multipurpose. One goal was to mollify the Americans. Additionally, Scandinavian cooperation was considered a means for strengthening the position of European Social Democracy at a time when the right and the center were gaining ground on the continent. Lastly, the Norwegians thought there might be economic advantages in closer Scandinavian economic cooperation.

However, the Labor government soon had second thoughts and by 1949 the Norwegian negotiators made it clear to their Scandinavian counterparts that Norway could not participate in any Scandinavian customs union. There were several reasons given that make it abundantly clear that the 1947 initiative was primarily of a tactical nature. The Norwegian economy suffered from decisive disadvantages when compared to those of Denmark and Sweden. In the first place, Norway had suffered more extensive war damages and had not properly recovered. Secondly, as far as the development of manufacturing industries was concerned, Norway was certainly a considerably less developed nation than Sweden. Thirdly, in agriculture Norwegian producers could in no way compete with the extremely efficient Danish farmers who had been geared to world market competition for a long time. The Norwegian negotiators concluded that Norway would lose to Sweden in the one field and to Denmark in the other. By and large, the three Scandinavian economies were considered competitive rather than complementary, thus losses from strong competition would not be compensated by advantages in other fields.

These objections of an economic nature were so strong and so widely shared across the board from the Labor party leadership to representatives of Norwegian industries that the issue was never really raised at the domestic political level. Labor and the economic interests groups were agreed that on the one hand advantages were too limited and the dangers too great for Norway to dare the Scandinavian venture. It was also pointed out that Norwegian trade was largely global, the combined trade with the two Scandinavian neighbors did not even approach 20 per cent of the total.

Why then did Norway reopen the issue of Scandinavian integration immediately after the first round had been closed? The economic position could hardly have changed all of a sudden? Fundamentally, there are two answers: In the first place, the Labor leadership thought in terms of more limited functional cooperation, where Norway would be better able to exploit her comparative advantages, such as in the field of hydroelectric power. Secondly, the Labor government wanted to make an effort to bridge as far as possible the split over NATO. The initiative was, however, to no avail. Neither Denmark nor Sweden appears to have been interested in limited functional cooperation. Domestically, the Labor Party was exposed to strong criticism from the bourgeois parties as well as from the economic interest groups.

The majority of non-Labor parliamentarians even voted against the establishment of the Nordic Council founded in 1952. The Council is an outstanding example of interstate, functional cooperation excluding such sensitive areas as defence, foreign affairs and economic policy. There is nothing even remotely supranational about the Nordic Council.

It is necessary to call attention to the fact that in 1952, Norway had been an independent nation for less than 50 years. Opposition to Scandinavian cooperation was so strong because of the pervasive fear of anything resembling a political union. That fear was clearly a potent force against European integration as well.

However, as the customs union was being buried for the second time, the labor party staged another resurrection. The Minister of Trade, Erik Brofoss [15], provided the main impetus for renewed negotiations. He advanced several arguments. In the first place, he was of the opinion that by the mid 1950s Norway had gained sufficient economic strength to enter more fully into Scandinavian competition. Secondly, the end of Marshall Aid had necessitated a new search for foreign investment capital.

Thirdly, Brofoss conceived of Nordic integration in the framework of economic planning. The three Scandinavian countries should join together to achieve a more rational organization of their economies, each exploiting their comparative advantages in a Scandinavian as well as a wider international setting. The Brofoss proposal led to renewed and prolonged investigations and negotiations lasting well into 1959. They gave evidence of continued Norwegian reluctance alongside the professed optimism. Labor was still pitted against both the bourgeois parties and private sector industries at this time. Thus, Norway was at best ambivalent, as were Denmark and Sweden.

The Nordic negotiations were at this time overtaken by developments in Western Europe. Brofoss had assumed that a Scandinavian Customs Union could be included in the Wider Free Trade Area, on par with the European Economic Community, or also as a subunit within European Free Trade Area [16]. The British, however, torpedoed the latter idea. Among other things, EFTA was also a British means of avoiding another European trading bloc. The Scandinavians thus had to give up in the summer of 1959, even before the domestic debates had been allowed to take off.

The Scandinavian negotiations were always woven into the larger North Atlantic and Western European web. The initiatives followed upon those of other states: the Marshall Plan in 1947 and the Schuman Plan in 1950, the European Political and Defence Communities [17] when Brofoss launched the final drive in 1953-54. Fear was a motive power. The planned Scandinavian economy was not least to function as a counterweight to the new Germany. In a memorandum in late 1953, Brofoss stated his fears and ambitions:

"Not least because of the political danger represented by the new German economic imperialism, it is necessary for the Nordic countries to try to consolidate their economic position by means of active cooperation." [18]

The complex interrelationship between the various integration and cooperation proposals is also demonstrated by the fact that the Scandinavian proposals in the late 1950s ran into opposition not only from the British and the bourgeois parties in Norway, but also from within the Labor party itself. By this time the new Minister of Trade, Arne Skaug [19], had become clearly sceptical of both the Scandinavian alternative and the planned approach to international economic cooperation. He plainly preferred Norway merely to join WFTA or EFTA without the Scandinavian

intermediary. He was as concerned as Brofoss with modernization and capital imports, but, it seems, did not find Scandinavian
cooperation particularly helpful if other alternatives were available. The EFTA memberships both foreclosed further exclusive
Scandinavian economic cooperation, and brought their economies closer together. Intra-Scandinavian trade grew dramatically
within EFTA.

In retrospect, we can by 1960 spot most of the elements that
made up the anti-EC coalition of 1970-72. We can also identify
the core supporters of a European alignment, the basically pragmatic and modernizing center and right of the Labor party on the
one hand, on the other the largely urban dominated and modernizing Conservative party with their kin among the Liberals.

Still temperatures were low during the 1950s. Integration and
international economic cooperation were questions discussed by
the very few. There was little ideological fervor on either side.
There are several reasons for this. Above all the foreign policy
ideological struggles were being fought over the issues of NATO
and nuclear weapons. Precisely for that reason the opposing
forces could not coalesce during the 1950s. The Norwegian
center parties as well as most of Labor were strongly anti-com-
munist. As long as western and West European economic cooperation was discussed within a Cold War context it would be
difficult to make a center-left coalition viable. As long as fear of
Communism rather than fear of the consequences of integration
or cooperation was the salient issue, only a small number of
Agrarians were able or willing to break ranks.

Two other factors should be emphasized. During the 1950s no
major political figure in Norway espoused supranational integration. Labor as well as the Conservatives supported inter-
governmental cooperation. Excepting the far left and elements
within the Agrarian party no Norwegian political party or group
advocated a move towards greater self-sufficiency. It was generally recognized that international liberalization was likely to
work to Norway's advantage. Labor explicitly favored loosely
organized North Atlantic cooperation; if that were not to be
achieved, then a loosely organized European cooperation that did
not involve agriculture and that excluded other nations from
Norwegian fishing ground demands. Cold War and the fear of
communism combined with an extremely vague threat probably
prevented the future anti-European allies from forging an alliance.

Indeed, while we, with the benefit of hindsight, can discern the elements of the future coalition, we can also see that there was neither need nor opportunity for it to appear at that time.

The British and Danish decisions that the creation of EFTA did not adequately safeguard their economic and political interests forced the Labor cabinet to decide on the issue of membership application as well. The Labor cabinet and party organization dithered for almost a year before deciding to follow suit. Prime Minister Gerhardsen and his advisors inside and outside the government knew that such a move would bring party and non-party opponents out in the open. Furthermore, as we have seen, there were not many real supporters of Western European integration in Norway. What had been achieved within the OEEC and EFTA was certainly acceptable if not always desirable, but Labor, and non-Labor as well, had spent the previous 15 years either denouncing or ignoring continental European integration. No Norwegian political party could be expected to join the race with great enthusiasm.

In 1962-63, until de Gaulle vetoed British membership in the EEC, there was some idealistic enthusiasm among the political youth movements for Europe as a force for peace. There were also some politically minded Europeanists within the parliamentary parties of both Labor and the opposition. Pro-Europeanism, however, counted for far less than the pervasive feeling that where Britain went Norway had to follow. Secondly, and possibly more important, the Labor government feared for the effects on Norwegian trade if the country decided to remain outside a group that would take some three-quarters of Norwegian exports. Finally, with Britain and Denmark joining, all the economically advanced European NATO members would belong to the EEC.

Such considerations must have played an important part. After all the Storting did amend the Constitution to make sure that with the necessary three-quarter majority, Norway could cede sovereignty to an international organization within a clearly specified field. There was also a sufficient majority in favor of seeking membership. However, if the Labor cabinet feared the effects of the membership application on the country and on the Labor party, it was certainly right to do so. While parliamentary opposition from both left and right was relatively modest, extra-parliamentary organizations both left and right, grew quite quickly.

Before the opposing forces could even explore the possibility of joining forces in opposition to Norwegian membership, the door to the EEC was closed when President de Gaulle vetoed

British membership. With Britain excluded there was no longer any need for Norway to ask for membership. The EFTA countries then concentrated on putting fully into effect their planned reduction of tariffs, in fact moving ahead of the EEC. The creation of EFTA had a dual purpose. It was to function as both a stepping stone to EEC membership and if necessary as an actual free trade arrangement. During the 1960s intra-EFTA trade grew considerably, particularly between the Scandinavian countries. Within EFTA in fact, the goals of a closer and more extensive Scandinavian economic community were to a considerable degree realized. Sweden for a period became Norway's most important trading partner.

For Britain and Denmark, however, eventual EEC membership remained the goal. Thus the possibility of a more extended integration struggle remained a time bomb within the Norwegian political system. Labor was faced with a potential opposition within its own ranks. The bourgeois parties, having formed a majority coalition government in 1965 were concerned lest the market issue rock the boat of cooperation. To introduce the Common Market issue would endanger the coalition between the modernizers within the Conservative party and the Eurosceptics of the center parties.

Political turmoil in France in 1968 caused the fall of de Gaulle and opened the door for Britain and other EFTA nations to EC membership again. The process was then launched which led to the protracted membership negotiations between the EC and Britain, Denmark and Norway. In 1972, the three were accepted as EC members. The agreement between the EC and Norway was subsequently made the subject of a referendum, and was rejected by 53.5 as against 46.5 percent of the vote. The Labor government that had negotiated the treaty resigned and a coalition made up of the Christian People's Party, the Agrarians and the majority of the Liberals negotiated a commercial treaty between Norway and the EC.

At the time the shattering defeat for the pro-marketeers was above all described as a victory of the grassroots over the political establishment. Secondly, it was seen as a victory for the political and economic interests of the peripheral districts over those of the center, a victory for the primary sector of the rural areas against the interests of urban Norway, a victory for anti-capitalism over capitalism. The interests of grassroots democracy had stopped the drift towards an international union largely run by a distant bureaucracy in Brussels. In this merger of domestic and foreign policy explanations, the left socialists in particular saw in the outcome a fundamental break with past Norwegian foreign policies. To the left and the right alike, EC membership represented a continuation of Norway's western alignment.

All of these explanations are to a degree valid. Considering the outcome of the referendum a disproportionate number of parliamentarians, newspapers and other media as well as upper echelon bureaucrats in the central administration were supporters of membership, as were the overwhelming majority of business interests in the secondary and tertiary sectors and a considerable number of trade union leaders. Yet there was no lack of elite representatives on the other side. More than a quarter of the parliamentarians were opponents; the businesses of the primary sectors furnished vast amounts of money as well as leadership. Leadership was provided by the universities and the trade unions as well.

The combined dichotomies of town versus country, center versus periphery, and primary versus secondary and tertiary sectors better account for the outcome. The anti-marketeers were the strongest in the fisheries districts of North Norway where hardly any supporters were to be found. Fishermen were adamant that Norwegians should have the exclusive right to exploit Norwegian waters. This demand was unacceptable to the EC, and was probably the strongest single reason for the victory of the opposition. Secondarily, the farmers insisted that the Norwegian agricultural market remain protected and the Norwegian system of subsidies be maintained, demands that were likewise not accepted in Brussels. Yet Norway in 1972 was a highly industrialized nation. The influence of primary sector industries cannot alone explain the outcome. Important also is the fact that workers that were employed in industries not primarily geared to the world or European markets were less inclined to support membership.

Most essential are the points that traditional worker radicalism militated against membership, and that the traditional Norwegian fear of a political union run from outside the country was strongest in more peripheral areas. The various causes for opposition were mutually re-enforcing, and the political and ideological ones were as strong as the economic.

A changing international context also played a role. Three factors deserve to be highlighted. In the first place we should recognize the growing importance of environmental issues and of increasing foreign aid to the non-Western world. The EC in

Norway was seen as primarily an engine for economic growth and as such likely to be a major cause for pollution and an opponent of strong environmental measures. As a capitalist, rich man's club, it was also seen as exploitative of the Third World. Thus the idealism of the youth movements, which in 1962 had turned them towards integration as a means for promoting peace in Europe, in 1972 turned them against Europe.

The security concerns which had caused Norway to align with the US and Britain throughout the postwar era were no longer such potent forces for integration. Britain's declining stature and ability to serve as protector reduced her importance as a model to follow. US warfare in Vietnam tended generally to diminish the usefulness of the arguments for western alignment. NATO, of course, was still necessary, but the third world policies of the US required Norway to keep some distance from dominant western powers. At the same time this was a period of international detente. As Europe was stabilized there was less reason to strengthen the Western European ties for security reasons.

The period of the late 1960s and early 1970s was one when new issues burst upon the political scene, when old truths were being questioned and when old political loyalties were being shattered by aggressive grassroots as well as elitist political movements. These movements and organizations, particularly concerned with Vietnam and the environment, contributed to the growth of extra-parliamentary activity beyond the control of political parties, activities that were so important for the victory of the anti-marketeers. Thus new elements had been added to the old equation. The old arguments against Europe, not least the fear that the EC was a means for German economic and political expansion, had lost little of their force among the voters. The new elements eroded traditional political loyalties, and made it more difficult particularly for the Labor leadership to carry the rank and file along.

Finally, within the elites of Labor and the Conservatives there was hardly much real enthusiasm for Europe; among their supporters even less. Membership was seen as a necessity, not as desirable in itself. The EC had initially been created to solve problems that were of no direct concern to Norway.

Reluctance continued to characterize even the supporters, who were unable to mobilize grassroot support to any significant degree. And as oil was struck by the beginning of the decade even the economic argument lost some potency. An oil-rich Norway would be better able to remain outside.

Thus as seen from the outside, and to a degree from the point of view of the supporters, no to Europe did imply a break with postwar foreign policy. If looked at from the inside and in a full postwar perspective, continuity is also apparent. Fear of political union, fear of Germany, fear of the continental kind of economic policies, desire for planning within the Norwegian context, concern for the fate of the primary sector were the constants within Norway. Labor and Conservative leaders and somewhat less than half of the electorate had moved beyond those constraints. No doubt they as well as Norway had changed course.

From 1972 until 1989 the issue of European integration vanished altogether from political discourse in Norway. The former supporters, Labor as well as Conservatives, tried with considerable success to recoup their political losses and rebuild their respective western-oriented political coalitions. To achieve success, both had to put Europe on the back burner. Integration was a fundamentally disruptive issue in the Norwegian political system.

At the same time it was also necessary to move to minimize the international damage wrought by the result of the referendum. A commercial treaty was negotiated with the EC, and both Labor and the bourgeois parties hastened to declare that in fact Norway's no to Europe did not imply a change in Norway's western alignment. Using again the dichotomy of integration and screening, Norwegian governments had to make sure that the screening with regard to economic cooperation did not cause damage to integration into the Western security system.

With the accelerating integration process in Europe, embodied in the agreement on the European Economic Area and the Maastrict agreement, and the breakdown of the Soviet empire, the integration issue is again threatening to disrupt the Norwegian political system through another struggle over membership. The opposing forces are nearly identical with those of the referendum campaign of the early seventies, the main exceptions being the flight of a number of leading intellectuals and as well of former Labor anti-marketeers to the camp of the supporters. Among the rank and file, however, the divisions do not seem to have been much affected. The country is fairly evenly divided among those who oppose, those who support and those who have not yet made up their minds. Labor is somewhat less divided than in 1972, primarily it would appear because those opposed are leaving the party. The Conservatives are solidly in favor, and again see the chances for creating a non-Labor coalition vanish.

"And I miss Norway". Newspaper cartoon depicting Norwegian Prime Minister, Gro Harlem Brundtland, a strong supporter of Norwegian membership of the European Community.

This last round of the integration struggle may yet create new and lasting cleavages in the Norwegian political system. If so, the reason will be found not the least in the strong emotions and idealism called forth among the opponents. The lack of enthusiasm so far evident among the supporters may on the other hand again reduce the permanent impact of the struggle. This lack of enthusiasm is not least due to the fact that the supporters, the main modernizing forces on the left and the right of the traditional divide, have only the desire for membership in common. The opponents, however, desire to preserve what they consider crucial elements of the Norwegian economy and culture which they consider at stake. The supporters have no such goal. That makes the EC issue fundamentally different from the NATO one. NATO was seen to be important to secure Norwegian values, and the opposition could present no viable alternative. Even with Sweden and Finland wanting to join the EC, the supporters have not succeeded in convincing the electorate that there is no viable alternative. The Labor government is now moving towards linking integration with security as the US presence in Europe is being reduced. That may prove to clinch the argument for the pro-marketeers. As yet it has not.

Decolonization and Foreign Aid: Good Things

The third world issues are fundamentally different from those of security and integration. From a realpolitik point of view and in terms of national interest, support for third world liberation movements and aid to third world nations have little direct relevance for Norwegian economic development or security. The material well-being, safety and political liberties of Norwegian citizens are not significantly affected by these policies. Norwegian trade with these parts of the world is limited, well below 10 percent of the total volume. Norway has no traditional interests in the former colonial areas, as it gained its own independence in 1905.

Such a definition of interests is certainly far too narrow to be acceptable. Citizens of most states have strong non-material interests, they have ideological or religious preferences that they want to express and, at times, to translate into international political action. Furthermore, while security and economic interests may not be at stake in the short run by developments on distant shores, long run consequences may be different. We should also not disregard the possibility that statesmen and politicians may feel as obliged to act by moral precepts, as by perceived economic and security demands.

Norwegian social democracy ideologically puts Norway on the side of the colonial peoples seeking to govern themselves. The government, however, dependent on Great Britain and other NATO colonial powers to defend Norway against the possible Soviet threat, had to be circumspect in its support of decolonization. Secondly, as the Cold War developed it also spread to non-European areas. Norway, as well as the United States and the colonial powers, saw the importance of meeting the assumed Communist threat outside of Europe. Not until the 1960s when it was appalled by French intransigence in North Africa, and impressed by the growing power of the non-aligned movement, did the Norwegian government argue its anticolonization more forthrightly. The Labor cabinet would have preferred France to follow the more peaceful and accommodationist decolonization policies of Great Britain. When the French, however, documented that they did not realize that the colonial era had come to an end, Labor decided it had to join the march of history and side with the opponents of its NATO ally.

The question of foreign aid was easier to handle. Together with the vast majority of western statesmen after World War II, the Labor party leadership shared the prevailing view that economic distress, poverty and a low level of development was likely to lead to political unrest and possibly to totalitarian rule. There was a pervasive fear in the West that the former colonial nations would turn to Communism if aid was not forthcoming from the West.

Throughout the entire postwar period, Norwegian aid has generally not been tied to domestic purchases. The guiding principle for Norway, unlike almost all other donors, has been to give the receivers freedom to purchase where they have found it most advantageous. From the late 1960s foreign aid increased dramatically and, as a percentage of GNP, Norway is today one of the world's leading contributors. At the same time Norway has shown little direct interest in exports to the Third World or economic activities in conjunction with foreign aid. The government has had only limited success in drawing private industry into aid programs. During the last decade, however, economic difficulties have contributed to creating greater interest in tied aid from Norway also.

Even though the consensus in Norway for foreign aid is considerable, it appears partly a matter of political expediency. There is aid scepticism within the Conservative Party, but aid is not a crucial issue on the right. However, for its traditional and prospective coalition partners, the Center Party and especially the Christian People's Party, it is. The Conservatives can use aid for political trade-offs in coalition building.

A large aid program gives Norway an important voice within international organizations. Norway thus stands out as an active promoter of greater international social justice.

A prominent Norwegian historian has characterized Norway as the nationalist internationalist, pointing out that Norwegian governments to an unusual degree in matters of security as well as integration, have insisted on special arrangements as well as on security guarantees and market access. The terms "integration" and "screening", of course, cover precisely that duality in Norwegian foreign policy. At the same time, Norwegian postwar governments have endeavored to project Norwegian goals into the external world: small state democratic idealism as well as the developmental ideals of social democracy and protestant missionary groups. In terms of foreign policy then, Norway to a considerable degree resembles the United States. Securing the integrity and sovereignty of the Norwegian state has been coupled with moralism in international affairs. Unlike the United States, of course, Norway as a small and relatively insignificant military power has only been able to project its foreign policy goals and ideals by seeking great power protection and by persuasion and foreign aid contributions.

While the Labor cabinets of the first two postwar decades primarily promoted Norwegian ideals and interests within the councils of the various western security and economic organizations, NATO, the OEEC and EFTA, later Labor and bourgeois governments have been more inclined to speak out on the public stage, particularly within the United Nations. We can discern a drift from an almost exclusively behind the scenes pragmatism to a somewhat more declaratory policy aimed at both a world and a domestic audience.

Norwegian foreign policy, when considered in an international perspective has been formed through an increasingly open policy debate and democratic political process. To a greater degree than is usual, foreign policy in Norway has not been the preserve of closed circles. Public opinion, as seen particularly in the debate over European integration, has been very important in Norway throughout the postwar years. We may assume that the relative openness of the foreign policy process, in combination with Norway's brief existence as an independent nation, go a long way towards explaining the strong moralism and nationalism that is so evident. In the field of security, nationalism was modified by the experience of the April 1940 German invasion. With regard to integration and relations with the Third World there have been few such inhibiting factors. These facts help explain both the outcome of the EC referendum and the increasing UN activism.

Notes

1 A US aid program offered to all European states for post World War II reconstruction and political stabilization. As a condition for aid the Europeans were required to set up an organizational framework for handling economic cooperation within the program. The Organization for European Economic Cooperation (OEEC) was established in April 1948. The Soviet Union, the Eastern bloc countries and Finland declined aid on such conditions. The Marshall Plan was launched by Secretary of State George C. Marshall in a speech at Harvard University in June 1947, hence the Marshall Plan.

2 Until World War I Norway had a common border with the Russian empire. After World War I the new Finnish state gained a narrow strip of land between Norway and Russia's successor state, the Soviet Union, giving Finland an outlet to the Barents Sea. After World War II Finland lost that territory as a consequence of having sided with Germany against the Soviet Union during the war.

3 Gunnar Jahn *Diaries*, The Oslo University Library, typescript, 17 September 1947; Lundestad, *America Scandinavia and the Cold War,* p. 61 for the scepticism of US senator Arthur H. Vandenberg, jr.

4 H.Ø. Pharo, «Bridgebuilding and Reconstruction», p. 136.

5 The Brussels Treaty Organization was formed in March 1948 by Belgium, France, Great Britain, Luxembourg and the Netherlands. After the creation of NATO the organization remained largely dormant until 1955. It was then reactivated as the Western Union with the inclusion of Italy and the Federal Republic of Germany. It was mainly intended to serve as a vehicle for West German rearmament. It is presently being tentatively changed into a military organization for the European Community.

6 The Vandenberg Resolution, a US Senate resolution of June 1948 paving the way for the US joining a North Atlantic Alliance. Self-help and mutual aid would be required of all participants.

7 Einar Gerhardsen, the outstanding leader of the Norwegian Labor Party. Prime Minister of four Cabinets; 1945, 1945-51, 1955-63, 1963-65. He was at the same time chairman of the Party. By the 1960s a father figure in Norwegian politics.

8 The concepts have been introduced by historian Rolf Tamnes. See his major work *The United States and the Cold War in the High North* (Oslo, 1991). For further works, see the bibliography.

9 The bases policy is the term used to denote the Norwegian decision not to allow the stationing of allied troops on Norwegian territory except during war or when war threatens. The bases declaration of 1949 has subsequently been added to but not changed in substance. It should be noted that it is a unilateral declaration and thus may be revoked unilaterally by Norway.

10 A formidable Russian military base in the proximity of the Norwegian-Russian border. It is presumably geared primarily to project Russian power globally, but still represents at least an implicit military threat against Norway.

11 The European Coal and Steel Community (ECSC) was proposed by French Foreign Minister Robert Schuman in 1950 and came into being in 1952, the member states being Belgium, the Federal Republic of Germany, France, Italy, Luxembourg and the Netherlands. The same six created Euratom which was to cater for atomic energy cooperation and the European Economic Community (EEC), a common market. Both agreements came into force in 1958. The EC, the European Community has accepted several new members since 1965.

12 Halvard Lange served as foreign minister from 1946 to 1965. He was widely respected within NATO.

13 H.M. Lange, «European Union: False Hopes and Realities», Foreign Affairs, 1949-50, pp. 441-50.
14 UD (Archives of the Norwegian Foreign Ministry) 44.3/5, IV, A. Skaug, memorandum for H.M. Lange, 20 July 1950.
15 Erik Brofoss, Minister of Finance 1945-1947, Minister of Trade 1947-54, President of the Bank of Norway from 1954. The main architect of Norway's postwar economic planning system.
16 The Wider Free Trade Area, WFTA, a planned OEEC-wide free trade area. Negotiations broke down in 1958. Great Britain, Austria, Denmark, Norway, Portugal,Sweden and Switzerland created the European Free Trade Area, EFTA, in 1960 instead.
17 The European Defence and Political Communities, EDC and EPC, were negotiated in the early 1950s between the members of the ECSC. Negotiations broke down in 1954.
18 E. Brofoss Papers, Archives of the Labor Movement, Oslo. Memorandum concerning «Issues of capital import and Nordic cooperation», (in Norwegian) dated 21 December 1953. Quoted from I. Sogner, «Norwegian Attitudes towards Nordic Economic Cooperation 1947-1959» (in Norwegian), Cand. philol. dissertation in History, University of Oslo, 1992. This is the basic work on Scandinavian economic cooperation, bringing forth a wealth of new materials and new points of view. I rely heavily on it.
19 Important Labor politician-bureaucrat who held a number of top level political and diplomatic posts from 1947 to 1974.

References

Allen, H. *Norway and Europe in the 1970s*. Oslo, 1979.
Angell, V. "Non-Aid Economic Relations with Developing Countries: The Case of Norway", in G. Helleiner, ed., *The Other Side of International Development Policy*. Toronto, 1989.
Blidberg, K. *Just Good Friends*. Nordic Social Democracy and Security Policy, 1945–50. (Oslo, IFS, 5/1987)
Bryceson, I., (ed.). *Fisheries Development. The Experience of Norway and her Partner Countries in the Context of Norwegian Assistance*. Oslo, 1985.
Di Nolfo, E. (ed.). *The Atlantic Pact Forty Years Later*. Berlin, 1991.
Eriksen, K.E. and Pharo, H.Ø. Norsk sikkerhetspolitikk som etterkrigshistorisk forskningsfelt, LOS-senter Notat, Bergen, 1992. (Norwegian security policies as a research field for historians: the postwar years).
Eriksen, T.L. *Norge og den tredje verden som etterkrigshistorisk forskningsfelt*, LOS-senter Notat 89/39 (Third World issues).
Haskel, B. *The Scandinavian Option*. Oslo, 1976.
Holst, J.J. (ed.). *Norwegian Foreign Policy for the 1980s*. Oslo, 1985.
Holst, J.J. Hunt, K., and Sjaastad, A.C., (eds.). *Deterrence and Defence in the North* Oslo, 1985.
Hveem, H. "Norway the Hesitant Reformer" in C. Pratt, ed., *Internationalism under Strain*. Toronto, 1989.
Lundestad, G. *America, Scandinavia and the Cold War, 1945–1949*. Oslo, 1980.
Ørvik, N. (ed.). *Fears and Expectations. Norwegian Attitudes toward European Integration*. Oslo, 1972.
Ørvik, N. (ed.). *The Scandinavian Allies and the European Community*. Kingston, 1978.
Hansen, S. *India. Development and Aid. Norway's Contribution and Future Options*. Oslo, 1987.
Havnevik, K.J. (ed.). *Tanzania. Country Study and Norwegian Aid Review*. Bergen, 1989.

Jacobsen, K., *The Nordic Countries in the UN.* (Oslo, 1967, dissertation, Department of Political Science, Oslo University).

Klausen, A.M. *Kerala Fishermen and the Indo-Norwegian Pilot Project.* Oslo, 1967.

Pharo, H.O. "Bridgebuilding and Reconstruction: Norway Faces the Marshall Plan", *Scandinavian Journal of History,* vol. 1, no. 1-2 (1976).

Pharo, H.O. *Domestic and International Implications of Norwegian Reconstruction,* European University Institute (EUI) Working Papers 81/1984, Florence.

Pharo, H.O. "The Cold War in Norwegian and International Historical Research", *Scandinavian Journal of History,* vol. 10, no. 3 (1985).

Pharo, H.O. *The Third Force, Atlanticism and Norwegian Attitudes towards European Integration* (EUI) Working Papers, 255/1986, Florence.

Pharo, H.O. "Conflict and Cooperation in the Indo-Norwegian Fisheries Project, 1952–1972", in C. Dewey, ed., *The State and the Market.* New Delhi, 1987.

Pharo, H.O. *Norwegian Social Democrats and European Integration in the 1950s* (EUI Colloquium Papers, 312/1988, Florence).

Pharo, H.O. "The Indo-Norwegian Project and the modernisation of Kerala Fisheries, 1950–1970", in M. Shepperdson and C. Simmons, eds., *The Indian National Congress and the Political Economy of India 1885–1985.* Aldershot, 1988.

Pharo, H.O. *Norge, Norden og europeisk integrasjon som etterkrigshistorisk forskningsfelt,* LOS-senter Notat 91/26 (Integration issues).

Pharo, H.O. "Scandinavia and the Cold War: An Overview" in D. Reynolds, ed., *The Origins of the Cold War in Europe* (New Haven, forthcoming).

Riste, O. (ed.). *Western Security.* Oslo, 1985.

Skodvin, M. *Nordic or North Atlantic Alliance. The Postwar Scandinavian Security Debate* (Oslo, Institute for Defence Studies (IFS) Occasional Papers, 3/ 1990).

Stokke, O. "The Determinants of Norwegian Aid Policy", In. O. Stokke, red., *Western Middle Powers and Global Poverty.* Uppsala, 1989.

Tamnes, R. *Integration and Screening. The Two Faces of Alliance Policy, 1945– 1986,* (Oslo, Institute for Defence Studies (IFS) Occasional Papers, 1987).

Tamnes, R. *The United States and the Cold War in the High North.* Oslo, 1991.

Udgaard, N.M. *Great Power Politics and Norwegian Foreign Policy.* Oslo, 1973.

Valen, H. "National Conflict Structure and Foreign Politics", *European Journal of Political Research,* 1976.

Wendt, F.W. *Cooperation in the Nordic Countries: Achievements and Obstacles.* Stockholm, 1981.

Glossary

Akademikernes Fellesforbund *(AF)* The Federation of Norwegian Professional Associations, established in 1976.

Bokmål See Standard Norwegian.

Bondepartiet See Center Party.

Brand A drama by Henrik Ibsen, where the protagonist is also called Brand. Ibsen allegedly used Christopher Bruun as a model when he developed the character of Brand.

Bretton Woods Monetary System This system is based on an agreement from 1944, to coordinate currency exchange rates between membership countries of the International Monetary Fund (IMP).

Brofoss, Erik (1908–) The main architect of Norway's postwar economic planning system. Minister of Finance 1945–1947, Minister of Trade 1947–54, President of the Bank of Norway from 1954—1970.

Brussels Treaty An organization formed in 1948. After the creation of NATO, it remained dormant until 1955. It was mainly intended to serve as a vehicle for West German Rearmament. It is tentatively being changed into a military organization for the European Community (EC).

Bruun, Christopher (1839–1920) Norwegian minister and educator. His teachings and ideas were influential in building a Norwegian national identity.

Center Party *Senterpartiet (SP)* The Center Party was founded in 1920. Formally called the Agrarian Party (Bondepartiet), it changed its name in 1959.

Christian Democratic Party – *Kristelig Folkeparti (KrF)* Political Party founded in 1933.

Chernobyl Chernobyl refers to the nuclear reactor accident near Kiev in the Soviet Union in 1988.

County – *fylke.*

Det Norske Arbeiderparti *(DNA)* – The Norwegian Labor Party.

Elder Edda See under Snorri.

European Community (EC) The EC is a common market resulting from the union of the European Economic Community (EEC), the European Coal and Steel Community (ECSC) and the European Atomic Energy Community (EURATOM) in 1970. The EC is a common market.

European Economic Area (EEA) Known as the *EØS avtalen* in Norwegian. Treaty between the EC and EFTA countries. Yet to be ratified by the respective member countries.

European Economic Community (EEC) The EEC was created by the member states of the European Coal and Steel Community (ECSC) in 1952. Member States were Belgium, the Federal Republic of Germany, France, Italy, Luxemborg and the Netherlands. In 1965, the EEC accepted several new members. In 1970, the EEC changed its name to the European Community (EC) after merging with the ECSC (European Coal and Steel Community) and EURATOM (European Atomic Energy Community).

European Free Trade Association *(EFTA)* Economic organization established in 1959.

Flor, Ellinor (1946–) Designer. Ellinor Flor is famous for her ability to transform traditional Norwegian patterns to contemporary haute couture.

Fremskrittspartiet *(FrP)* See under The Progress Party.

General Agreement on Tariffs and Trade (GATT) International customs and trade agreement ratified 1947. Norway is one of the many countries included in the agreement.

Gerhardsen, Einar (1897–1987) The leading figure in the Norwegian Labor Party. Prime Minister of four cabinets; 1945, 1945–51, 1955–63, 1963–65. By the 1960s, Gerhardsen was a father figure in Norwegian politics. His son, Rune, is also a front figure in the Norwegian Labor Party.

Gross Domestic Product (GDP) The value of the production in any given country.

Gruntvig, N.F.S. (1783–1872) Danish theologian. Folk high schools in Denmark were built upon Gruntvig's ideals, and they became important vehicles for the identity and culture building of the peasantry.

Higher Chamber of the National Assembly – *Lagting*.

Holberg, Ludvig (1684–1754) Norwegian-Danish poet and author.

Ibsen, Henrik (1828–1906) Internationally known Norwegian playwright and critic of modern society. He is most known for dramas such as, A Doll's House, Brand, Peer Gynt, etc.

Jensen, P. A. (1812–1867) Theologian and author. He is well known for publishing Jensen's reader (Jensens lesebok).

Keynesianism Macroeconomic management through government manipulation of the demand side of the economy. Named after the economist, John Maynard Keynes.

Kielland, Alexander (1849–1906) Lawyer and writer.

King in Council – *Kongen i statsråd.*

King and the Council of State – *Statsrådet.*

Kristelig folkepartiet (KrF) See under The Christian Democratic Party.

Labor Party, The Norwegian – *Det norske arbeiderparti (DNA).*

Law of Jante *(Janteloven)* The law of the mythical village of Jante in Axel Sandemose's book, *En flyktning krysser sitt spor* (Oslo 1962).

Landsorganisasjonen (LO) The Norwegian Confederation of Trade Unions.

Lower Chamber of the National assembly – *Odelstinget.*

Marshall Plan A US aid program offered to all European states for post World War II reconstruction and political stabilization. The plan was named after Secretary of State, George C. Marshall who launched the plan in 1947.

Municipality – *kommune.*

NAF see *Næringslivets hovedorganisasjon* (NHO).

Nansen, Fritjof (1861–1930) Internationally known for his Arctic research and for his leadership in international humanitarian work.

National Insurance Scheme – *(folketrygden)* All social rights for Norwegian citizens and residents of Norway are compiled into the National Insurance Scheme. The scheme was established in 1966 with additions made in the 1970s.

New Norwegian *(Nynorsk)* One of the two official Norwegian languages. It was developed by Ivar Aasen, primarily from the dialects of western Norway. Up until 1929, New Norwegian was called Landsmål (Country language).

Nissen, Hartvig (1815–1874) Educator and interparliamentary union established in 1952.

Næringslivets Hovedorganisasjon (NHO) The Confederation of Norwegian Business and Industry.

North Atlantic Treaty Organization (NATO) A military alliance founded in 1949.

Norwegian Language See under Standard Norwegian, New Norwegian and the State Language.

Norwegian National Assembly, The – *Stortinget.*

Nynorsk See New Norwegian.

Old Norwegian *(Gammelnorsk)* Old Norwegian, also known as Old Norse, is a dead language, however it is similar to present day Icelandic.

Organization of Economic Cooperation and Development (OECD) An extension of the Organization for European Economic Cooperation (OEEC) which was a Western European organization. OEEC originated in 1948 in connection with the Marshall Plan. In 1961, the name changed to OECD when the United States, Canada, Australia, Turkey, Japan and New Zealand became members.

Progress Party, The Fremskrittspartiet (FrP) Founded in 1973.
Regional Policies (RP) – *Distriktspolitikk.*
Riksmål See State language.
Senterpartiet *(SP)* See under Center Party.
Sami Parliament *(Sametinget)* In 1989, King Olav V inaugurated the Sami Parliament. The Parliament has real, but limited power.
Sami The large sub-Arctic ethnic group formally known as the Lapps. The Sami are Norway's oldest ethnic minority. While the largest group of Sami live in Norway, they live also in Finland, Sweden and the Russian Kola peninsula.
Snorri (Snorre Sturlason) (1179–1241) Snorre refers to the person, as well as to his works.
Standard Norwegian *(Bokmål)* One of Norway's two official languages. Standard Norwegian, literally translated as Book language, is a modified form of *riksmål* (State language) which is based upon the Danish written tradition. It became an official language in 1929.
State language *(Riksmål)* From ca. 1900 to 1929, *Riksmål* was the term used for the most common written and spoken language in Norway (as opposed to *landsmål*). In 1929, the government changed *riksmål* to *bokmål*, and *landsmål* to *nynorsk*. Today, however, *bokmål* is the term used for the more archaic Norwegian based upon Danish tradition.
Stortinget The Norwegian National Assembly.
Trygvason, Olav A viking hero and king portrayed in Snorre's sagas.
United Kingdom Scandinavian Economic Cooperation (UNISCAN) Established in 1950 as a forum for economic and trade discussions. The agreement had little practical importance.
United Nations (UN) Universal organization established in 1945.
Wider Free Trade Area (WFTA) A planned OEEC-wide free trade area. Negotiations broke down in 1958. In 1960, the European Free Trade Association (EFTA), was created instead by Great Britain, Austria, Denmark, Norway, Portugal, Sweden and Switzerland.
Wotan God in Norse mythology.
Yrkesorganisasjonenes Sentralforbund *(YS)* Confederation of Vocational Trade Unions, founded in 1977.

Abbrevations

AF	–	Akademikernes Fellesforbund
EC	–	European Community
EEA	–	European Economic Area
EEC	–	European Economic Community
EFTA	–	European Free Trade Association
EØS	–	Europeisk Økonomisk Sone (see EEA)
GATT	–	General Agreement on Tariffs and Trade
GDP	–	Gross Domestic Product
KrF	–	Kristelig Folkeparti
LO	–	Landsorganisasjonen
NAF	–	Norges Arbeidsgiverforening
NATO	–	North Atlantic Treaty Organisation
NHO	–	Næringslivets Hovedorganisasjon
OECD	–	Organisation for Economic Cooperation and Development
OEEC	–	Organisation for European Economic Cooperation
RP	–	Regional Politics
SP	–	Senterpartiet
UNISCAN	–	United Kingdom Scandinavian Economic Cooperation
UN	–	United Nations
WFTA	–	Wider Free Trade Area
YS	–	Yrkesorganisasjonenes Sentralforbund

Photo Acknowledgements

p. 20 Signe Dons
p. 23 Anne Cohen Kiel
p. 42 The University of Oslo Library (Universitetsbiblioteket i Oslo)
p. 48 The University of Oslo Library (Universitetsbiblioteket i Oslo)
p. 49 The National Gallery, Oslo
p. 63 Oslo City Transport
p. 64 Jiri Havran
p. 65 The Munch Museum, Oslo
p. 98 Ruth Ensby
p. 98 Dag Grundseth
p. 143 Per Svensson
p. 154 Per Svensson
p. 169 Svein E. Furulund
p. 178 Anne Cohen Kiel
p. 194 L. Thorsrud
p. 213 Rolf Øhman
p. 255 Inge Grødum

Contributors

Berggreen, Brit. (1940–) Ph.D. Cultural Historian affiliated to the Norwegian Institute in Athens, Greece.

Cohen Kiel, Anne. (1960–) Editor of this volume, Anthropologist. Teacher and Advisor for a centre for immigrants and refugees under the auspices of the Labour Directorate (IFF-Holmlia).

Eriksen, Erik Oddvar. (1955–) Associate Professor of Political Science at the University of Tromsø.

Eriksen, Thomas Hylland. (1962–) Associate Professor of Anthropology at the University of Oslo.

Fliflet, Arne (1946–) Supreme Court Barrister and Parliamentary Ombudsman of Norway.

Hagen, Kåre. (1958–) Research Director at the Norwegian Trade Union Center for Social Research (FAFO), Oslo.

Hindar, Kjetil. (1954–) Researcher at the Norwegian Institute for Nature Research (NINA), Trondheim.

Hippe, Jon M. (1959–) Research Director at the Norwegian Trade Union Center for Social Research (FAFO), Oslo.

Holter, Øystein Gulvåg. (1952–) Researcher at the Work Research Institute (AFI), Oslo.

Long, Litt Woon. (1958–) Anthropologist and Senior Executive Officer at the Ministry of Local Government and Labour.

Malinowski, Richard. (1946–) Deputy Chief Executive for the Municipality of Ski (Ski Kommune)

Mjøset, Lars. (1954–) Research Director at the Institute for Social Research, Oslo.

Pharo, Helge O. (1943–) Professor of International History at the University of Oslo (Ph.D).

Skotvedt, Tove. (1944–) Former Board Member of the International Work Group for Indigenous Affairs (IWGIA), Senior Executive Officer at the Ministry of Local Government and Labour.

Vormeland, Oddvar (1924–) Inspector of Schools and later Chief Officer of Education in Oslo. Former Director General of the Norwegian Ministry of Education (KUFD). Presently Professor at the Institute for Special Education.